THE PRENTICE HALL

ATLAS

of

WORLD HISTORY

Produced in Collaboration with Dorling Kindersley

DORLING KINDERSLEY
LONDON • NEW YORK • MUNICH
MELBOURNE • DELHI
www.dk.com

PEARSON
Prentice Hall

UPPER SADDLE RIVER, NJ 07458

CREDITS

 THE TEAM AT DK:

PROJECT EDITOR Andrew Szudek
SENIOR ART EDITOR Carole Oliver
PROJECT MANAGER Nigel Duffield
CARTOGRAPHY Selected maps taken from the *DK Atlas of World History*
(ISBN: 0-7513-0719-X)

 THE TEAM AT PRENTICE HALL:

EDITORIAL DIRECTOR Charlyce Jones-Owen
EXECUTIVE EDITOR Charles Cavaliere
EDITORIAL ASSISTANT Shannon Corliss
EXECUTIVE MARKETING MANAGER Heather Shelstad
MARKETING ASSISTANT Cherron Gardner
MANAGING EDITOR Joanne Riker
PRINT BUYER Ben Smith
FORMATTER Scott Garrison

MAP CONSULTANTS:
Gayle Brunelle, California State University, Fullerton
R. Scott Moore, Indiana Universtiy of Pennsylvania
Linda Bregstein Scherr, Mercer County Community College

CONTENTS

CONTENTS

HOW TO USE THIS ATLAS

MAPS USE A UNIQUE VISUAL language to convey a great deal of detailed information in a relatively simple form. The maps in this atlas use a variety of different projections – techniques used to show the Earth's curved surface on a flat map – to trace the geographical, physical, and social development of humans, from over 4 million years ago to the present. This page explains how to look for different features on the maps and how to unravel the different layers of information you can find on them.

Projection

Projections, which show the world at global, continental, or country scale, vary with each map. The projections for this atlas have been carefully chosen, ensuring that there is as little distortion as possible.

Scalebar

When using a map to work out what distances are in reality, it is necessary to refer to the scale of that particular map. The maps in this atlas use a linear scale. This only works on equal-area maps (where distances are true); on all other maps the scalebar is omitted.

Map Key

Maps use symbols to both show the location of a feature, and to give information about that feature. The symbols used in this atlas are explained in the key that accompanies each map.

Timeline

Many of the maps featured in this atlas are accompanied by timelines. Various important events and developments are plotted along a historical line, which shows the order in which they occured during a certain period in history. Where a place or event shown on the map and colored in the key is also named on the timeline, the corresponding section on the timeline is given the same color as that on the key, to allow for cross-referencing.

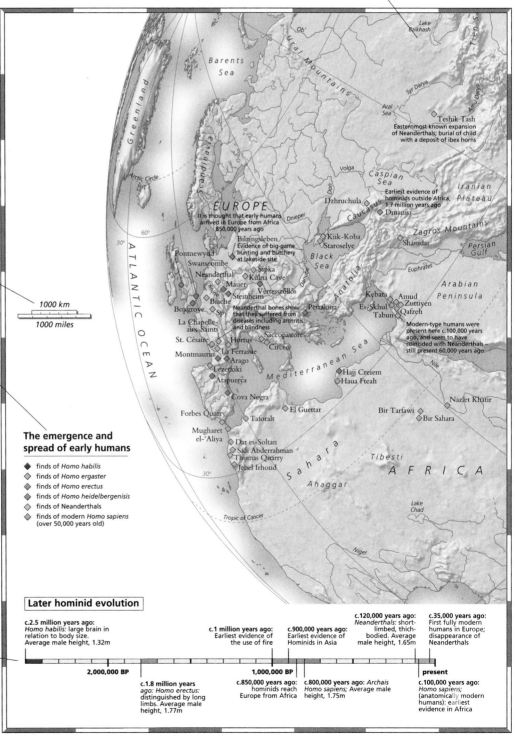

1000 km
1000 miles

The emergence and spread of early humans

- ◆ finds of *Homo habilis*
- ◇ finds of *Homo ergaster*
- ◇ finds of *Homo erectus*
- ◇ finds of *Homo heidelbergenisis*
- ◇ finds of Neanderthals
- ◇ finds of modern *Homo sapiens* (over 50,000 years old)

Later hominid evolution

c.2.5 million years ago: *Homo habilis*: large brain in relation to body size. Average male height, 1.32m.

c.1 million years ago: Earliest evidence of the use of fire

c.900,000 years ago: Earliest evidence of Hominids in Asia

c.120,000 years ago: *Neanderthals*: short-limbed, thick-bodied. Average male height, 1.65m

c.35,000 years ago: First fully modern humans in Europe; disappearance of Neanderthals

2,000,000 BP

1,000,000 BP

present

c.1.8 million years ago: *Homo erectus*: distinguished by long limbs. Average male height, 1.77m.

c.850,000 years ago: hominids reach Europe from Africa

c.800,000 years ago: *Archais Homo sapiens*; Average male height, 1.75m

c.100,000 years ago: *Homo sapiens*; (anatomically modern humans): earliest evidence in Africa

5

EARLY HOMINIDS

THE EARLIEST IDENTIFIABLE human ancestors date to over 4.5 million years ago, and were upright walking hominids with many apelike characteristics. *Australopithecus afarensis*, represented by an adult female known as "Lucy," flourished in the Hadar region of Ethiopia 3.4 million years ago. This Australopithecine, or "southern ape," evolved into several forms by 2.5 million years ago, among them a larger brained *Homo*, the ancestor of all later humans. Until about 1.8 million years ago, these humans were confined to their continent of origin, tropical Africa.

How did Australopithicenes adapt to the African landscape?

Aramis ◇

S a h a r a

Lake Chad

Recent discoveries of a new australopithecine (*A. bahrelchazali*) stretch the geographical range 3800 km west of Great Rift Valley

Equator

C o n g o

B a s i n

Congo

A F R I C A

Cunene

Kalahari Desert

Tropic of Capricorn

Swartkrans ◇

Taung ◆

ATLANTIC OCEAN

Orange River

Drakensberg

500 km

500 miles

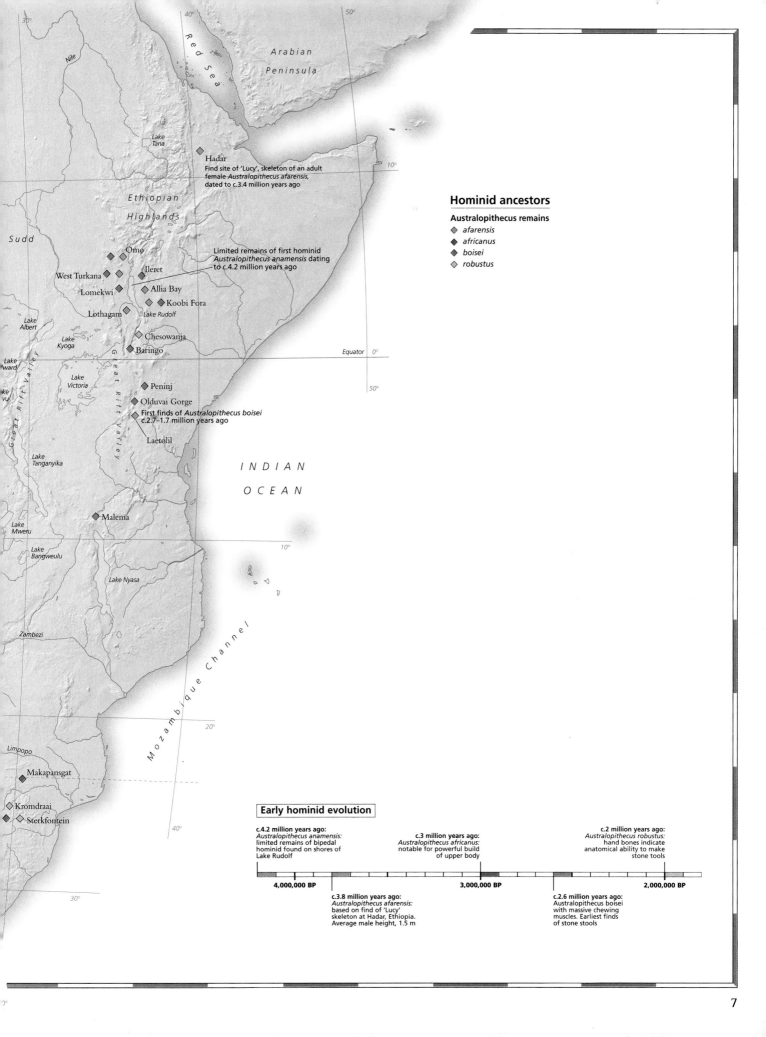

Red Sea

Nile

Lake Tana

Arabian Peninsula

◆ **Hadar**
Find site of 'Lucy', skeleton of an adult female *Australopithecus afarensis*, dated to c.3.4 million years ago

Ethiopian Highlands

Sudd

◆ Omo
◆ Ileret
West Turkana ◆◆
Lomekwi
◆ Allia Bay
Lothagam ◆ Koobi Fora
Lake Rudolf

Limited remains of first hominid *Australopithecus anamensis* dating to c.4.2 million years ago

Lake Albert
Lake Kyoga
Lake Victoria
Lake ...ward
...ke vu...

◆ Chesowanja
◆ Baringo

Equator   0°

Great Rift Valley

50°

◆ Peninj
◆ Olduvai Gorge
First finds of *Australopithecus boisei* c.2.7–1.7 million years ago

Laetolil

Lake Tanganyika

INDIAN

OCEAN

◆ Malema
Lake Mweru
Lake Bangweulu
Lake Nyasa

10°

Zambezi

Mozambique Channel

Limpopo

20°

◆ Makapansgat

◇ Kromdraai
◆ ◇ Sterkfontein

30°

40°

Hominid ancestors

Australopithecus remains
◆ *afarensis*
◆ *africanus*
◆ *boisei*
◇ *robustus*

Early hominid evolution

c.4.2 million years ago:
Australopithecus anamensis: limited remains of bipedal hominid found on shores of Lake Rudolf

c.3 million years ago:
Australopithecus africanus: notable for powerful build of upper body

c.2 million years ago:
Australopithecus robustus: hand bones indicate anatomical ability to make stone tools

| 4,000,000 BP | | 3,000,000 BP | | 2,000,000 BP |

c.3.8 million years ago:
Australopithecus afarensis: based on find of 'Lucy' skeleton at Hadar, Ethiopia. Average male height, 1.5 m

c.2.6 million years ago:
Australopithecus boisei with massive chewing muscles. Earliest finds of stone stools

THE EMERGENCE OF MODERN HUMANS

THE FIRST REPRESENTATIVE of the *Homo* genus, *Homo habilis* ("handy person"), emerged about 2.5 million years ago and was distinguished by its toolmaking abilities. *Homo erectus*, which appeared in Africa about 1.9 million years ago, had a larger brain capacity, long-legged physique, and adapted successfully to a wide range of environments, spreading from Africa to Asia and Europe over the next 1.25 million years. The earliest fossil remains of fully modern humans, *Homo sapiens sapiens*, found in Africa, date to c.150,000 years ago. Resourceful and inventive, modern humans colonized all kinds of environments, and became the sole surviving human species.

What environmental factors influenced the diffusion of early modern humans?

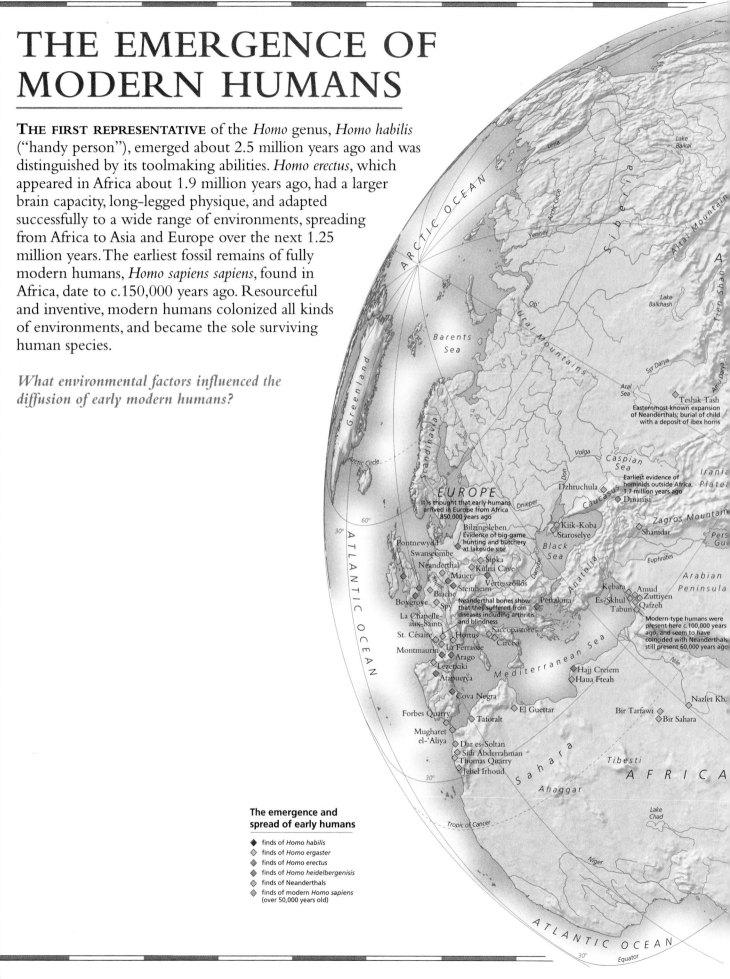

Teshik-Tash
Easternmost known expansion of Neanderthals; burial of child with a deposit of ibex horns

Earliest evidence of hominids outside Africa, 1.7 million years ago
Dmanisi

Dzhruchula

It is thought that early humans arrived in Europe from Africa 850,000 years ago

Bilzingsleben
Evidence of big-game hunting and butchery at lakeside site

Kiik-Koba
Staroselye
Shanidar

Pontnewydd
Swanscombe
Neanderthal
Mauer
Steinheim
Šipka
Kulna Cave
Vertesszöllos
Biache
Boxgrove
Spy
La Chapelle-aux-Saints
Neanderthal bones show that they suffered from diseases including arthritis and blindness
Petralona
Kebara
Amud
Zuttiyen
Es-Skhul
Tabun
Qafzeh

Modern-type humans were present here c.100,000 years ago, and seem to have coincided with Neanderthals still present 60,000 years ago

St. Césaire
Hortus
Saccopastore
Montmaurin
La Ferrassie
Arago
Circeo
Lezetxiki
Atapuerça
Cova Negra
Hajj Creiem
Haua Fteah
Forbes Quarry
El Guettar
Bir Tarfawi
Nazlet Kha
Taforalt
Bir Sahara
Mugharet el-'Aliya
Dar es-Soltan
Sidi Abderrahman
Thomas Quarry
Jebel Irhoud
Tibesti
AFRICA
Sahara
Ahaggar

The emergence and spread of early humans

- ◆ finds of *Homo habilis*
- ◇ finds of *Homo ergaster*
- ◆ finds of *Homo erectus*
- ◆ finds of *Homo heidelbergenisis*
- ◇ finds of Neanderthals
- ◇ finds of modern *Homo sapiens* (over 50,000 years old)

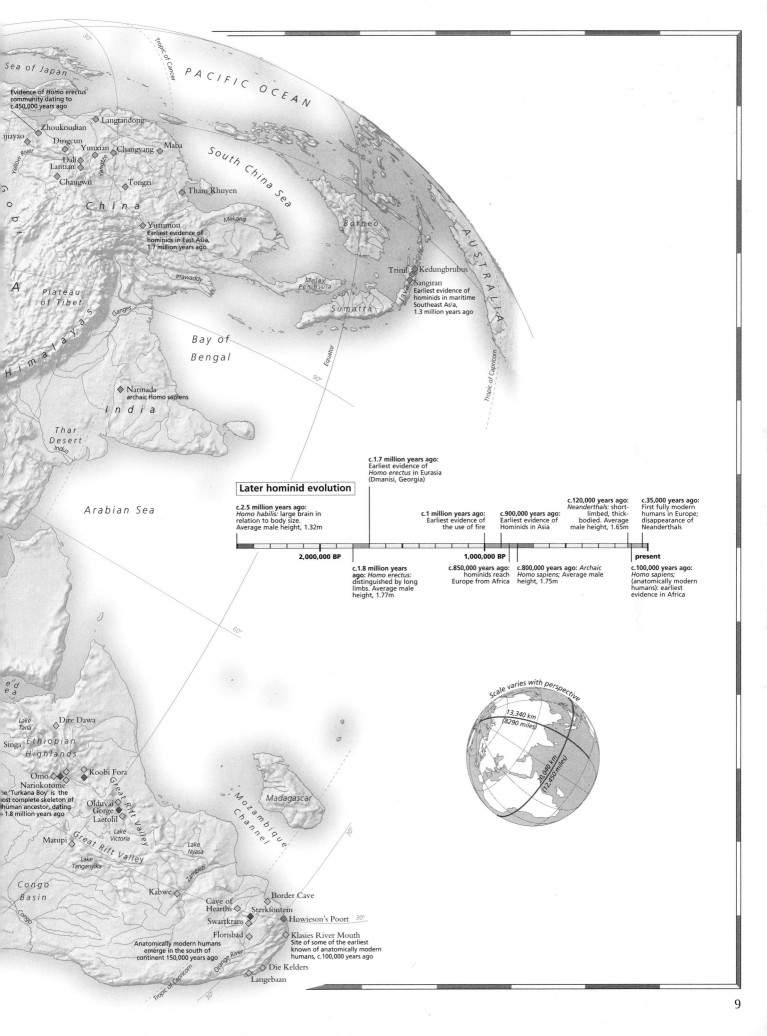

Sea of Japan

PACIFIC OCEAN

Evidence of *Homo erectus* community dating to c.450,000 years ago

Zhoukoudian

Langtandong

djiayao

Dingcun

Yunxian

Changyang

Maba

Dali

Lantian

Changwu

Tongzi

China

Tham Khuyen

South China Sea

Borneo

AUSTRALIA

Yuanmou
Earliest evidence of hominids in East Asia, 1.7 million years ago

Mekong

Malay Peninsula

Sumatra

Trinil

Kedungbrubus

Sangiran
Earliest evidence of hominids in maritime Southeast Asia, 1.3 million years ago

Irrawaddy

Plateau of Tibet

Himalayas

Ganges

Bay of Bengal

Narmada
archaic Homo sapiens

India

Thar Desert

Indus

Arabian Sea

Gobi

A

Later hominid evolution

c.1.7 million years ago:
Earliest evidence of *Homo erectus* in Eurasia (Dmanisi, Georgia)

c.2.5 million years ago:
Homo habilis: large brain in relation to body size. Average male height, 1.32m

c.1 million years ago:
Earliest evidence of the use of fire

c.900,000 years ago:
Earliest evidence of Hominids in Asia

c.120,000 years ago:
Neanderthals: short-limbed, thick-bodied. Average male height, 1.65m

c.35,000 years ago:
First fully modern humans in Europe; disappearance of Neanderthals

2,000,000 BP   1,000,000 BP   present

c.1.8 million years ago: *Homo erectus:* distinguished by long limbs. Average male height, 1.77m

c.850,000 years ago: hominids reach Europe from Africa

c.800,000 years ago: *Archaic Homo sapiens;* Average male height, 1.75m

c.100,000 years ago: *Homo sapiens;* (anatomically modern humans): earliest evidence in Africa

Lake Tana

Dire Dawa

Singa

Ethiopian Highlands

Omo

Koobi Fora

Nariokotome
he 'Turkana Boy' is the ost complete skeleton of human ancestor, dating 1.8 million years ago

Olduvai Gorge

Laetolil

Matupi

Great Rift Valley

Lake Victoria

Great Rift Valley

Lake Nyasa

Lake Tanganyika

Zambezi

Congo Basin

Congo

Kabwe

Cave of Hearths

Sterkfontein

Swartkrans

Florisbad

Border Cave

Howieson's Poort

Klasies River Mouth
Site of some of the earliest known of anatomically modern humans, c.100,000 years ago

Die Kelders

Langebaan

Anatomically modern humans emerge in the south of continent 150,000 years ago

Madagascar

Mozambique Channel

Scale varies with perspective

13,340 km
(8290 miles)

20,040 km
(12,450 miles)

9

THE WORLD: PREHISTORY TO 10,000 BCE

By 30,000 YEARS AGO, humans had colonized much of the globe. When the last Ice Age reached its peak 20,000 years ago, they were forced to adapt to survive the harsh conditions. As the temperatures rose and ice sheets retreated, plants and animals became more abundant and new areas were settled.

How did climate change affect the spread of modern humans?

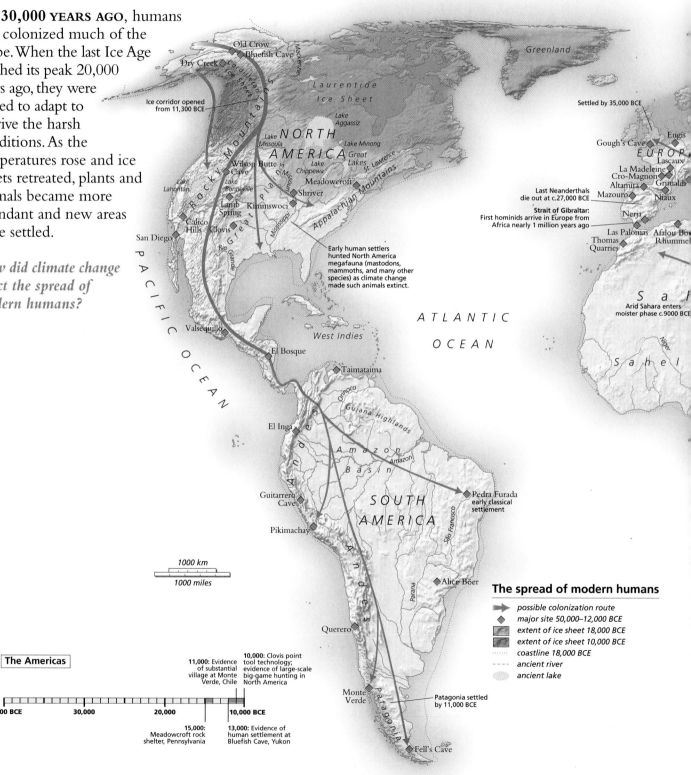

Europe

35,000: Fully modern humans settle continent. Extinction of Neanderthals. New tool technology

10,000: Retreat of glaciers; temperate deciduous woodland spreads northwards. Rich array of marine and land resources

110,000 BCE 90,000 70,000 50,000 30,000 10,000 BCE

120,000: Neanderthals present from western Europe to Central Asia

10,000: Large mammals, such as woolly rhinoceros, giant deer, and mammoth gradually become extinct

Greenland

Old Crow
Bluefish Cave
Dry Creek
Coahuiltecan Ice Sheet

Ice corridor opened from 11,300 BCE

MacKenzie

Laurentide Ice Sheet

Lake Agassiz

Lake Missoula
NORTH AMERICA
Lake Minong

Rocky Mountains

Wilson Butte Cave
Lake Bonneville
Lake Lahontán

Lake Chippewa
Great Lakes
St. Lawrence

Missouri

Meadowcroft
Shriver

Appalachian Mountains

Lamb Spring
Kimmswoci

Calico Hills Clovis

San Diego

Great Plains

Mississippi

Rio Grande

Early human settlers hunted North America megafauna (mastodons, mammoths, and many other species) as climate change made such animals extinct.

Settled by 35,000 BCE

Engis
Gough's Cave EUROP
Lascaux
La Madeleine Grimaldi
Cro-Magnon
Altamira Niaux
Mazouco
Nerja
Last Neanderthals die out at c.27,000 BCE
Strait of Gibraltar: First hominids arrive in Europe from Africa nearly 1 million years ago
Las Palomas Afalou Bo
Thomas Quarries Rhummel

S a
Arid Sahara enters moister phase c.9000 BCE

Niger

Sahel

ATLANTIC OCEAN

Valsequillo

El Bosque

West Indies

Taimataima

Orinoco

Guiana Highlands

El Inga

Amazon Basin
Amazon

Guitarrero Cave

SOUTH AMERICA

Pedra Furada early classical settlement

São Francisco

Pikimachay

Andes

Alice Böer

Paraná

Querero

1000 km

1000 miles

Monte Verde

Patagonia

Patagonia settled by 11,000 BCE

Fell's Cave

The spread of modern humans

➤ *possible colonization route*
◆ *major site 50,000–12,000 BCE*
▨ *extent of ice sheet 18,000 BCE*
▨ *extent of ice sheet 10,000 BCE*
⋯ *coastline 18,000 BCE*
– – *ancient river*
░ *ancient lake*

The Americas

11,000: Evidence of substantial village at Monte Verde, Chile

10,000: Clovis point tool technology; evidence of large-scale big-game hunting in North America

40,000 BCE 30,000 20,000 10,000 BCE

15,000: Meadowcroft rock shelter, Pennsylvania

13,000: Evidence of human settlement at Bluefish Cave, Yukon

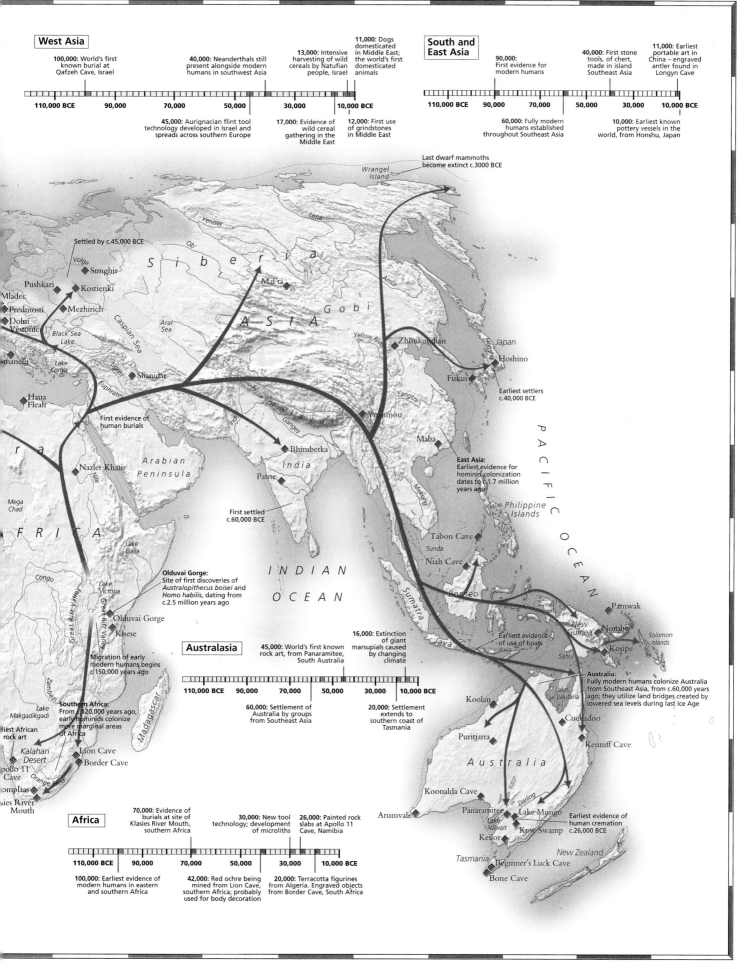

100,000: World's first known burial at Qafzeh Cave, Israel

40,000: Neanderthals still present alongside modern humans in southwest Asia

13,000: Intensive harvesting of wild cereals by Natufian people, Israel

11,000: Dogs domesticated in Middle East; the world's first domesticated animals

110,000 BCE   90,000   70,000   50,000   30,000   10,000 BCE

45,000: Aurignacian flint tool technology developed in Israel and spreads across southern Europe

17,000: Evidence of wild cereal gathering in the Middle East

12,000: First use of grindstones in Middle East

South and East Asia

90,000: First evidence for modern humans

40,000: First stone tools, of chert, made in island Southeast Asia

11,000: Earliest portable art in China – engraved antler found in Longyn Cave

110,000 BCE   90,000   70,000   50,000   30,000   10,000 BCE

60,000: Fully modern humans established throughout Southeast Asia

10,000: Earliest known pottery vessels in the world, from Honshu, Japan

Last dwarf mammoths become extinct c.3000 BCE

Wrangel Island

Yenisey

Lena

Settled by c.45,000 BCE

Volga

◆ Sunghir

Siberia

Mal'ta ◆

Amur

Pushkari ◆
◆ Kostienki
Mladec ◆   ◆ Mezhirich
◆ Predmosti
◆ Dolní
Věstonice

ASIA   *Gobi*

Black Sea Lake

Aral Sea

Yellow River

Zhoukoudian ◆

Japan

◆ Hoshino

Caspian Sea

...anelli
Lake Konya
◆ Shanidar

Tigris   *Euphrates*

Himalayas

Yangtze

Fukui ◆

Earliest settlers c.40,000 BCE

◆ Haua Fleah

First evidence of human burials

Indus   *Ganges*

◆ Yuanmou

...ra

◆ Nazlet Khatir

Nile

Arabian Peninsula

India

Bhimbetka ◆

Maba ◆

East Asia: Earliest evidence for hominid colonization dates to c.1.7 million years ago

Mega Chad

Patne ◆

Philippine Islands

PACIFIC OCEAN

First settled c.60,000 BCE

Tabon Cave ◆

Sunda

Niah Cave ◆

Congo

Lake Victoria

Olduvai Gorge: Site of first discoveries of *Australopithecus boisei* and *Homo habilis*, dating from c.2.5 million years ago

Lake Galla

INDIAN OCEAN

Borneo

Mekong

Sumatra

◆ Panwak

New Guinea

Nombe ◆

AFRICA

Great Rift Valley

◆ Olduvai Gorge
◆ Kisese

Solomon Islands

◆ Kosipe

Migration of early modern humans begins c.150,000 years ago

Australasia

45,000: World's first known rock art, from Panaramitee, South Australia

Java

Sahul

16,000: Extinction of giant marsupials caused by changing climate

Earliest evidence of use of boats

Southern Africa: From c.120,000 years ago, early hominids colonize more marginal areas of Africa

Zambezi

Lake Makgadikgadi

Lake Curpeutaria

Australia: Fully modern humans colonize Australia from Southeast Asia from c.60,000 years ago; they utilize land bridges created by lowered sea levels during last Ice Age

110,000 BCE   90,000   70,000   50,000   30,000   10,000 BCE

60,000: Settlement of Australia by groups from Southeast Asia

20,000: Settlement extends to southern coast of Tasmania

Koolan ◆

...liest African rock art

Kalahari Desert

◆ Lion Cave
◆ Border Cave

Cuckadoo ◆

...pollo 11 Cave

Orange River

◆ Kenniff Cave

Puritjarra ◆

...omplaas

Australia

...ies River Mouth

Koonalda Cave ◆

Africa

70,000: Evidence of burials at site of Klasies River Mouth, southern Africa

30,000: New tool technology; development of microliths

26,000: Painted rock slabs at Apollo 11 Cave, Namibia

Darling

Arumvale ◆

Panaramitee ◆
Lake Nitwait

Lake Mungo ◆

Earliest evidence of human cremation c.26,000 BCE

Keilor ◆   Kow Swamp ◆

110,000 BCE   90,000   70,000   50,000   30,000   10,000 BCE

Tasmania

Beginner's Luck Cave ◆

New Zealand

100,000: Earliest evidence of modern humans in eastern and southern Africa

42,000: Red ochre being mined from Lion Cave, southern Africa; probably used for body decoration

20,000: Terracotta figurines from Algeria. Engraved objects from Border Cave, South Africa

Bone Cave ◆

EARLY PEOPLES OF NORTH AMERICA

THE FIRST HUMAN SETTLERS of North America crossed from Siberia into Alaska around 15,000 years ago—the date is uncertain. They traveled south along the Pacific continental shelf as Ice Age glaciers melted, settling throughout the Americas. Over the millennia, their descendants adapted to every environment imaginable, from deserts to tropical rainforest. By 2,500 BCE, sedentary villages flourished in Mesoamerica, where maize and bean cultivation developed.

Why did complex societies first appear in Mesoamerica before other areas of North America?

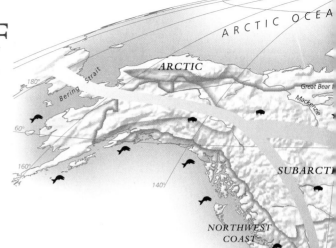

Subsistence and agriculture in early North America

▨	Native American culture areas
▨	southern extent of ice cover at height of Wisconsin glaciation 18,000 BCE
→	possible migration routes of first human settlers
◇	important Archaic sites in North America (to 2500 BCE)
◇	important Archaic sites in Central America (7000–c.2000 BCE)

Major types of subsistence

🐗	game animals
🐟	fishing
⚘	wild plants

The development of agriculture c.7000 BCE–c.700 CE

▨	core region of agricultural development
▨	first expansion of agricultural practice
▨	later expansion of agricultural practice
→	primary routes for diffusion of agriculture
→	subsequent routes for diffusion of agriculture

Domestication of plants and animals

○	beans	🎃	pumpkin
🦃	turkey	○	squash
⌀	chilli pepper	✳	sunflower
⚘	tobacco	🐕	dog
◐	avocado	◊	bottle gourd
🌾	maize	⬭	peanut
⚘	cotton	○	sweet potato
⚘	amaranth	○	tomato

Symbols in red denote core areas of plant and animal domestication; symbols in green denote dispersal of domesticated plants and animals

---

Early human settlement of North and Central America

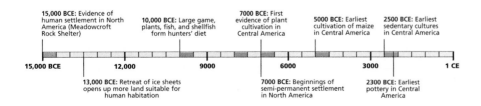

15,000 BCE: Evidence of human settlement in North America (Meadowcroft Rock Shelter)

10,000 BCE: Large game, plants, fish, and shellfish form hunters' diet

7000 BCE: First evidence of plant cultivation in Central America

5000 BCE: Earliest cultivation of maize in Central America

2500 BCE: Earliest sedentary cultures in Central America

| 15,000 BCE | 12,000 | 9000 | 6000 | 3000 | 1 CE |

13,000 BCE: Retreat of ice sheets opens up more land suitable for human habitation

7000 BCE: Beginnings of semi-permanent settlement in North America

2300 BCE: Earliest pottery in Central America

Greenland

ARCTIC

Great Slave Lake

Lake Athabasca

Hudson Bay

ARCTIC

60°

40°

SUBARCTIC

NORTH AMERICA

Lake Superior

GREAT PLAINS

Lake Michigan

Lake Huron

Lake Ontario

Lake Erie

Missouri

Meadowcroft Rock Shelter
c.15,000 BCE

NORTHEAST

40°

Koster
c.6000–8000 BCE

Ohio

Russell Cave
c.7000–8000 BCE

Stallings Island
2500 BCE: Earliest pottery in North America

Appalachian Mountains

Red River

REAT
ASIN

Watson Brake Mounds
c.3500 BCE

SOUTHEAST

Rio Grande

500 km

500 miles

Rocky Mountains

SOUTHWEST

Gulf of Mexico

ATLANTIC OCEAN

Lower California

Ocampo

Armadillo

Cueva Humida

Cuba

Hispaniola

20°

20°

PACIFIC OCEAN

100°

Coxcatlan Cave

CIRCUM-CARIBBEAN

60°

Yanhuitlan

MESOAMERICA

Santa Marta

Comitan

Caribbean Sea

Islona de Chantuto

El Chayal

Isthmus of Panama

60°

SOUTH
AMERICA

Equator

80°

Scale varies with perspective

8900 km (5550 miles)

12,070 km (7530 miles)

EARLY PEOPLES OF SOUTH AMERICA

SOUTH AMERICA was settled from the north, possibly more than 13,000 years ago. By 10,000 BCE, hunter-gatherers had colonized the entire subcontinent. Cereal and root cultivation developed before 3000 BCE. Successful agriculture led to growing populations and increasingly stratified societies. By 1800 BCE, large temples appeared on the Peruvian coast, and a distinctive religious iconography spread from Chavín de Huantar after 900 BCE.

How did the environment of South America affect the spread of agriculture?

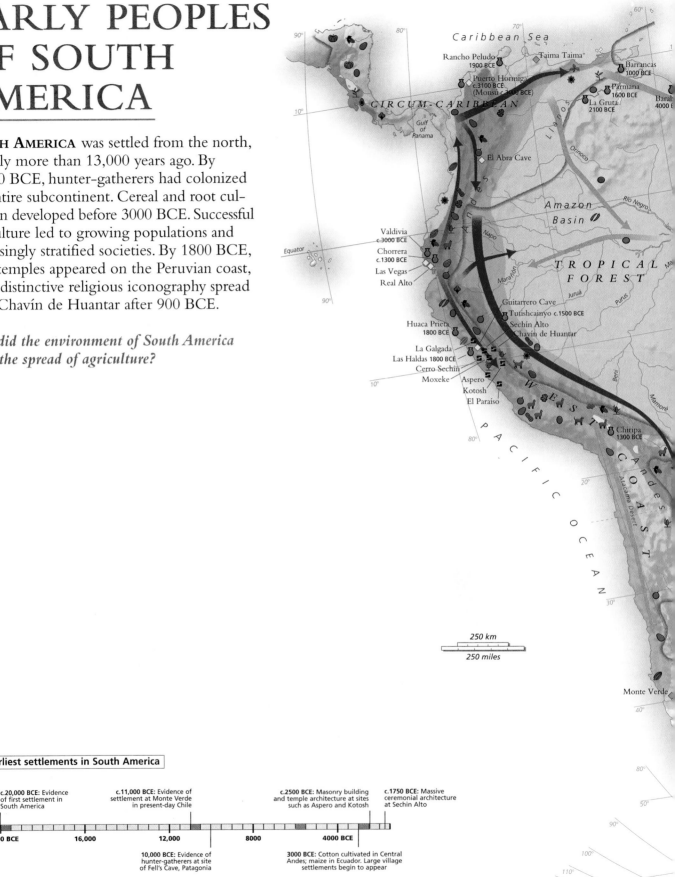

Earliest settlements in South America

c.20,000 BCE: Evidence of first settlement in South America

c.11,000 BCE: Evidence of settlement at Monte Verde in present-day Chile

c.2500 BCE: Masonry building and temple architecture at sites such as Aspero and Kotosh

c.1750 BCE: Massive ceremonial architecture at Sechín Alto

| 20,000 BCE | 16,000 | 12,000 | 8000 | 4000 BCE |

10,000 BCE: Evidence of hunter-gatherers at site of Fell's Cave, Patagonia

3000 BCE: Cotton cultivated in Central Andes; maize in Ecuador. Large village settlements begin to appear

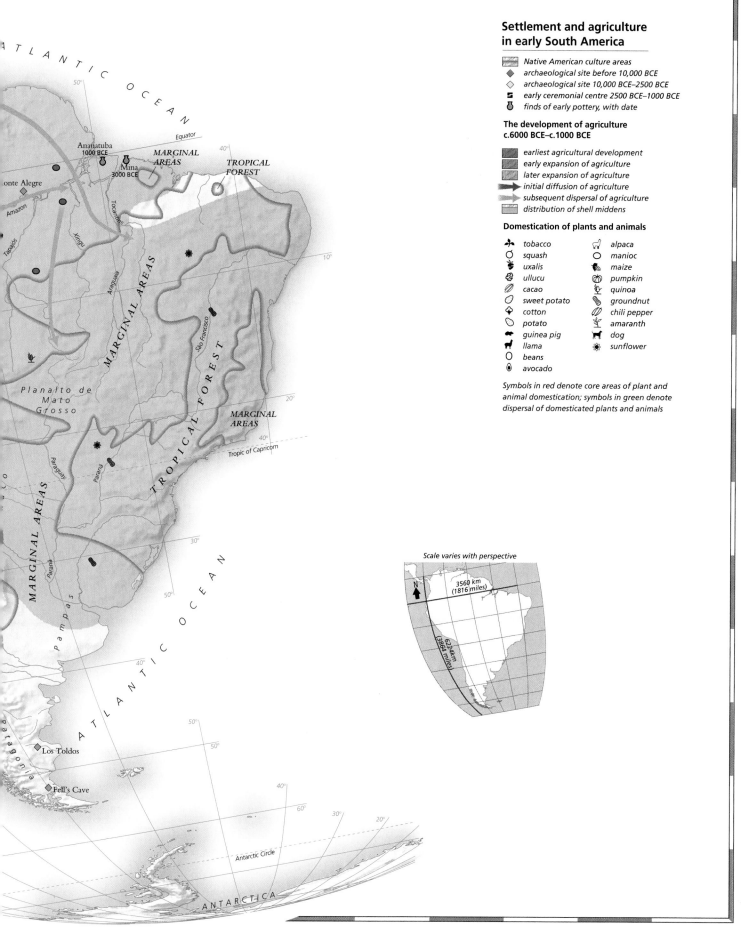

Settlement and agriculture in early South America

- ▨ Native American culture areas
- ◆ archaeological site before 10,000 BCE
- ◇ archaeological site 10,000 BCE–2500 BCE
- ⌇ early ceremonial centre 2500 BCE–1000 BCE
- ⚱ finds of early pottery, with date

The development of agriculture c.6000 BCE–c.1000 BCE

- ■ earliest agricultural development
- ▨ early expansion of agriculture
- ▨ later expansion of agriculture
- ➡ initial diffusion of agriculture
- ⇨ subsequent dispersal of agriculture
- ▨ distribution of shell middens

Domestication of plants and animals

☘ tobacco		⬛ alpaca	
○ squash		○ manioc	
⚘ uxalis		🐗 maize	
◉ ullucu		🍎 pumpkin	
⬭ cacao		⚘ quinoa	
○ sweet potato		⬮ groundnut	
♤ cotton		⬯ chili pepper	
○ potato		⚘ amaranth	
🐖 guinea pig		🐕 dog	
🐐 llama		✻ sunflower	
○ beans			
◉ avocado			

Symbols in red denote core areas of plant and animal domestication; symbols in green denote dispersal of domesticated plants and animals

Map labels

ATLANTIC OCEAN

Equator

Anatuba 1000 BCE

MARGINAL AREAS

TROPICAL FOREST

Mina 3000 BCE

Monte Alegre

Amazon

Tapajós

Xingu

Tocantins

Araguaia

MARGINAL AREAS

São Francisco

TROPICAL FOREST

Planalto de Mato Grosso

Paraguay

Paraná

MARGINAL AREAS

MARGINAL AREAS

Tropic of Capricorn

Paraná

Pampas

ATLANTIC OCEAN

Patagonia

◇ Los Toldos

◇ Fell's Cave

ATLANTIC OCEAN

Antarctic Circle

ANTARCTICA

Scale varies with perspective

N

3560 km (1816 miles)

6224 km (3864 miles)

THE WORLD: 10,000–5000 BCE

By 7000 BCE, farming was the main means of subsistence in West Asia, although hunter-gathering remained the most common form of subsistence elsewhere. Over the next 5,000 years farming became established independently in other areas.

What were the reasons for the transition from hunting and gathering to agriculture?

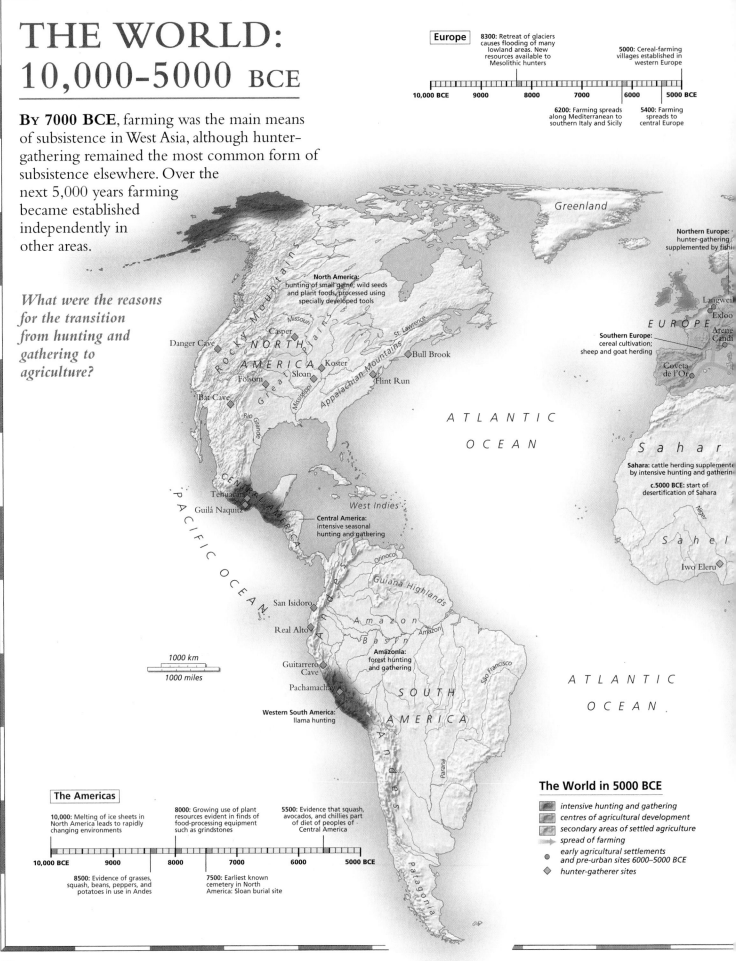

Europe

8300: Retreat of glaciers causes flooding of many lowland areas. New resources available to Mesolithic hunters

5000: Cereal-farming villages established in western Europe

10,000 BCE   9000   8000   7000   6000   5000 BCE

6200: Farming spreads along Mediterranean to southern Italy and Sicily

5400: Farming spreads to central Europe

Northern Europe: hunter-gathering supplemented by fishing

Southern Europe: cereal cultivation; sheep and goat herding

Langwei[?]
Exloo
Atene
Candi
Coveta de l'Or

EUROPE

Greenland

North America: hunting of small game; wild seeds and plant foods, processed using specially developed tools

Danger Cave
Casper
Folsom
Sloan
Koster
Bull Brook
Flint Run
Bat Cave

ROCKY Mountains
NORTH AMERICA
Great Plains
Missouri
St. Lawrence
Appalachian Mountains
Mississippi
Rio Grande

ATLANTIC OCEAN

Sahara
Sahel

Sahara: cattle herding supplemented by intensive hunting and gathering

c.5000 BCE: start of desertification of Sahara

Niger

Iwo Eleru

Central America: intensive seasonal hunting and gathering

Tehuacan
Guilá Naquitz
CENTRAL AMERICA
West Indies

PACIFIC OCEAN

San Isidoro
Real Alto
Guitarrero Cave
Pachamachay

Andes
Orinoco
Guiana Highlands
Amazon Basin
Amazon
São Francisco
SOUTH AMERICA
Paraná
Patagonia

Amazonia: forest hunting and gathering

Western South America: llama hunting

1000 km
1000 miles

ATLANTIC OCEAN

The Americas

10,000: Melting of ice sheets in North America leads to rapidly changing environments

8000: Growing use of plant resources evident in finds of food-processing equipment such as grindstones

5500: Evidence that squash, avocados, and chillies part of diet of peoples of Central America

10,000 BCE   9000   8000   7000   6000   5000 BCE

8500: Evidence of grasses, squash, beans, peppers, and potatoes in use in Andes

7500: Earliest known cemetery in North America: Sloan burial site

The World in 5000 BCE

- intensive hunting and gathering
- centres of agricultural development
- secondary areas of settled agriculture
- spread of farming
- • early agricultural settlements and pre-urban sites 6000–5000 BCE
- ◆ hunter-gatherer sites

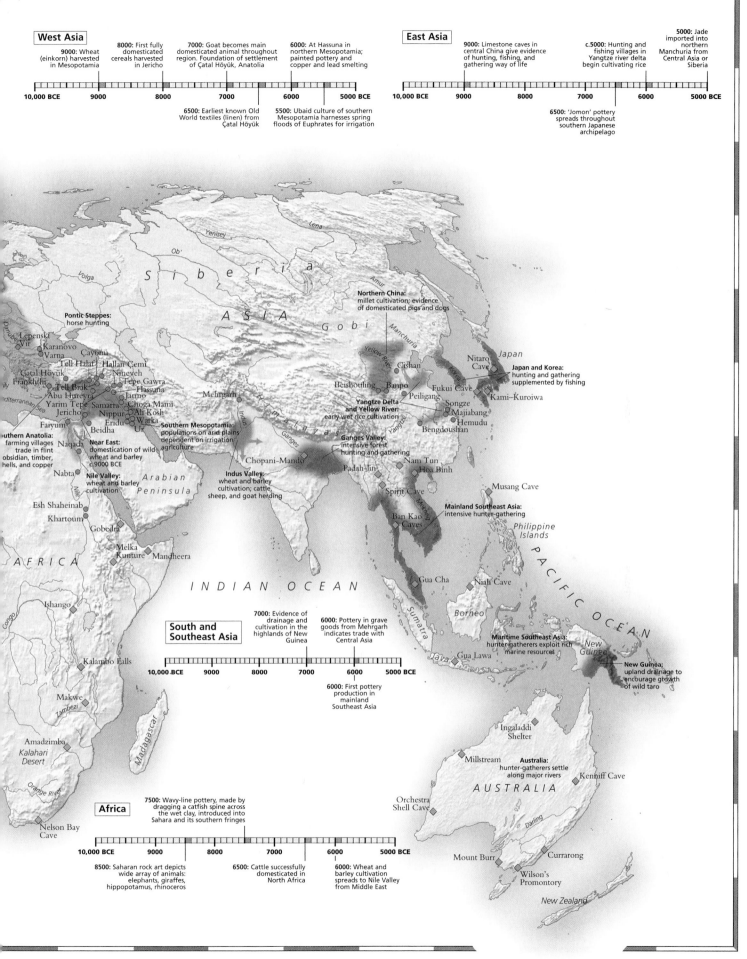

West Asia

9000: Wheat (einkorn) harvested in Mesopotamia

8000: First fully domesticated cereals harvested in Jericho

7000: Goat becomes main domesticated animal throughout region. Foundation of settlement of Çatal Höyük, Anatolia

6000: At Hassuna in northern Mesopotamia; painted pottery and copper and lead smelting

6500: Earliest known Old World textiles (linen) from Çatal Höyük

5500: Ubaid culture of southern Mesopotamia harnesses spring floods of Euphrates for irrigation

10,000 BCE — 9000 — 8000 — 7000 — 6000 — 5000 BCE

East Asia

9000: Limestone caves in central China give evidence of hunting, fishing, and gathering way of life

c.5000: Hunting and fishing villages in Yangtze river delta begin cultivating rice

5000: Jade imported into northern Manchuria from Central Asia or Siberia

6500: 'Jomon' pottery spreads throughout southern Japanese archipelago

10,000 BCE — 9000 — 8000 — 7000 — 6000 — 5000 BCE

Yenisei

Lena

Ob'

Volga

S i b e r i a

A S I A

Gobi

Amur

Manchuria

Yellow River

Japan

Korea

Pontic Steppes: horse hunting

Northern China: millet cultivation; evidence of domesticated pigs and dogs

Lepenski Vir
Karanovo
Varna
Çayönü
Tell Halaf
Hallan Çemi
Nineveh
Tepe Gawra
Abu Hureyra
Jarmo
Hassuna
Samarra
Choga Mami
Ali Kosh
Nippur
Eridu
Warka
Ur
Beidha
Jericho
Yarim Tepe
Çatal Höyük
Franchthi
Tell Brak
Faiyum
Naqada
Nabta

Mehrgarh

Cishan
Beishoutling
Banpo
Peiligang
Songze
Majiabang
Hemudu
Bengdoushan

Nitaro Cave
Fukui Cave
Kami-Kuroiwa

Japan and Korea: hunting and gathering supplemented by fishing

Yangtze Delta and Yellow River: early wet rice cultivation

Southern Anatolia: farming villages trade in flint, obsidian, timber, shells, and copper

Near East: domestication of wild wheat and barley c.9000 BCE

Southern Mesopotamia: populations on arid plains dependent on irrigation agriculture

Nile Valley: wheat and barley cultivation

Indus Valley: wheat and barley cultivation; cattle, sheep, and goat herding

Ganges Valley: intensive forest hunting and gathering

Chopani-Mando
Padah-lin
Nam Tun
Hoa Binh
Spirit Cave

Musang Cave

Mainland Southeast Asia: intensive hunter-gathering

Ban Kao Caves

Himalaya
Indus
Ganges
Yangtze
Mekong

Arabian Peninsula

Esh Shaheinab
Khartoum
Gobedra
Melka Kunture
Mandheera

AFRICA

Congo
Nile

Ishango

Kalambo Falls

Makwe
Zambezi

Amadzimba
Kalahari Desert

Orange River

Nelson Bay Cave

Madagascar

INDIAN OCEAN

South and Southeast Asia

7000: Evidence of drainage and cultivation in the highlands of New Guinea

6000: Pottery in grave goods from Mehrgarh indicates trade with Central Asia

10,000 BCE — 9000 — 8000 — 7000 — 6000 — 5000 BCE

6000: First pottery production in mainland Southeast Asia

Sumatra
Borneo
Java

Philippine Islands

PACIFIC OCEAN

Gua Cha
Niah Cave
Gua Lawa

Maritime Southeast Asia: hunter-gatherers exploit rich marine resources

New Guinea

New Guinea: upland drainage to encourage growth of wild taro

Ingaladdi Shelter
Millstream

Australia: hunter-gatherers settle along major rivers

Kenniff Cave

Orchestra Shell Cave

AUSTRALIA

Darling

Africa

7500: Wavy-line pottery, made by dragging a catfish spine across the wet clay, introduced into Sahara and its southern fringes

10,000 BCE — 9000 — 8000 — 7000 — 6000 — 5000 BCE

8500: Saharan rock art depicts wide array of animals: elephants, giraffes, hippopotamus, rhinoceros

6500: Cattle successfully domesticated in North Africa

6000: Wheat and barley cultivation spreads to Nile Valley from Middle East

Mount Burr
Currarong
Wilson's Promontory

New Zealand

17

THE ADVENT OF AGRICULTURE

THE APPEARANCE OF FARMING transformed the face of the
Earth. It was not merely a change in subsistence – it also
transformed the way in which our ancestors lived.
Agriculture, and the vastly greater crop yields it produced,
enabled large groups of people to live in permanent
villages, surrounded by material goods and equipment.
Specialized craftsmen produced these goods,
supported by the community as a whole –
the beginnings of social differentiation.

*What common features
characterize the areas
where agriculture
first appeared?*

The spread of agriculture

▨ areas of early
agriculture, with
dates of first
domestication of
plants and animals

➤ diffusion of
agricultural skills

Staple crops under cultivation by c.4000 BCE

🌿 wheat
🌿 barley
🌿 millet
🌽 maize
🌾 rice

Wild ancestors of domesticated animals

🐗 aurochs (wild cattle)
🐖 pig
🐑 sheep
🐐 ass
🐪 dromedary camel
🐎 horse
🐫 bactrian camel
🐃 gaur (wild ox)
🐂 buffalo
🐓 chicken
🐐 goat
🐂 yak
🦃 turkey
🦙 guanaco (llama)
🐹 guinea pig
🦙 alpaca
🐃 banteng

Greenland

Iceland

*Briti
Isle*

NORTH
AMERICA

Rocky Mountains

Great Plains

Missouri

Mississippi

Rio Grande

Great Lakes

St Lawrence

Appalachian Mountains

ATLANTIC

OCEAN

c.4500
BCE

Eastern North America:
sunflower
sumpweed
tepary bean

c.4750 BCE

Gulf of
Mexico

Caribbean Sea

Central America:
maize
sweet potato
manioc
squash
bottle gourd
tomato
avocado
cotton

PACIFIC

OCEAN

Orinoco

c.1000 BCE

Guiana Highlands

c.3000 BCE

Amazon

Amazon Basin

Andes

c.4500 BCE

SOUTH
AMERICA

São Francisco

South America:
manioc
potato
cotton
peanut
squash
bottle gourd
chilli pepper
lima bean

Paraná

Andes

ATLANTIC

OCEAN

Patagonia

1000 km

1000 miles

c.9000: Einkorn wheat grown in northern Syria: first evidence of true cultivation

c.7000: Farming in northern India; barley is main crop

c.6500: Farming spreads to Balkans from Near East

c.6000: Farming spreads to Nile Valley from Near East

c.4500: Cultivation of maize in eastern North America

c.4000: Plants domesticated in sub-Saharan Africa

9000 BCE 8000 7000 6000 5000 4000 BCE

c.8500: Rice domesticated in southern China

c.7750: Broomcorn and foxtail millets domesticated on North China Plain

c.6500: Cattle domesticated in Saharan region

c.4750: First evidence of plant and animal domestication in Central America

c.4500: Evidence of agriculture in south-central Andes

Northern Europe: oats, rye

Mediterranean: olive, grape, turnip, leek, plum, pear, cabbage, lettuce, rapeseed

Sahara: bones of domesticated cattle dating from c.6500 BCE found in areas which are now desert

Sub-Saharan Africa: yam, sorghum, millet, ensete, peas, black-eyed beans, okra

Central Asia: alfalfa, taro, carrot

Southwest Asia: wheat, barley, pea, lentil, onion, date palm

Indus Valley: cotton

Northern China: millet, soyabean, buckwheat, barley, adzuki bean, peach, cucumber, rapeseed

Southeast Asia: rice, taro, sago palm, orange, lemon, banana, coconut, breadfruit, sugar cane

c.3500 BCE, c.4200 BCE, 3500 BCE, c.5000 BCE, c.7000 BCE, 5000 BCE, c.6000 BCE, c.6000 BCE, c.9000 BCE, c.4500 BCE, c.6000 BCE, c.4500 BCE, c.6000 BCE, c.8500 BCE, c.7750 BCE, c.500 BCE, c.2500 BCE, c.2500 BCE, c.1000 BCE, c.1000 AD, c.4000 BCE

EUROPE · ASIA · AFRICA · AUSTRALIA

Siberia · Gobi · Arabian Peninsula · Kalahari Desert

Scandinavia · Japan · East China Sea · Philippine Islands · South China Sea · New Guinea · Borneo · Sumatra · Java · Madagascar · New Zealand

Black Sea · Caspian Sea · Mediterranean Sea · Red Sea · Arabian Sea · Bay of Bengal · INDIAN OCEAN · PACIFIC OCEAN

Rhine · Danube · Volga · Euphrates · Tigris · Nile · Niger · Congo · Zambezi · Orange River · Ob' · Yenisey · Lena · Amur · Yellow River · Yangtze · Indus · Ganges · Mekong · Darling

c.10,5000: Earliest pottery in the world, from southern Japan

9000: Earliest Chinese pottery

7000: First pottery in the Near East

7000: Foundation of Çatal Höyük, Anatolia, the largest neolithic site in the Near East

6500: Small-scale copper smelting at Çatal Höyük

5500: World's earliest irrigation system, at Choga Mami, Mesopotamia

5000: Gold and copper metallurgy in the Balkans

10,000 BCE 9000 8000 7000 6000 5000 BCE

c.8500: Saharan rock art depicts wild animals, long since extinct in the region

c.7500: Characteristic 'wavy line' pottery of the Sahara is produced

6500: Linen from Çatal Höyük is earliest known textile in the world

6000: Pottery produced at Mehrgarh, Central Asia; First pottery in mainland Southeast Asia

5200: Bandkeramik pottery produced by farmers of central Europe

THE WORLD: 5000–2500 BCE

THE FERTILE VALLEYS of the Nile, Tigris, Euphrates, Indus, and Yellow rivers were able to support very large populations, and it was here that the great urban civilizations of the ancient world emerged. Urban societies were hierarchical, with complex labor divisions. They were administered, economically and spiritually, by an elite literate class, and in some cases, were subject to a divine monarch. Monuments came to symbolize and represent the powers of the ruling elite.

Why did urban civilizations develop in some regions and not in others?

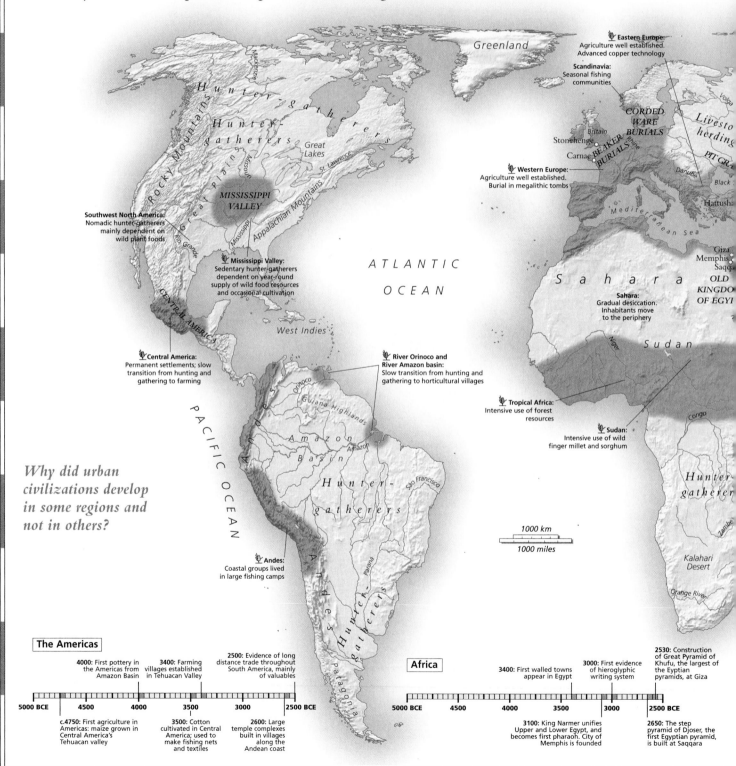

Eastern Europe: Agriculture well established. Advanced copper technology

Scandinavia: Seasonal fishing communities

Western Europe: Agriculture well established. Burial in megalithic tombs

Southwest North America: Nomadic hunter-gatherers mainly dependent on wild plant foods

Mississippi Valley: Sedentary hunter-gatherers dependent on year-round supply of wild food resources and occasional cultivation

Central America: Permanent settlements; slow transition from hunting and gathering to farming

River Orinoco and River Amazon basin: Slow transition from hunting and gathering to horticultural villages

Sahara: Gradual desiccation. Inhabitants move to the periphery

Tropical Africa: Intensive use of forest resources

Sudan: Intensive use of wild finger millet and sorghum

Andes: Coastal groups lived in large fishing camps

1000 km
1000 miles

The Americas

4000: First pottery in the Americas from Amazon Basin

3400: Farming villages established in Tehuacan Valley

2500: Evidence of long distance trade throughout South America, mainly of valuables

| 5000 BCE | 4500 | 4000 | 3500 | 3000 | 2500 BCE |

c.4750: First agriculture in Americas: maize grown in Central America's Tehuacan valley

3500: Cotton cultivated in Central America; used to make fishing nets and textiles

2600: Large temple complexes built in villages along the Andean coast

Africa

3400: First walled towns appear in Egypt

3000: First evidence of hieroglyphic writing system

2530: Construction of Great Pyramid of Khufu, the largest of the Eyptian pyramids, at Giza

| 5000 BCE | 4500 | 4000 | 3500 | 3000 | 2500 BCE |

3100: King Narmer unifies Upper and Lower Egypt, and becomes first pharaoh. City of Memphis is founded

2650: The step pyramid of Djoser, the first Egyptian pyramid, is built at Saqqara

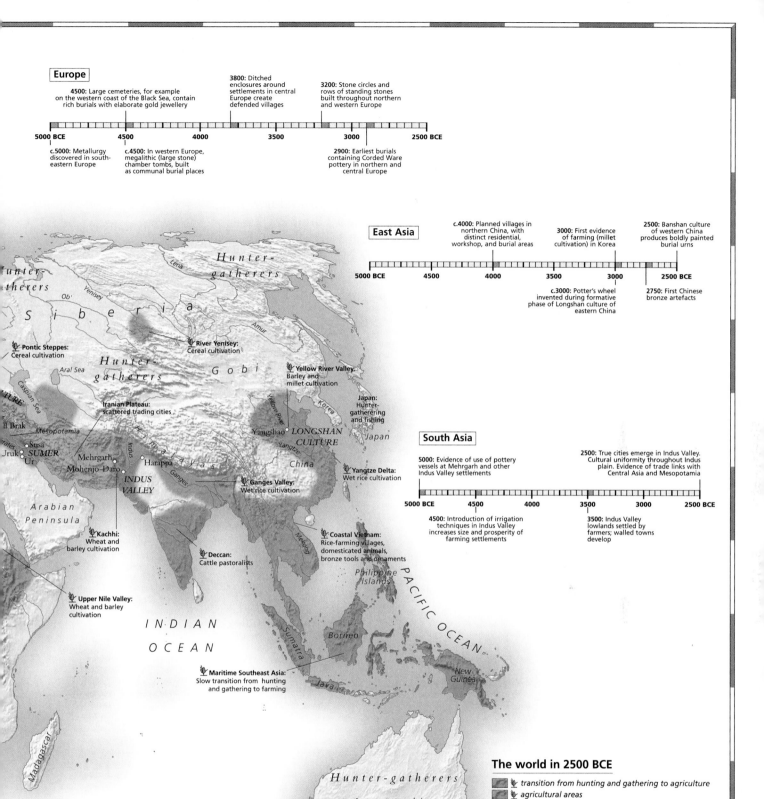

Europe

4500: Large cemeteries, for example on the western coast of the Black Sea, contain rich burials with elaborate gold jewellery

3800: Ditched enclosures around settlements in central Europe create defended villages

3200: Stone circles and rows of standing stones built throughout northern and western Europe

| 5000 BCE | 4500 | 4000 | 3500 | 3000 | 2500 BCE |

c.5000: Metallurgy discovered in south-eastern Europe

c.4500: In western Europe, megalithic (large stone) chamber tombs, built as communal burial places

2900: Earliest burials containing Corded Ware pottery in northern and central Europe

East Asia

c.4000: Planned villages in northern China, with distinct residential, workshop, and burial areas

3000: First evidence of farming (millet cultivation) in Korea

2500: Banshan culture of western China produces boldly painted burial urns

| 5000 BCE | 4500 | 4000 | 3500 | 3000 | 2500 BCE |

c.3000: Potter's wheel invented during formative phase of Longshan culture of eastern China

2750: First Chinese bronze artefacts

South Asia

5000: Evidence of use of pottery vessels at Mehrgarh and other Indus Valley settlements

2500: True cities emerge in Indus Valley. Cultural uniformity throughout Indus plain. Evidence of trade links with Central Asia and Mesopotamia

| 5000 BCE | 4500 | 4000 | 3500 | 3000 | 2500 BCE |

4500: Introduction of irrigation techniques in Indus Valley increases size and prosperity of farming settlements

3500: Indus Valley lowlands settled by farmers; walled towns develop

West Asia

c.3250: Pictographic clay tablets from Tell Brak: earliest evidence of writing

2500: City-states present throughout Mesopotamia and Levant

| 5000 BCE | 4500 | 4000 | 3500 | 3000 | 2500 BCE |

3500: Emergence of Uruk, the first city-state

2500: Rich array of grave goods at Royal Graves at Ur indicate extensive trade links

Map labels:
Hunter-gatherers
Siberia
Lena
Ob'
Yenisey
Amur
Hunter-gatherers
Gobi
Aral Sea
Caspian Sea
Iranian Plateau: scattered trading cities
Pontic Steppes: Cereal cultivation
River Yenisey: Cereal cultivation
Yellow River Valley: Barley and millet cultivation
Yellow River
Korea
Japan: Hunter-gathering and fishing
Japan
Yangtze
Yangshao
LONGSHAN CULTURE
China
Mesopotamia
Il Brak
Euphrates
Susa
Uruk
SUMER
Ur
Mehrgarh
Mohenjo-Daro
Harappa
Indus
INDUS VALLEY
Ganges
Himalayas
Ganges Valley: Wet rice cultivation
Yangtze Delta: Wet rice cultivation
Arabian Peninsula
Kachhi: Wheat and barley cultivation
Deccan: Cattle pastoralists
Coastal Vietnam: Rice-farming villages, domesticated animals, bronze tools and ornaments
Mekong
Philippine Islands
PACIFIC OCEAN
Upper Nile Valley: Wheat and barley cultivation
INDIAN OCEAN
Sumatra
Borneo
New Guinea
Madagascar
Maritime Southeast Asia: Slow transition from hunting and gathering to farming
Java
Hunter-gatherers Australia
Darling
New Zealand

The world in 2500 BCE

- transition from hunting and gathering to agriculture
- agricultural areas
- urban areas
- urban hinterland

21

THE FIRST EAST ASIAN CIVILIZATIONS

THE EMERGENCE OF ORGANIZED CULTURES in East Asia took a variety of forms. The fertile soils of the Yellow River basin and the Yangtze valley provided the potential for the development of the first agricultural communities in the region 8000 years ago. Pottery working with kilns and bronze technology developed, accompanied by the first Chinese states and empires; the region remains to this day the heartland of China's culture and population. In Japan, the abundance of natural resources, especially fish and seafood, meant that hunter-gathering persisted, alongside features normally associated with sedentary agriculture – the world's earliest pottery is found here. Across the steppe grasslands of Central Asia, communities developed a mobile culture now revealed through elaborate burials and decorated grave goods.

Ural Mountains

Yenisey

Kokshetau   Petropavlovsk

Karaganda

S t e p p e s

Tomsk

Lake Balkhash

Barnaul

Siberia

Kuratoy   Orak   Chernovaya

Biysk

Kara-Ukok   Okunev   Karasuk   Andronovo

Aleksandrovka   Sukhoye   Angara

Ozero

Altai Mountains

Tien Shan

Zhigalovo

Takla Makan Desert

Irkutsk   Lake Baikal

Altun Shan

Lop Nor

Gobi

Indus

Qilian Shan

Himalayas

Plateau of Tibet

Yellow River   Ordos Desert

c.9000 BCE: earliest Chinese pottery

Amur

Sungari

Manchuria

Dadiwan   Majiayao

Banshan

Ganges

Brahmaputra

Banpo   Cishan

Jiangzhai   Hougang   Bo Hai

Erlitou   Dawenkou

Yangshaocun   Dahecun

Peiligang

India

Yangtze   China

Huai He

c.6000 BCE: cultivation of rice in Yangtze valley

Korea   c.6000 BCE: earliest pottery in Korea

Sea of Japan

Amsa-dong   c.10 500 BCE: earliest known pottery in Japan

Honshu

Zengpiyan   Liangzhu

Yellow Sea

Bay of Bengal

Xianréndong   Majiabang   Senpukuji   Fudodo   Umatak

Hemudu   Fukui Cave   Togariishi

Baozitou   Kami-Kuroiwa   Idojiri

Southeast Asia

East China Sea

Shikoku   Japan

Kyushu

Ryukyu Islands

Taiwan

Hainan

Tropic Of Cancer

Mekong

South China Sea

Malay Peninsula

INDIAN OCEAN

What role did rice cultivation play in early East Asian civilizations?

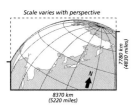

Scale varies with perspective

7780 km
(4830 miles)

8370 km
(5220 miles)

N

The agricultural revolution 6000–2000 BCE

 distribution of Yellow River loess soils

 northern limit of wild rice distribution

 spread of rice cultivation

 area of early wet rice cultivation

 area of early millet cultivation

● early farming site

● Japanese hunter-gatherer site

◆ pottery site before 10,000 BCE

◆ pottery site before 8000 BCE

◇ pottery site before 6000 BCE

● steppe site c.4500–2000 BCE

○ steppe site c.2000–1000 BCE

Domesticated plants and animals

◯	rapeseed		coconut
◉	soybean		breadfruit
◉	adzuki bean		tea
✺	cucumber		sago palm
✿	ginger		sugar cane
◗	taro		jute
◕	arrowroot		nutmeg
✾	turnip		buffalo
◯	lemon		banteng
◔	peach		yak
◖	grapefruit		pig
✇	banana		

Lena

ARCTIC OCEAN

80°

Indigirka

Arctic Circle

60°

180°

Kamchatka

Sea of
Okhotsk

Sakhalin

160°

Kurile Islands

kkaido

PACIFIC OCEAN

40°

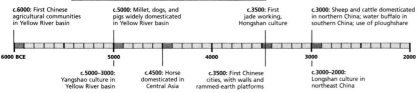

Early technology and agriculture in East Asia

c.6000: First Chinese agricultural communities in Yellow River basin

c.5000: Millet, dogs, and pigs widely domesticated in Yellow River basin

c.3500: First jade working, Hongshan culture

c.3000: Sheep and cattle domesticated in northern China; water buffalo in southern China; use of ploughshare

6000 BCE   5000   4000   3000   2000

c.5000–3000: Yangshao culture in Yellow River basin

c.4500: Horse domesticated in Central Asia

c.3500: First Chinese cities, with walls and rammed-earth platforms

c.3000–2000: Longshan culture in northeast China

POLYNESIAN MIGRATIONS

THE FIRST WAVE OF COLONIZATION of the Pacific, between 2000 and 1500 BCE, took settlers from New Guinea and neighbouring islands as far as the Fiji Islands. From there, they sailed on to Tonga and Samoa. In about 200 BCE, the Polynesians embarked on a series of far longer voyages, crossing vast tracts of empty ocean to settle the Marquesas, the Society Islands, Hawaii, Rapa Nui (Easter Island), and New Zealand.

How were the Polynesians able to migrate without the aid of modern technology?

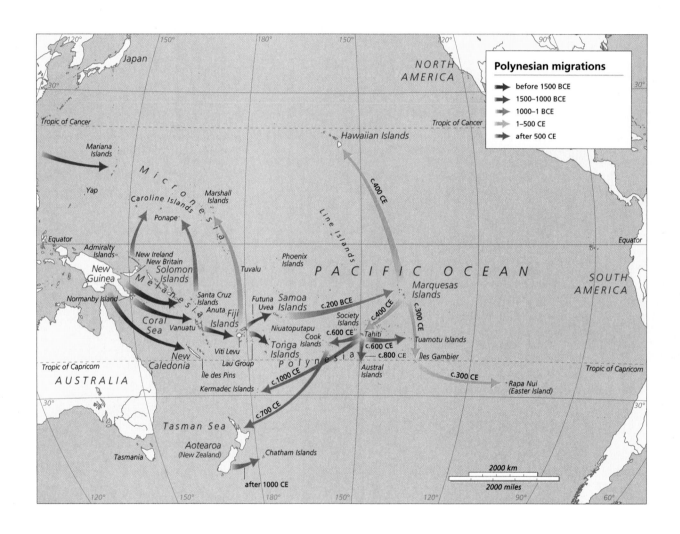

Polynesian migrations

→ before 1500 BCE
→ 1500–1000 BCE
→ 1000–1 BCE
→ 1–500 CE
→ after 500 CE

Polynesian voyages 1500 BCE–1000 CE

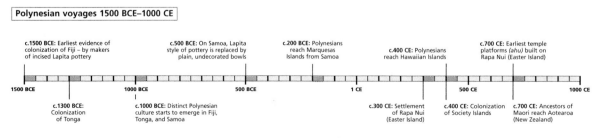

c.1500 BCE: Earliest evidence of colonization of Fiji – by makers of incised Lapita pottery

c.500 BCE: On Samoa, Lapita style of pottery is replaced by plain, undecorated bowls

c.200 BCE: Polynesians reach Marquesas Islands from Samoa

c.400 CE: Polynesians reach Hawaiian Islands

c.700 CE: Earliest temple platforms (*ahu*) built on Rapa Nui (Easter Island)

c.1300 BCE: Colonization of Tonga

c.1000 BCE: Distinct Polynesian culture starts to emerge in Fiji, Tonga, and Samoa

c.300 CE: Settlement of Rapa Nui (Easter Island)

c.400 CE: Colonization of Society Islands

c.700 CE: Ancestors of Maori reach Aotearoa (New Zealand)

1500 BCE — 1000 BCE — 500 BCE — 1 CE — 500 CE — 1000 CE

THE FERTILE CRESCENT

THE "FERTILE CRESCENT" is traditionally seen as the cradle of civilization. Here the first farming settlements were established, expanding into fortified walled towns. By 3500 BCE the first city-states, centers of population and trade, had grown up in Mesopotamia. Each had at its heart a mud-brick temple raised on a high platform. These structures later became ziggurats.

How was irrigation central to the development of civilization in the Fertile Crescent?

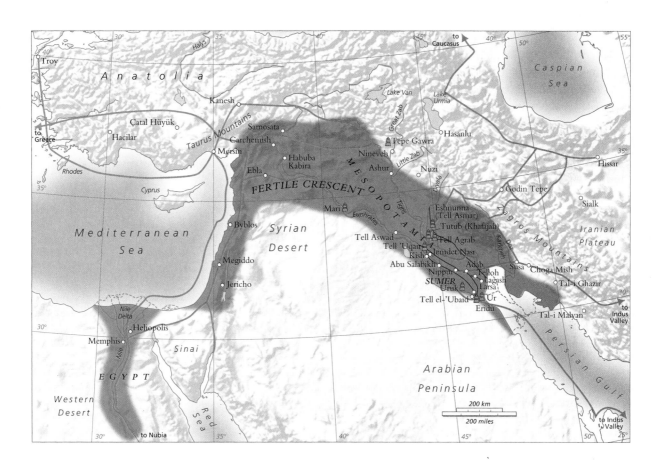

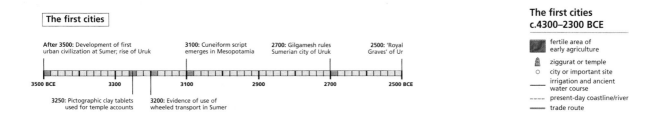

The first cities

After 3500: Development of first urban civilization at Sumer; rise of Uruk

3100: Cuneiform script emerges in Mesopotamia

2700: Gilgamesh rules Sumerian city of Uruk

2500: 'Royal Graves' of Ur

3500 BCE — 3300 — 3100 — 2900 — 2700 — 2500 BCE

3250: Pictographic clay tablets used for temple accounts

3200: Evidence of use of wheeled transport in Sumer

The first cities
c.4300–2300 BCE

- fertile area of early agriculture
- ziggurat or temple
- ○ city or important site
- irrigation and ancient water course
- ---- present-day coastline/river
- trade route

URBAN CENTERS
AND TRADE ROUTES

BY 2500 BCE cities were established in three major centers: the Nile Valley, Mesopotamia, and the Indus Valley, with a scattering of other cities across the intervening terrain. The culmination of a long process of settlement and expansion – some early cities had populations tens of thousands strong – the first urban civilizations all relied on rich agricultural lands to support their growth. In each case, lack of the most important natural resources – timber, metal, and stone – forced these urban civilizations to establish trading networks which ultimately extended from the Hindu Kush to the Mediterranean.

What is the impact of trade on the development of cities and civilizations?

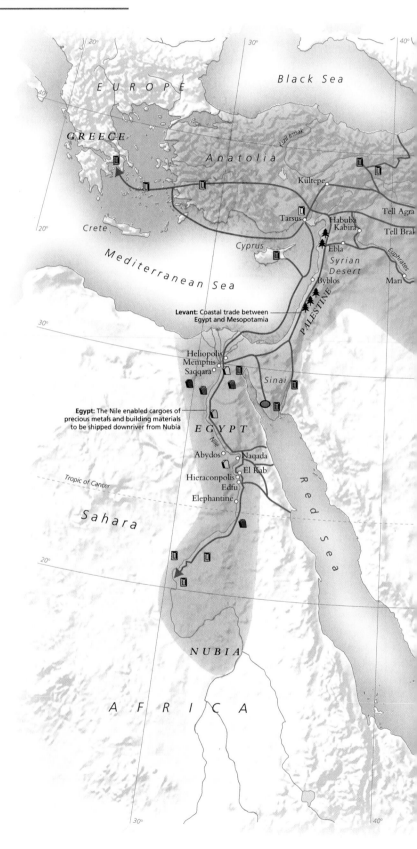

Levant: Coastal trade between Egypt and Mesopotamia

Egypt: The Nile enabled cargoes of precious metals and building materials to be shipped downriver from Nubia

250 km

250 miles

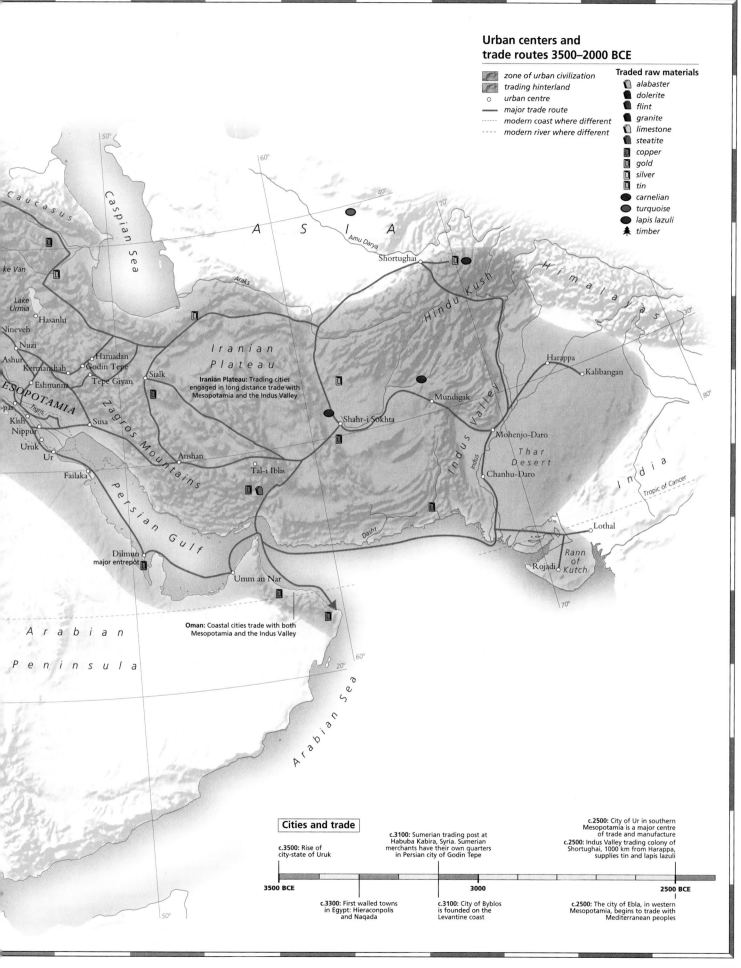

Urban centers and trade routes 3500–2000 BCE

Traded raw materials

- zone of urban civilization
- trading hinterland
- ○ urban centre
- major trade route
- modern coast where different
- modern river where different

- alabaster
- dolerite
- flint
- granite
- limestone
- steatite
- copper
- gold
- silver
- tin
- carnelian
- turquoise
- lapis lazuli
- timber

Caucasus

Caspian Sea

ke Van

Lake Urmia

Hasanlu

Nineveh

Nuzi

Ashur

Kermanshah

Hamadan

Godin Tepe

Tepe Giyan

Eshnunna

ESOPOTAMIA

Sialk

par

Kish

Nippur

Uruk

Ur

Failaka

Tigris

Susa

Anshan

Zagros Mountains

Persian Gulf

Dilmun
major entrepôt

Umm an Nar

Oman: Coastal cities trade with both Mesopotamia and the Indus Valley

Arabian Peninsula

A S I A

Amu Darya

Araks

Iranian Plateau

Iranian Plateau: Trading cities engaged in long distance trade with Mesopotamia and the Indus Valley

Tal-i Iblis

Dasht

Shahr-i Sokhta

Shortughai

Hindu Kush

Himalayas

Mundigak

Indus Valley

Indus

Harappa

Kalibangan

Mohenjo-Daro

Thar Desert

Chanhu-Daro

Tropic of Cancer

Lothal

Rann of Kutch

Rojadi

India

Arabian Sea

Cities and trade

c.3500: Rise of city-state of Uruk

c.3100: Sumerian trading post at Habuba Kabira, Syria. Sumerian merchants have their own quarters in Persian city of Godin Tepe

c.2500: City of Ur in southern Mesopotamia is a major centre of trade and manufacture

c.2500: Indus Valley trading colony of Shortughai, 1000 km from Harappa, supplies tin and lapis lazuli

3500 BCE	3000	2500 BCE

c.3300: First walled towns in Egypt: Hieraconpolis and Naqada

c.3100: City of Byblos is founded on the Levantine coast

c.2500: The city of Ebla, in western Mesopotamia, begins to trade with Mediterranean peoples

27

THE FIRST EMPIRES

IN ABOUT 2300 BCE, Akkadian King Sargon I came to power at Kish. Subsequently, he conquered the independent city-states of the south, and created an empire by conquering Elam and parts of Syria and Anatolia. However, Sargon's empire soon collapsed. Ur became the dominant power, to be replaced by the Babylonian empire of Hammurabi c. 2004 BCE. The Hittites rose to prominence in Anatolia after 1650 BCE, extending their empire into Syria and competing with the Egyptians and Mitanni.

Why were the first empires of West Asia located in Mesopotamia and Anatolia?

The first empires ▶
c.2300–1750 BCE

- *Sumer during Early Dynastic period C.3000–2360*
- *Empire of Sargon I of Akkad c.2360–2230*
- *Ur III Empire c.2112–2004*
- *Kingdom of Shamshi-Adad c.1813-1781*
- *Babylonian Empire of Hammurabi c.1782–50*
- *migration of Semites*
- *campaigns of Sargon*
- *campaigns of Naram Sin c.2330-2270*
- *invasion by Gutians*
- *present day coastline/river*

Black Sea
Hattians
Halys
Hattushash
CAPPADOCIA
Gordium
Anatolia
Kanesh
Purush Khaddum
Taurus Mountains
Hacilar
Catal Höyük
Harran
Carchemish
Mersin
Tarsus
Karaman
Halab
Ebla
Ugarit
Cyprus
SYRIA
Palmyra
Mediterranean Sea
Syrian Desert
Byblos
Damascus
150 km
150 miles
Migration of Semites to Sumer
Dead Sea
35°
30°
40°

The first empires of West Asia

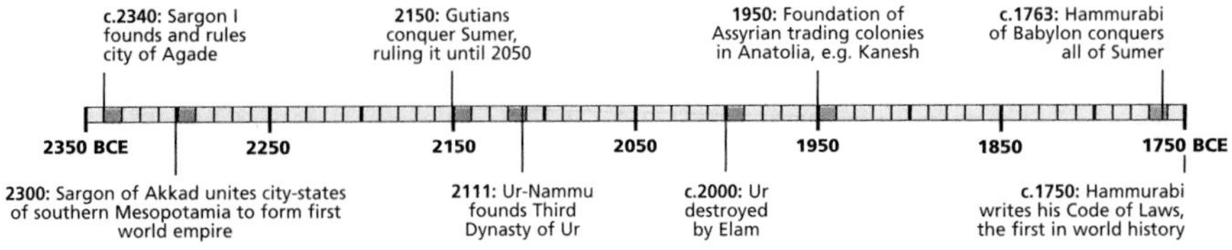
c.2340: Sargon I founds and rules city of Agade
2150: Gutians conquer Sumer, ruling it until 2050
1950: Foundation of Assyrian trading colonies in Anatolia, e.g. Kanesh
c.1763: Hammurabi of Babylon conquers all of Sumer
2350 BCE
2250
2150
2050
1950
1850
1750 BCE
2300: Sargon of Akkad unites city-states of southern Mesopotamia to form first world empire
2111: Ur-Nammu founds Third Dynasty of Ur
c.2000: Ur destroyed by Elam
c.1750: Hammurabi writes his Code of Laws, the first in world history

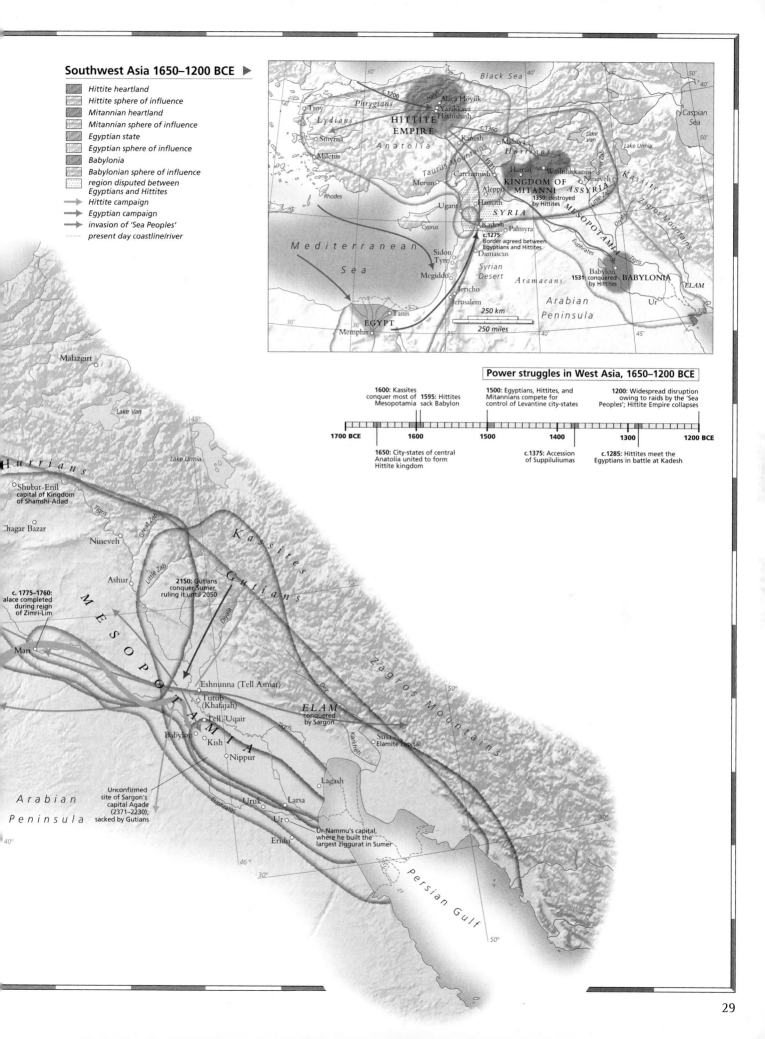

Southwest Asia 1650–1200 BCE ▶

- ▨ Hittite heartland
- ▨ Hittite sphere of influence
- ▨ Mitannian heartland
- ▨ Mitannian sphere of influence
- ▨ Egyptian state
- ▨ Egyptian sphere of influence
- ▨ Babylonia
- ▨ Babylonian sphere of influence
- ▨ region disputed between Egyptians and Hittites
- → Hittite campaign
- → Egyptian campaign
- → invasion of 'Sea Peoples'
- --- present day coastline/river

Black Sea

Troy
c.1200
Phrygians
Lydians
Hayaşa
Alaca Höyük
Yazılıkaya
Hattushash
Anatolia
HITTITE EMPIRE
c.1360
Kanesh
Lake Van
Lake Urmia
Caspian Sea
Smyrna
Miletus
Taurus Mountains
Malatya
Hurrians
Kassites
Mersin
Carchemish
Harran
Washshukanni
Nineveh
KINGDOM OF MITANNI
ASSYRIA
Rhodes
Aleppo
1350: destroyed by Hittites
MESOPOTAMIA
Zagros Mountains
Ugarit
Hamath
SYRIA
Little Zab
Great Zab
Cyprus
Kadesh
Palmyra
c.1275: Border agreed between Egyptians and Hittites
Euphrates
Tigris
Mediterranean Sea
Sidon
Tyre
Damascus
Syrian Desert
Aramaeans
1531: Babylon conquered by Hittites
Babylon
BABYLONIA
ELAM
Megiddo
Jericho
Jerusalem
Tanis
EGYPT
250 km
250 miles
Ur
Memphis

Power struggles in West Asia, 1650–1200 BCE

1600: Kassites conquer most of Mesopotamia
1595: Hittites sack Babylon
1500: Egyptians, Hittites, and Mitannians compete for control of Levantine city-states
1200: Widespread disruption owing to raids by the 'Sea Peoples'; Hittite Empire collapses

1700 BCE — 1600 — 1500 — 1400 — 1300 — 1200 BCE

1650: City-states of central Anatolia united to form Hittite kingdom
c.1375: Accession of Suppiluliumas
c.1285: Hittites meet the Egyptians in battle at Kadesh

Malazgirt

Lake Van

Lake Urmia

Hurrians

Shubat-Enil capital of Kingdom of Shamshi-Adad

Chagar Bazar

Tigris

Nineveh

Great Zab

Kassites

Ashur

Little Zab

Gutians

2150: Gutians conquer Sumer, ruling it until 2050

Diyala

c. 1775–1760: palace completed during reign of Zimri-Lim

MESOPOTAMIA

Mari

Eshnunna (Tell Asmar)

Tutub (Khafajah)

Tell Uqair

Zagros Mountains

Dez

Babylon

Kish

ELAM conquered by Sargon

Tigris

Karkheh

Susa Elamite capital

Nippur

Unconfirmed site of Sargon's capital Agade (2371–2230); sacked by Gutians

Arabian Peninsula

Lagash

Uruk

Larsa

Euphrates

Ur

Eridu

Ur-Nammu's capital, where he built the largest ziggurat in Sumer

Persian Gulf

THE GROWTH OF THE CITY

ALL CITIES THAT DEVELOPED during the two thousand years
after 3500 BCE symbolized a social chasm between the ruler
and the ruled, the sacred and the secular. The early expansion of
urban civilization in southern Mesopotamia created a swathe of
cities, from Ur to Mycenae, which thrived on trade and contact,
supplemented by taxes, tolls, and tributes. Major urban areas
flourished in southern and eastern Asia, and were
developing in the southeast.

*Where are most cities at
this time located?
Why?*

Lake Baikal

Russian steppes: Populated by
nomadic peoples, specializing in
horse-rearing, cattle and sheep
herding, supplemented by hunting

*Aral
Sea*

Amu Darya

Volga

EUROPE

Hindu Kush

Europe: Urbanism spreads
in early centuries CE with
Roman imperialism

Black Sea

Caucasus

*Caspian
Sea*

Elburz Mountains

Danube

c.750 BCE
Hattushash • Alaca Hüyük

Northern Greece
c.750 BCE • Troy
Acemhüyük • Kanesh

*Aegean
Sea* • Beycesultan • *Anatolia*
Italy
c.750 BCE • Athens • Karahüyük
Mycenae • • Tiryns • Miletus *Taurus Mountains*
Pylos •

Carchemish
• Tell Brak
Aleppo • *MESOPOTAMIA*
Ugarit • Mari
Byblos • Qadesh

Eshnunna
Tigris
Euphrates Kish
Babylon • Nippur
Uruk • Lagash
Larsa • Ur

Susa •
• Anshan

Persia
c.500 BCE

*Iranian
Plateau*

Shahr-i Sokhta •

*Zagros
Mountains*

Knossos • Mallia
Phaistos • Zakro

Hazor •
Lachish • Megiddo

*Syrian
Desert*

Mediterranean Sea

*Persian
Gulf*

Buto • Pi-Ramesse
Sais • Bubastis
Memphis • Heliopolis
El-Lisht •

*Arabian
Peninsula*

Phoenicia
c.750 BCE

El-Amarna •

EGYPT

Arabian Peninsula: Harsh
desert terrain is sparsely
populated by desert
pastoralists

Nile
Thebes • Luxor
Edfu •

Tropic of Cancer

*Red
Sea*

**Southern
Arabia**
c.500 BCE

1,000 km

1,000 miles

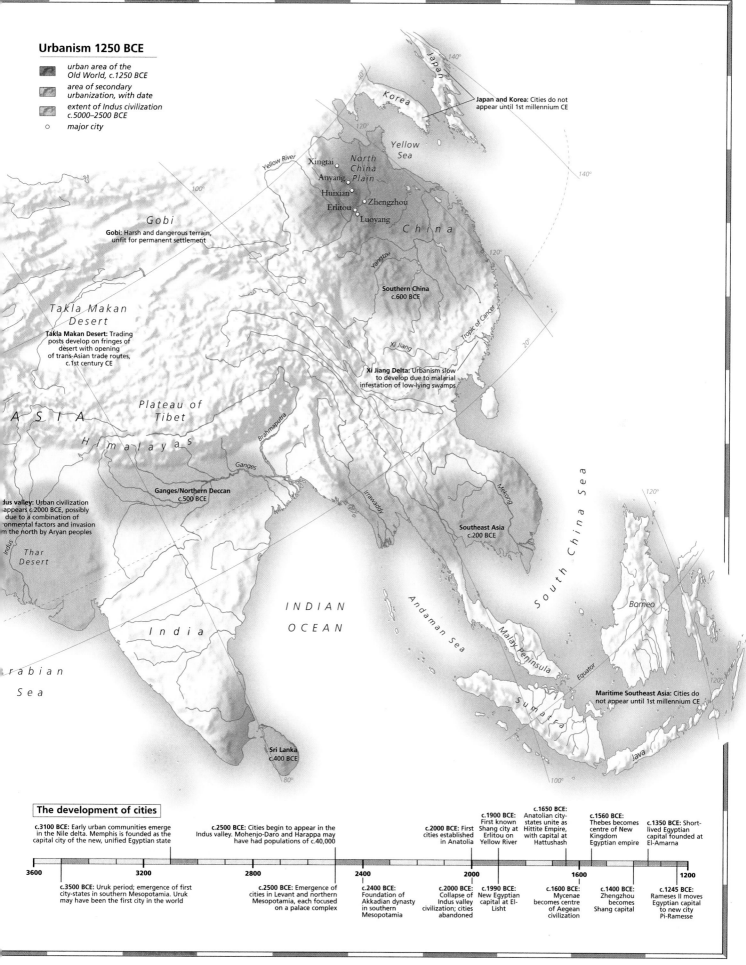

Urbanism 1250 BCE

- urban area of the Old World, c.1250 BCE
- area of secondary urbanization, with date
- extent of Indus civilization c.5000–2500 BCE
- ○ major city

Japan and Korea: Cities do not appear until 1st millennium CE

Gobi: Harsh and dangerous terrain, unfit for permanent settlement

Takla Makan Desert: Trading posts develop on fringes of desert with opening of trans-Asian trade routes, c.1st century CE

Xi Jiang Delta: Urbanism slow to develop due to malarial infestation of low-lying swamps

Indus valley: Urban civilization appears c.2000 BCE, possibly due to a combination of environmental factors and invasion from the north by Aryan peoples

Ganges/Northern Deccan c.500 BCE

Southern China c.600 BCE

Southeast Asia c.200 BCE

Maritime Southeast Asia: Cities do not appear until 1st millennium CE

Sri Lanka c.400 BCE

Xingtai
Anyang
Huixian
Erlitou
Zhengzhou
Luoyang

North China Plain

Gobi

Takla Makan Desert

Plateau of Tibet

Himalayas

Thar Desert

India

Yellow River

Yangtze

Xi Jiang

China

Korea

Japan

Yellow Sea

ASIA

Ganges

Brahmaputra

Irrawaddy

Mekong

Malay Peninsula

Andaman Sea

INDIAN OCEAN

Arabian Sea

South China Sea

Borneo

Sumatra

Java

Tropic of Cancer

Equator

The development of cities

c.3100 BCE: Early urban communities emerge in the Nile delta. Memphis is founded as the capital city of the new, unified Egyptian state

c.2500 BCE: Cities begin to appear in the Indus valley. Mohenjo-Daro and Harappa may have had populations of c.40,000

c.2000 BCE: First cities established in Anatolia

c.1900 BCE: First known Shang city at Erlitou on Yellow River

c.1650 BCE: Anatolian city-states unite as Hittite Empire, with capital at Hattushash

c.1560 BCE: Thebes becomes centre of New Kingdom Egyptian empire

c.1350 BCE: Short-lived Egyptian capital founded at El-Amarna

3600 3200 2800 2400 2000 1600 1200

c.3500 BCE: Uruk period; emergence of first city-states in southern Mesopotamia. Uruk may have been the first city in the world

c.2500 BCE: Emergence of cities in Levant and northern Mesopotamia, each focused on a palace complex

c.2400 BCE: Foundation of Akkadian dynasty in southern Mesopotamia

c.2000 BCE: Collapse of Indus valley civilization; cities abandoned

c.1990 BCE: New Egyptian capital at El-Lisht

c.1600 BCE: Mycenae becomes centre of Aegean civilization

c.1400 BCE: Zhengzhou becomes Shang capital

c.1245 BCE: Rameses II moves Egyptian capital to new city Pi-Ramesse

THE WORLD: 750-500 BCE

CIVILIZATIONS OF EURASIA now lay in a more or less continuous belt from the Mediterranean to China. Both trade and cultural contact were well-established; understanding of iron metallurgy had spread from the Middle East as far as China and sub-Saharan Africa, and by the 6th century BCE Chinese silk was beginning to appear in Europe. All these civilizations, however, were increasingly subjected to incursions by tribes of nomadic pastoralists who were rapidly spreading across Central Asia, eastern Europe, and Siberia.

What factors favored expansion of empires and states worldwide? What factors limited expansion?

Europe

700: Scythians from Central Asia begin to settle in eastern Europe and Black Sea area

600: Foundation of Greek colony of Massalia. Trade between Greeks and Celts

505: Establishment of democracy in Athens

| 750 BCE | 700 | 650 | 600 | 550 | 500 BCE |

750: First evidence of use of Greek alphabet

c.600: Defensive hill-top fortresses built throughout southern Germany and eastern France

510: Romans expel Etruscan overlords and establish a republic

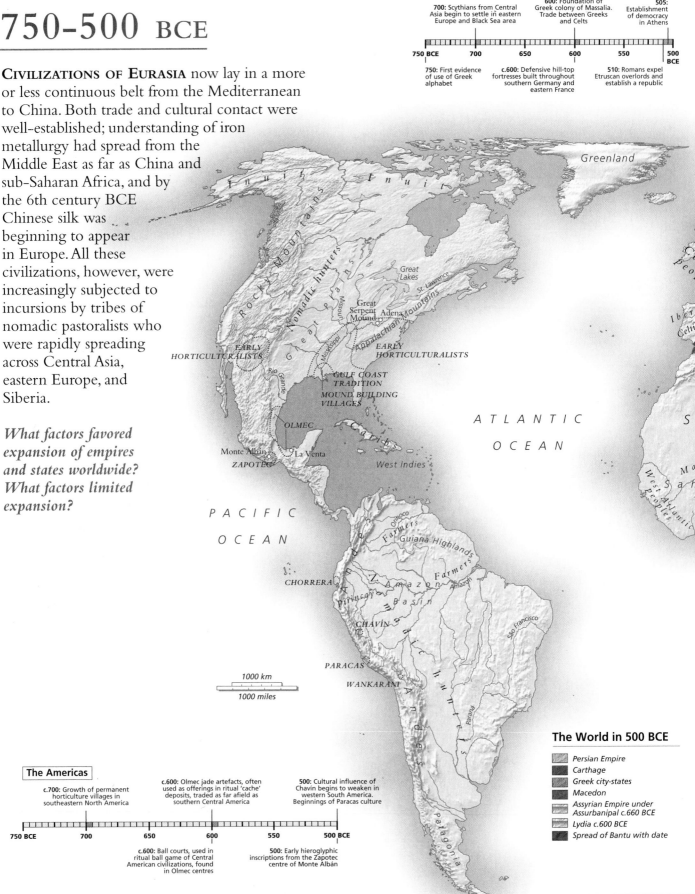

Greenland

Inuit   Inuit

Rocky Mountains

Nomadic hunters

Great Lakes   St. Lawrence

Great Plains

Missouri   Mississippi   Appalachian Mountains

Great Serpent Mound   Adena

EARLY HORTICULTURALISTS

EARLY HORTICULTURALISTS

Rio Grande

GULF COAST TRADITION
MOUND BUILDING VILLAGES

OLMEC

Caribbean

Monte Albán   La Venta
ZAPOTEC

West Indies

ATLANTIC OCEAN

Iberia
Celtiberi

Mande

West Saharan Peoples

PACIFIC OCEAN

Orinoco   Farmers
Guiana Highlands

CHORRERA
Amazon Basin   Farmers   Amazon

Pirincay   Nomadic hunters

CHAVÍN

São Francisco

Paraná

PARACAS
WANKARANI

Andes

Patagonia

1000 km
1000 miles

The World in 500 BCE

	Persian Empire
	Carthage
	Greek city-states
	Macedon
	Assyrian Empire under Assurbanipal c.660 BCE
	Lydia c.600 BCE
	Spread of Bantu with date

The Americas

c.700: Growth of permanent horticulture villages in southeastern North America

c.600: Olmec jade artefacts, often used as offerings in ritual 'cache' deposits, traded as far afield as southern Central America

500: Cultural influence of Chavín begins to weaken in western South America. Beginnings of Paracas culture

| 750 BCE | 700 | 650 | 600 | 550 | 500 BCE |

c.600: Ball courts, used in ritual ball game of Central American civilizations, found in Olmec centres

500: Early hieroglyphic inscriptions from the Zapotec centre of Monte Albán

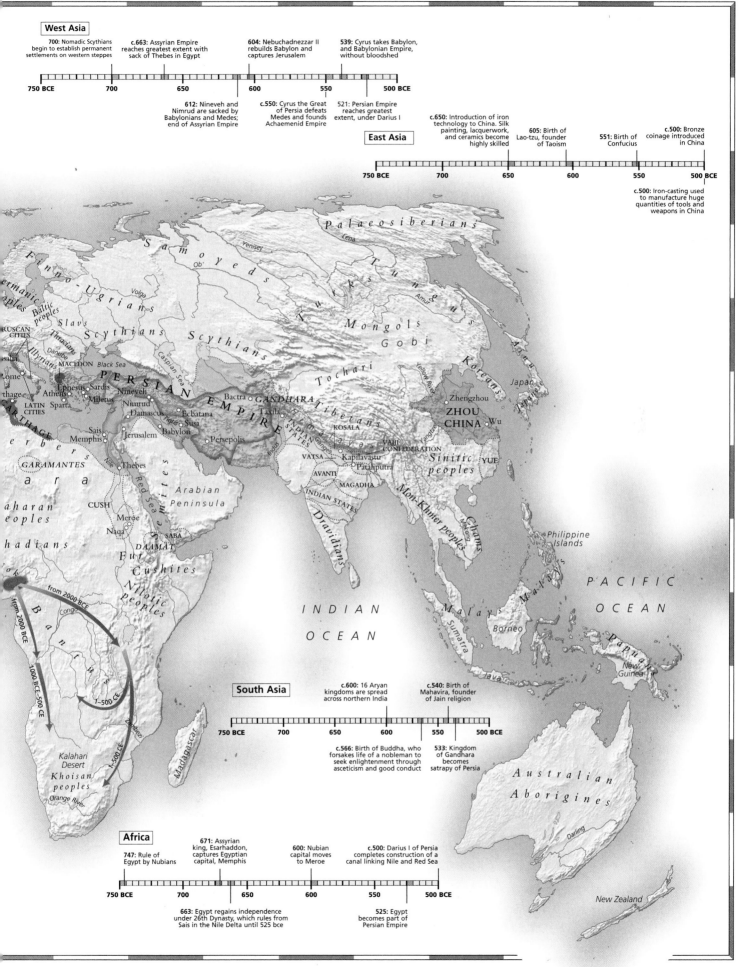

West Asia

700: Nomadic Scythians begin to establish permanent settlements on western steppes

c.663: Assyrian Empire reaches greatest extent with sack of Thebes in Egypt

604: Nebuchadnezzar II rebuilds Babylon and captures Jerusalem

539: Cyrus takes Babylon, and Babylonian Empire, without bloodshed

750 BCE   700   650   600   550   500 BCE

612: Nineveh and Nimrud are sacked by Babylonians and Medes; end of Assyrian Empire

c.550: Cyrus the Great of Persia defeats Medes and founds Achaemenid Empire

521: Persian Empire reaches greatest extent, under Darius I

East Asia

c.650: Introduction of iron technology to China. Silk painting, lacquerwork, and ceramics become highly skilled

605: Birth of Lao-tzu, founder of Taoism

551: Birth of Confucius

c.500: Bronze coinage introduced in China

750 BCE   700   650   600   550   500 BCE

c.500: Iron-casting used to manufacture huge quantities of tools and weapons in China

Palaeosiberians

Samoyeds
Finno-Ugrians
Germanic peoples
Baltic peoples
Slavs
Thracians
Illyrians
ETRUSCAN CITIES
Rome
Carthage
LATIN CITIES
Athens
Sparta
Ephesus
Sardis
Miletus
Macedon
Black Sea
Caspian Sea
Scythians
Scythians
Volga
Ob
Yenisei
Lena
Tungus
Turks
Mongols
Gobi
Amur
Koreans
Japan
Tochari
Tibetans
Zhengzhou
ZHOU CHINA
Wu
Yellow River
Sinitic peoples
YUE
Chams
Mon-Khmer peoples
Mekong
Yangtze
PERSIAN EMPIRE
Nineveh
Nimrud
Damascus
Babylon
Ecbatana
Susa
Persepolis
Bactra
GANDHARA
Taxila
Indus
INDIAN STATES
KOSALA
VAJJI CONFEDERATION
Kapilavastu
Pataliputra
VATSA
AVANTI
MAGADHA
Ganges
INDIAN STATES
Dravidians
Jerusalem
Sais
Memphis
GARAMANTES
Berbers
Sahara
Saharan peoples
Chadians
Nile
Thebes
Red Sea
CUSH
Meroë
Naqa
SABA
DAAMAT
Fut
Cushites
Nilotic peoples
Arabian Peninsula
Semites
Tigris
Euphrates
Bantu
from 2000 BCE
from 2000 BCE
1000 BCE–500 CE
1–500 CE
1–500 CE
Congo
Zambezi
Kalahari Desert
Khoisan peoples
Orange River
Madagascar
INDIAN OCEAN
Philippine Islands
Malays
Malays
Borneo
Sumatra
Java
PACIFIC OCEAN
Papuans
New Guinea
Australian Aborigines
Darling
New Zealand

South Asia

c.600: 16 Aryan kingdoms are spread across northern India

c.540: Birth of Mahavira, founder of Jain religion

750 BCE   700   650   600   550   500 BCE

c.566: Birth of Buddha, who forsakes life of a nobleman to seek enlightenment through asceticism and good conduct

533: Kingdom of Gandhara becomes satrapy of Persia

Africa

747: Rule of Egypt by Nubians

671: Assyrian king, Esarhaddon, captures Egyptian capital, Memphis

600: Nubian capital moves to Meroe

c.500: Darius I of Persia completes construction of a canal linking Nile and Red Sea

750 BCE   700   650   600   550   500 BCE

663: Egypt regains independence under 26th Dynasty, which rules from Sais in the Nile Delta until 525 bce

525: Egypt becomes part of Persian Empire

THE MEDITERRANEAN WORLD 700–300 BCE

Between 700 and 300 BCE the Mediterranean world shaped Western civilization. Though the Phoenicians were active in maritime trade and colonization, the impact of Classical Greek ideas on art, philosophy, science, and politics was far more profound.

How were colonies and colonization central to the ancient Mediterranean world?

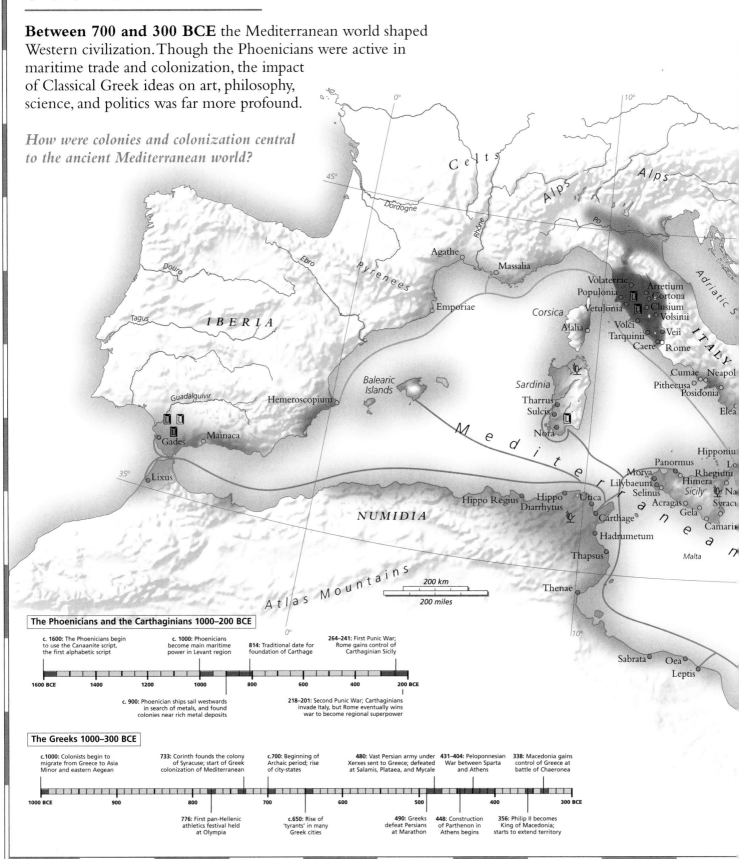

The Phoenicians and the Carthaginians 1000–200 BCE

c. 1600: The Phoenicians begin to use the Canaanite script, the first alphabetic script

c. 1000: Phoenicians become main maritime power in Levant region

814: Traditional date for foundation of Carthage

264–241: First Punic War; Rome gains control of Carthaginian Sicily

| 1600 BCE | 1400 | 1200 | 1000 | 800 | 600 | 400 | 200 BCE |

c. 900: Phoenician ships sail westwards in search of metals, and found colonies near rich metal deposits

218–201: Second Punic War; Carthaginians invade Italy, but Rome eventually wins war to become regional superpower

The Greeks 1000–300 BCE

c.1000: Colonists begin to migrate from Greece to Asia Minor and eastern Aegean

733: Corinth founds the colony of Syracuse; start of Greek colonization of Mediterranean

c.700: Beginning of Archaic period; rise of city-states

480: Vast Persian army under Xerxes sent to Greece; defeated at Salamis, Plataea, and Mycale

431–404: Peloponnesian War between Sparta and Athens

338: Macedonia gains control of Greece at battle of Chaeronea

| 1000 BCE | 900 | 800 | 700 | 600 | 500 | 400 | 300 BCE |

776: First pan-Hellenic athletics festival held at Olympia

c.650: Rise of 'tyrants' in many Greek cities

490: Greeks defeat Persians at Marathon

448: Construction of Parthenon in Athens begins

356: Philip II becomes King of Macedonia; starts to extend territory

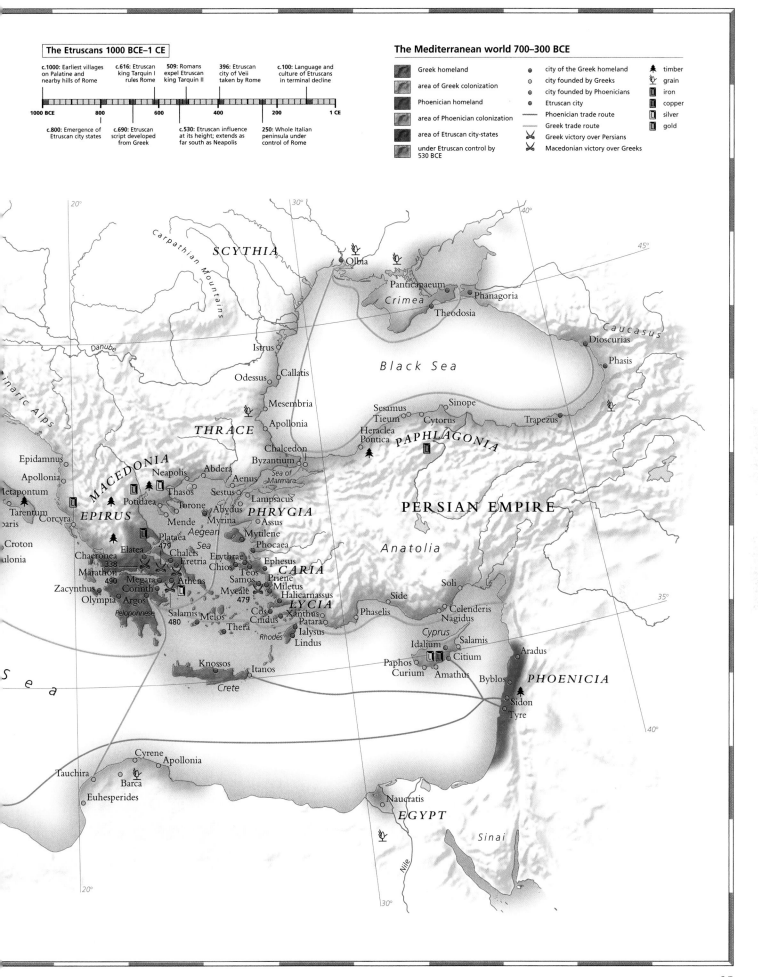

The Etruscans 1000 BCE–1 CE

c.1000: Earliest villages on Palatine and nearby hills of Rome | **c.616:** Etruscan king Tarquin I rules Rome | **509:** Romans expel Etruscan king Tarquin II | **396:** Etruscan city of Veii taken by Rome | **c.100:** Language and culture of Etruscans in terminal decline

1000 BCE — 800 — 600 — 400 — 200 — 1 CE

c.800: Emergence of Etruscan city states | **c.690:** Etruscan script developed from Greek | **c.530:** Etruscan influence at its height; extends as far south as Neapolis | **250:** Whole Italian peninsula under control of Rome

The Mediterranean world 700–300 BCE

- Greek homeland
- area of Greek colonization
- Phoenician homeland
- area of Phoenician colonization
- area of Etruscan city-states
- under Etruscan control by 530 BCE

- ● city of the Greek homeland
- ○ city founded by Greeks
- ◑ city founded by Phoenicians
- ● Etruscan city
- —— Phoenician trade route
- —— Greek trade route
- ✕ Greek victory over Persians
- ✕ Macedonian victory over Greeks

- 🌲 timber
- 🌾 grain
- iron
- copper
- silver
- gold

SCYTHIA

Carpathian Mountains

Dinaric Alps

Danube

Olbia

Panticapaeum

Crimea

Phanagoria

Theodosia

Caucasus

Dioscurias

Istrus

Black Sea

Phasis

Odessus
Callatis

Mesembria
Apollonia

THRACE

Sesamus
Tieum
Heraclea
Pontica

Sinope
Cytorus

Trapezus

PAPHLAGONIA

Chalcedon
Byzantium

Epidamnus

Apollonia

Abdera
Aenus

MACEDONIA
Neapolis

Sea of Marmara

Sestus
Lampsacus

PERSIAN EMPIRE

Metapontum
baris
Tarentum

Thasos
Torone
Potidaea

Abydus

PHRYGIA

Corcyra

EPIRUS

Mende
Myrina

Assus

Anatolia

Croton
ulonia

Plataea
479

Aegean
Sea

Mytilene
Phocaea

Chaeronea
338
Elatea
Marathon
490

Chalcis
Eretria

Erythrae
Chios

Ephesus
Teos

CARIA

Zacynthus

Megara
Corinth

Athens

Samos
Mycale
479

Priene
Miletus

Side

Soli

Celenderis
Nagidus

Olympia
Argos

Peloponnese

Salamis
480

Melos

Halicarnassus

LYCIA

Phaselis

Cos
Cnidus

Xanthus
Patara

Thera

Rhodes

Ialysus
Lindus

Cyprus

Idalium
Paphos
Curium

Salamis
Citium
Amathus

Aradus

Knossos
Itanos

Byblos

PHOENICIA

Crete

Sidon
Tyre

Sea

Cyrene
Apollonia

Tauchira
Barca

Euhesperides

Naucratis

EGYPT

Sinai

Nile

THE EMPIRE OF ALEXANDER

THE CONQUESTS OF ALEXANDER OF MACEDON (356–323 BCE) took Greek armies as far east as India, and forced Persia, the most powerful empire in the world, into submission. This audacious military feat, accomplished in just ten years, created a truly cosmopolitan civilization, known as Hellenism, which spread Greek culture from Egypt to the Hindu Kush.

Why is the Empire of Alexander considered a global empire?

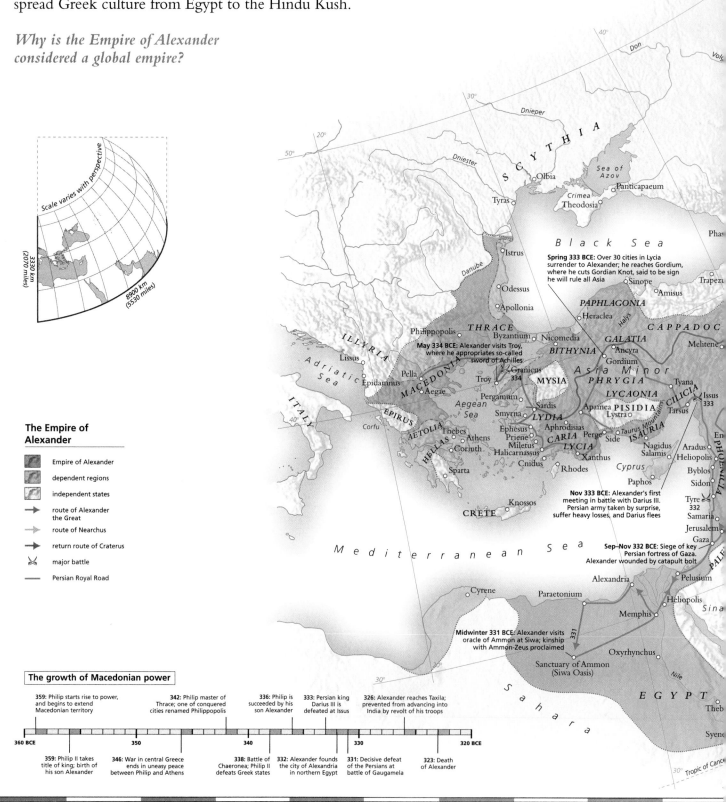

Scale varies with perspective

3330 km (2070 miles)

8900 km (5530 miles)

The Empire of Alexander

- Empire of Alexander
- dependent regions
- independent states
- → route of Alexander the Great
- → route of Nearchus
- → return route of Craterus
- ✂ major battle
- — Persian Royal Road

Spring 333 BCE: Over 30 cities in Lycia surrender to Alexander; he reaches Gordium, where he cuts Gordian Knot, said to be sign he will rule all Asia

May 334 BCE: Alexander visits Troy, where he appropriates so-called sword of Achilles

Nov 333 BCE: Alexander's first meeting in battle with Darius III. Persian army taken by surprise, suffer heavy losses, and Darius flees

Sep–Nov 332 BCE: Siege of key Persian fortress of Gaza. Alexander wounded by catapult bolt

Midwinter 331 BCE: Alexander visits oracle of Ammon at Siwa; kinship with Ammon-Zeus proclaimed

The growth of Macedonian power

359: Philip starts rise to power, and begins to extend Macedonian territory

342: Philip master of Thrace; one of conquered cities renamed Philippopolis

336: Philip is succeeded by his son Alexander

333: Persian king Darius III is defeated at Issus

326: Alexander reaches Taxila; prevented from advancing into India by revolt of his troops

359: Philip II takes title of king; birth of his son Alexander

346: War in central Greece ends in uneasy peace between Philip and Athens

338: Battle of Chaeronea; Philip II defeats Greek states

332: Alexander founds the city of Alexandria in northern Egypt

331: Decisive defeat of the Persians at battle of Gaugamela

323: Death of Alexander

360 BCE — 350 — 340 — 330 — 320 BCE

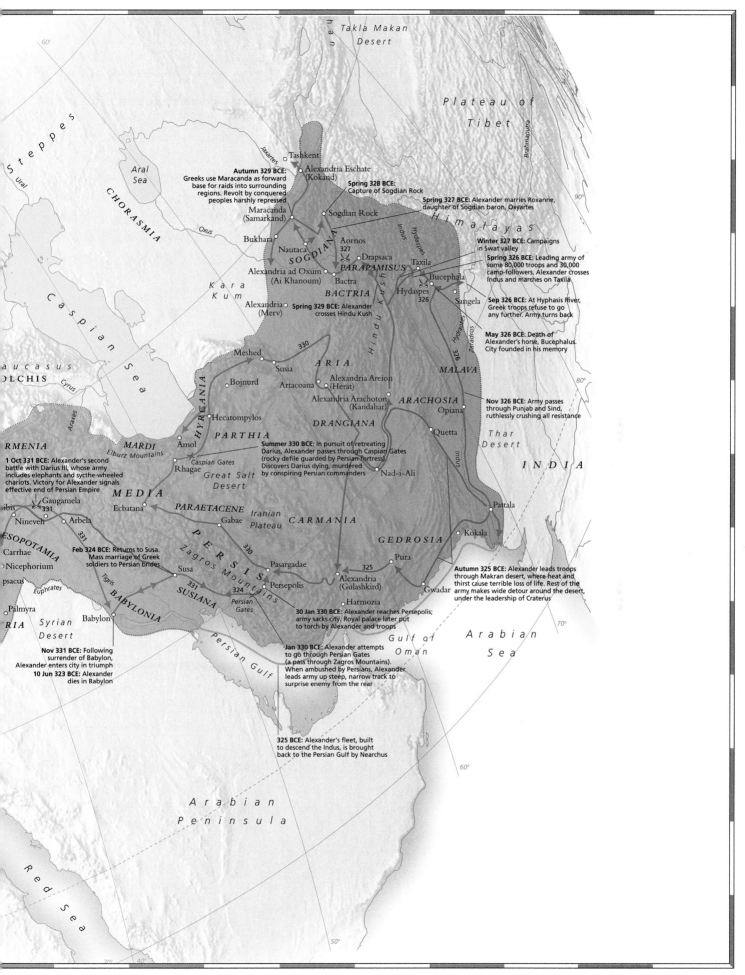

Takla Makan Desert

Plateau of Tibet

Brahmaputra

Steppes

Ural

Aral Sea

CHORASMIA

Oxus

Autumn 329 BCE: Greeks use Maracanda as forward base for raids into surrounding regions. Revolt by conquered peoples harshly repressed

Maracanda (Samarkand)

Bukhara

Nautaca

Alexandria ad Oxum (Ai Khanoum)

Bactra

Alexandria (Merv)

Tashkent
Jaxartes

Alexandria Eschate (Kokand)

Spring 328 BCE: Capture of Sogdian Rock

Sogdian Rock

Aornos 327

Drapsaca

SOGDIANA

PARAPAMISUS

BACTRIA

Himalayas

90°

Spring 327 BCE: Alexander marries Roxanne, daughter of Sogdian baron, Oxyartes

Indus

Hydaspes

Taxila

Bucephala

Hydaspes 326

Hindu Kush

Spring 329 BCE: Alexander crosses Hindu Kush

Winter 327 BCE: Campaigns in Swat valley

Spring 326 BCE: Leading army of some 80,000 troops and 30,000 camp-followers, Alexander crosses Indus and marches on Taxila

Sangela

MALAVA

Zaradros

Hydaspes

Sep 326 BCE: At Hyphasis River, Greek troops refuse to go any further. Army turns back

May 326 BCE: Death of Alexander's horse, Bucephalus. City founded in his memory

80°

Caspian Sea

aucasus

OLCHIS

Cyrus

Araxes

RMENIA

1 Oct 331 BCE: Alexander's second battle with Darius III, whose army includes elephants and sycthe-wheeled chariots. Victory for Alexander signals effective end of Persian Empire

ibis
Gaugamela
331
Nineveh   Arbela

331

MESOPOTAMIA
Carrhae
Nicephorium

psacus

Euphrates

Palmyra

Tigris

Babylon

Syrian Desert

RIA

Nov 331 BCE: Following surrender of Babylon, Alexander enters city in triumph

10 Jun 323 BCE: Alexander dies in Babylon

Meshed

Susia

Bojnurd

Artacoana

HYRCANIA

PARTHIA

Hecatompylos

Amol

MARDI
Elburz Mountains

Caspian Gates

Rhagae

Great Salt Desert

MEDIA

Ecbatana

PARAETACENE

Gabae

Iranian Plateau

P E R S I S

Zagros Mountains

Susa

SUSIANA

BABYLONIA

Persian Gates

Feb 324 BCE: Returns to Susa. Mass marriage of Greek soldiers to Persian brides

330

Pasargadae

330

Persepolis

Persian Gulf

324
331

Jan 330 BCE: Alexander attempts to go through Persian Gates (a pass through Zagros Mountains). When ambushed by Persians, Alexander leads army up steep, narrow track to surprise enemy from the rear

A R I A

Alexandria Areion (Herat)

Alexandria Arachoton (Kandahar)

DRANGIANA

ARACHOSIA

Opiana

Quetta

Nad-i-Ali

Kara Kum

Summer 330 BCE: In pursuit of retreating Darius, Alexander passes through Caspian Gates (rocky defile guarded by Persian fortress). Discovers Darius dying, murdered by conspiring Persian commanders

Thar Desert

I N D I A

Nov 326 BCE: Army passes through Punjab and Sind, ruthlessly crushing all resistance

Indus

Pattala

Kokala

CARMANIA

GEDROSIA

Pura

325

Alexandria (Gulashkird)

Harmozia

30 Jan 330 BCE: Alexander reaches Persepolis; army sacks city. Royal palace later put to torch by Alexander and troops

Gwadar

Autumn 325 BCE: Alexander leads troops through Makran desert, where heat and thirst cause terrible loss of life. Rest of the army makes wide detour around the desert, under the leadership of Craterus

Gulf of Oman

A r a b i a n   S e a

70°

60°

325 BCE: Alexander's fleet, built to descend the Indus, is brought back to the Persian Gulf by Nearchus

Red Sea

A r a b i a n   P e n i n s u l a

50°

20°   40°

THE WORLD: 500–250 BCE

Europe

490: Greeks defeat Persians at Marathon
443–429: Athens flourishes under rule of Pericles
390: Celts sack Rome
336: Alexander embarks on conquest of Persian Empire
323: Death of Alexander the Great
264: Rome leads single Italian confederacy

500 BCE   450   400   350   300   250 BCE

c.450: Celts expand into British Isles and to east and south
431–404: Peloponnesian Wars between Athens and Sparta
338: Philip II of Macedon defeats Greek states
260: Start of Roman conflict with Carthage

THE 5TH CENTURY BCE was an age of enlightened and innovative thought. It was the climax of the Classical Age in Greece. At the same time the Buddhist religion, based on the precepts of Siddhartha Gautama (c. 566–486 BCE), was spreading throughout the Indian subcontinent. In China, the teachings of Confucius (551–479 BCE) were concerned with ethical conduct and propriety in human relations. Yet the ensuing centuries would be a time of conflict and conquest.

What is the connection between political developments and philosophical and religious thinking?

The World in 250 BCE

- Qin Empire
- Carthage
- Massalia
- Greek city-states
- Macedon
- Mauryan Empire
- Seleucid Empire
- ◆ Ptolemaic Empire
- Empire of Alexander the Great 323 BCE

The Americas

c.500: Paracas culture of southern Peru, famed for brightly coloured textiles, emerges
c.350: Beginnings of Nazca culture in southern Peru

500 BCE   450   400   350   300   250 BCE

c.400: Early Zapotec culture flourishing around city of Monte Albán
c.300: Hopewell culture in eastern North America develops traditions of earlier Adena culture

Africa

c.500: First iron-working in sub-Saharan Africa. Beginning of period of Nok culture in Niger Delta
332: Alexander the Great conquers Egypt. He lays the foundations of Alexandria
302: Ptolemy I declares himself king of Egypt. The Ptolemies took pharaonic titles and worshipped Egyptian deities

500 BCE   450   400   350   300   250 BCE

c.500: Iron-using Bantus begin to spread from Niger to East African lakes region and down west coast of Africa
c.250: Settlement of Jenne-jeno is founded on inland Niger Delta

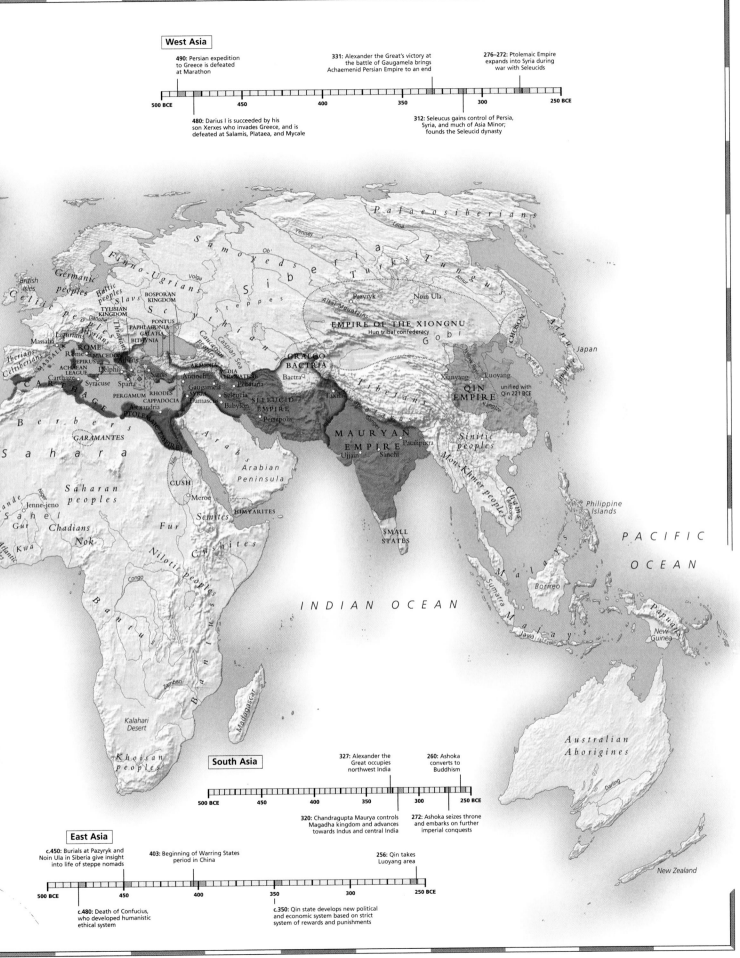

West Asia

490: Persian expedition
to Greece is defeated
at Marathon

331: Alexander the Great's victory at
the battle of Gaugamela brings
Achaemenid Persian Empire to an end

276–272: Ptolemaic Empire
expands into Syria during
war with Seleucids

500 BCE   450   400   350   300   250 BCE

480: Darius I is succeeded by his
son Xerxes who invades Greece, and is
defeated at Salamis, Plataea, and Mycale

312: Seleucus gains control of Persia,
Syria, and much of Asia Minor;
founds the Seleucid dynasty

West Asia map labels: *Palaeosiberians*, Lena, *Samoyeds*, Yenisey, Ob', *Finno-Ugrians*, *Germanic peoples*, British Isles, *Celtic peoples*, Volga, *Baltic peoples*, *Slavs*, *Siberia*, *Turks*, *Tungus*, *Amur*, Danube, BOSPORAN KINGDOM, TYLISIAN KINGDOM, *Scythians*, *Steppes*, Altai Mountains, Pazyryk, Noin Ula, *Ainu*, PAPHLAGONIA, PONTUS, GALATIA, BITHYNIA, **EMPIRE OF THE XIONGNU** Hun tribal confederacy, *Gobi*, CHOSON, Japan, Massalia, *Illyrians*, *Ligurians*, *Thracians*, Caucasus Mtns, Caspian Sea, Korea, Japanese Isles, **ROME**, Rome, MACEDON, ARMENIA, MEDIA ATROPATENE, **GRAECO-BACTRIA**, Bactra, *Tibetans*, Xianyang, Luoyang, EPIRUS, ACHAEAN LEAGUE, Delphi, Athens, Sardis, Antioch, MEDIA, Ecbatana, *Himalayas*, **QIN EMPIRE**, unified with Qin 221 BCE, **CARTHAGE**, Carthage, Syracuse, Sparta, PERGAMUM, RHODES, CAPPADOCIA, SYRIA, Damascus, Gaugamela, Seleucia, Babylon, **SELEUCID EMPIRE**, Taxila, Yellow River, Yangtze, *Iberians*, *Celtiberians*, Alexandria, **PTOLEMAIC EMPIRE**, Persepolis, *Arabs*, **MAURYAN EMPIRE**, Pataliputra, *Sinitic peoples*, *Berbers*, GARAMANTES, *Arabian Peninsula*, Ujjain, Sanchi, *Sahara*, Nile, *Saharan peoples*, CUSH, Meroe, *Semites*, HIMYARITES, *Mon-Khmer peoples*, *Chams*, *Mekong*, Philippine Islands, *Mande*, Jenne-jeno, Niger, Sahel, Gur, Kwa, *Chadians*, Nok, *Fur*, *Cushites*, **SMALL STATES**, *Nilotic peoples*, *Malays*, Sumatra, Borneo, Java, Papua, New Guinea, Congo, **INDIAN OCEAN**, **PACIFIC OCEAN**, *Bantus*, Zambezi, Madagascar, Kalahari Desert, *Khoisan peoples*, *Australian Aborigines*, Darling, New Zealand

South Asia

327: Alexander the
Great occupies
northwest India

260: Ashoka
converts to
Buddhism

500 BCE   450   400   350   300   250 BCE

320: Chandragupta Maurya controls
Magadha kingdom and advances
towards Indus and central India

272: Ashoka seizes throne
and embarks on further
imperial conquests

East Asia

c.450: Burials at Pazyryk and
Noin Ula in Siberia give insight
into life of steppe nomads

403: Beginning of Warring States
period in China

256: Qin takes
Luoyang area

500 BCE   450   400   350   300   250 BCE

c.480: Death of Confucius,
who developed humanistic
ethical system

c.350: Qin state develops new political
and economic system based on strict
system of rewards and punishments

TRADE IN THE CLASSICAL WORLD

BY THE BEGINNING of the 1st millennium CE, a series of commercial and political networks had evolved which combined to form a nexus of trade linking the eastern shores of the Atlantic Ocean, the Indian Ocean, and the western shores of the Pacific.

How did trade connect the Roman Empire and Han China to each other and the rest of the Old World?

Eurasian and African trade c.1 CE

	Roman Empire and client states		
	Han Empire		
	Sinkiang (Han protectorate 73–94 CE)		

Trade routes
- —— Roman
- —— Trans–Saharan (rudimentary route)
- —— Indian Ocean
- —— Silk Road
- —— Scythian (rudimentary route)
- —— China
- —— East Africa
- —— amber
- —— incense
- —— other (rudimentary route)

Goods traded
- amber
- animals
- clothing
- gold
- silver
- grain
- horses
- incense
- ivory
- olive oil
- precious stones
- silk
- slaves
- spices
- timber
- tin
- tortoiseshell
- wine

Scale varies with perspective

7720 km (4490 miles)

17,810 km (11,070 miles)

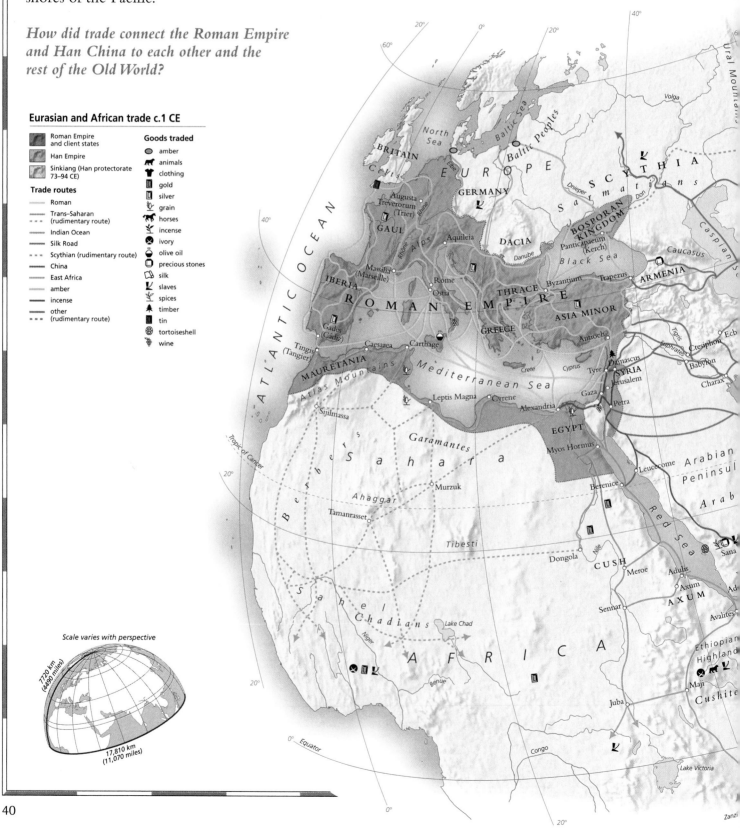

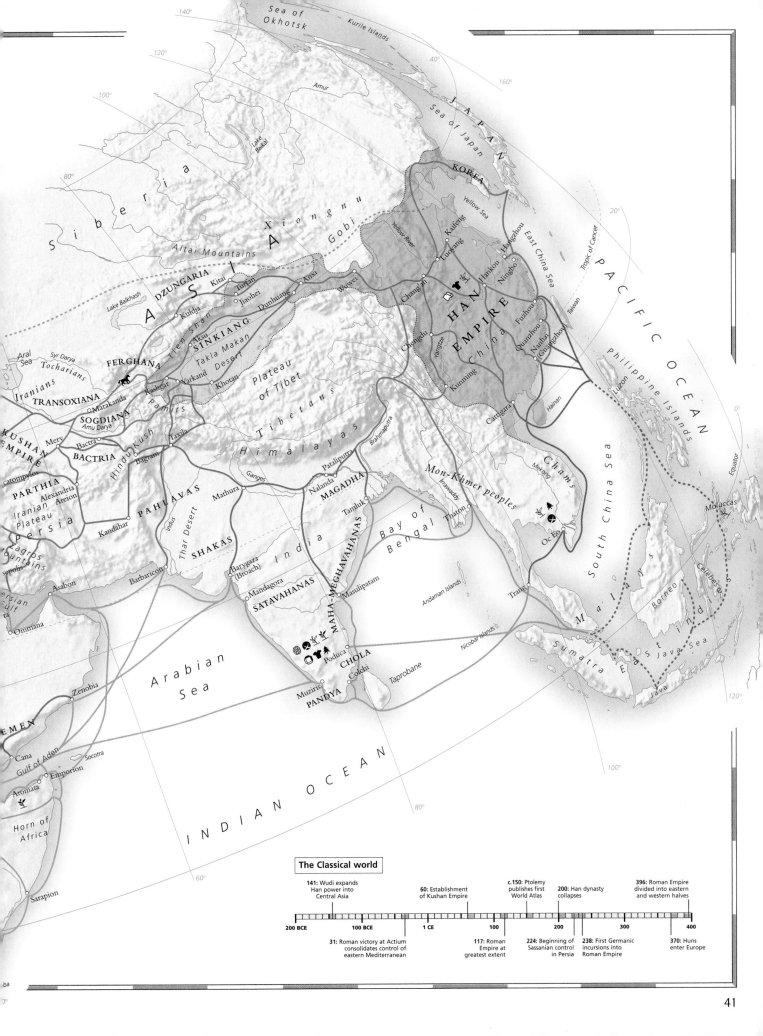

Sea of
Okhotsk

Kurile Islands

PACIFIC OCEAN

Sea of Japan

JAPAN

KOREA

Yellow Sea

East China Sea

Taiwan

Philippine Islands

HAN EMPIRE

Kaifeng
Luoyang
Hankou
Ningbo
Changʼan
Fuzhou
Yangtze
Quanzhou
Chengdu
Nanhai (Guangzhou)

China

Kunming

Hainan

Cattigara

South China Sea

Luzon

Equator

Moluccas

Yellow River

Wuwei

Siberia

Altai Mountains

ASIA

Xiongnu

Gobi

Lake Baikal

Amur

DZUNGARIA

Kuldja
Kitai
Turfan
Aksu
Jiaohei
Ainu
Dunhuang

Tien Shan

SINKIANG

Takla Makan
Desert

Yarkand
Khotan

Plateau
of Tibet

Tibetans

Himalayas

Brahmaputra

Kashgar

Pamirs

Lake Balkhash

FERGHANA

Aral
Sea

Syr Darya

Tocharians

Iranians

TRANSOXIANA

Marakanda

SOGDIANA

Amu Darya

KUSHAN
EMPIRE

Merv
Bactra

BACTRIA

Hindu Kush

Bagram
Taxila

PAHLAVAS

Mathura

Ganges

Nalanda
Pataliputra
MAGADHA
Tamluk

Bay of
Bengal

Mon-Khmer peoples

Irrawaddy

Thaton

Chams

Mekong

Malaya

Sumatra

East Indies

Borneo

Celebes Sea

Java Sea

Java

PARTHIA

Alexandria
Areion
catompylos

Iranian
Plateau

Persia

Kandahar

Indus

Thar Desert

SHAKAS

India

Barygaza
(Broach)

MAHA-MEGHAVAHANAS

SATAVAHANAS

Mandagora

Masulipatam

Andaman Islands

Trang

Oc Eo

Zagros
Mountains

sepolis

Asabon

Barbaricon

Poduca

CHOLA
Colchi

Taprobane

Nicobar Islands

Persian
Gulf

ta

Ommana

Zenobia

Muziris

PANDYA

Arabian
Sea

EMEN

Cana

Gulf of Aden

Emporion

Socotra

Aromata

Horn of
Africa

Sarapion

INDIAN OCEAN

ba

The Classical world

141: Wudi expands Han power into Central Asia

60: Establishment of Kushan Empire

c.150: Ptolemy publishes first World Atlas

200: Han dynasty collapses

396: Roman Empire divided into eastern and western halves

200 BCE — 100 BCE — 1 CE — 100 — 200 — 300 — 400

31: Roman victory at Actium consolidates control of eastern Mediterranean

117: Roman Empire at greatest extent

224: Beginning of Sassanian control in Persia

238: First Germanic incursions into Roman Empire

370: Huns enter Europe

THE ROMAN EMPIRE

AT THE HEIGHT OF ITS POWER in the 2nd century, Rome ruled over some 50 million people scattered in over 5000 administrative units. For the most part, the subjects of the Empire accepted Roman rule, and, at least in the west, many adopted Roman culture and the Latin language. After 212 CE, all free inhabitants of the Empire had the status of Roman citizens.

What were the limitations on the expansion of the Roman Empire?

The Roman Empire under Hadrian c.120 CE

......	boundary of Roman Empire c.120 CE
DACIA	province in reign of Hadrian
45 CE	date of conquest or annexation by Rome
◉	provincial capital
⚑	legion headquarters
⚓	major naval base
ᴸᴸᴸ	fortified frontier *(limes)*
——	major road
▨	region temporarily held by Rome, with dates

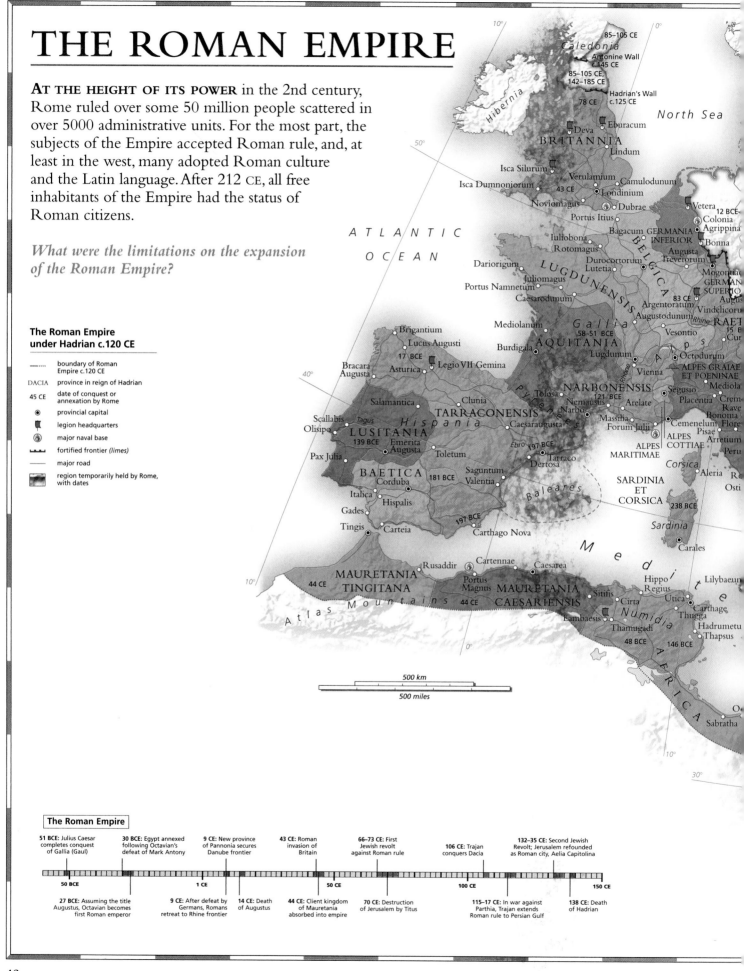

The Roman Empire

51 BCE: Julius Caesar completes conquest of Gallia (Gaul)

30 BCE: Egypt annexed following Octavian's defeat of Mark Antony

9 CE: New province of Pannonia secures Danube frontier

43 CE: Roman invasion of Britain

66–73 CE: First Jewish revolt against Roman rule

106 CE: Trajan conquers Dacia

132–35 CE: Second Jewish Revolt; Jerusalem refounded as Roman city, Aelia Capitolina

27 BCE: Assuming the title Augustus, Octavian becomes first Roman emperor

9 CE: After defeat by Germans, Romans retreat to Rhine frontier

14 CE: Death of Augustus

44 CE: Client kingdom of Mauretania absorbed into empire

70 CE: Destruction of Jerusalem by Titus

115–17 CE: In war against Parthia, Trajan extends Roman rule to Persian Gulf

138 CE: Death of Hadrian

50 BCE   1 CE   50 CE   100 CE   150 CE

Burgundians

ermania

arcomanni

Quadi

Sarmatians

Vindobona
Carnuntum
Brigetio
RICUM
Noviomagum
Virunum
Aquincum
15 BCE
9 CE
PANNONIA
INFERIOR
PANNONIA
SUPERIOR
Siscia
Mursa
Sirmium
Apulum
Sarmizegethusa
DACIA
107 CE
Singidunum
Viminacium
Roxolani
Troesmis

Caspian Sea

Caucasus

BOSPORAN
KINGDOM
vassal of Rome
from 63 BCE

Black Sea

ARMENIA
114–117 CE

PARTHIAN
EMPIRE

minum
Ancona
Salonae
rfinium
ALIA
ia
Puteoli
Neapolis
num
Brundisium
Tarantum

DALMATIA
33 BCE
MOESIA
SUPERIOR
29 BCE
Oescus
Serdica
THRACIA
Philippopolis
45 CE
Nicopolis
Dyrrhachium
Stobi
Heraclea
MACEDONIA
148 BCE
Thessalonica

Danube
Novae
MOESIA INFERIOR
Tomi
Durostorum

Sinope
Heraclea
Pontica
Cyzicus
Nicomedia
Prusa
Byzantium
Hadrianopolis

Pompeiopolis
BITHYNIA ET PONTUS
74 BCE
Ancyra
GALATIA
25 BCE
Gangra
Zela
18 CE

Trapezus

Satala
Nicopolis

EPIRUS
140 BCE
Nicopolis

Delphi
Corinth
Athens
ACHAIA
146 BCE
Sparta

Pergamum
ASIA
133 BCE
Ephesus
Miletus
Laodicea
Cnidus

Dorylaeum
Antiochia
Iconium

LYCIA
74 CE
Attalia
101 CE

CAPPADOCIA
Caesarea
Samosata

Melitene

ASSYRIA
116–117 CE

rmus
Messana
gentum
Rhegium
SICILIA
Syracuse

CILICIA
Tarsus
Seleucia

Zeugma
Cyrrhus
Antioch
Laodicea
Raphanaea
SYRIA
64 BCE

Euphrates

115 CE

MESOPOTAMIA
115–117 CE

Tigris

Ctesiphon

Rhodus
74 CE
Myra

Salamis
CYPRUS
Paphus
58 BCE

Tripolis

Heliopolis

Dura
Europos

Creta
67 BCE
Gortyn

anean
Sea

Caparcotna
Caesarea Maritima

Damascus
Tyrus

Bostra

Syrian
Desert

Arabian

Peninsula

is Magna

Ptolemais
Cyrene
74 BCE

CYRENE
ET CRETA

Alexandria
Nicopolis

JUDAEA
6 CE
Jerusalem
(Aelia Capitolina)

ARABIA
106 CE

Petra

Memphis

20 BCE

AEGYPTUS
30 BCE

Nile

Red
Sea

43

HAN CHINA

THE UNIFICATION OF CHINA by the Qin in 221 BCE paved the way for the Han, who assumed control in 206 BCE. The Han established a domain by far the greatest the world had ever seen, and provided a template for Chinese territorial aspirations for the next two millennia.

What factors limited Han expansion?

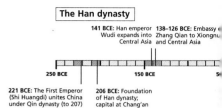

The Han dynasty	
141 BCE: Han emperor Wudi expands into Central Asia	**138–126 BCE:** Embassy of Zhang Qian to Xiongnu and Central Asia

| 250 BCE | 150 BCE | 5 |

221 BCE: The First Emperor (Shi Huangdi) unites China under Qin dynasty (to 207)

206 BCE: Foundation of Han dynasty; capital at Chang'an

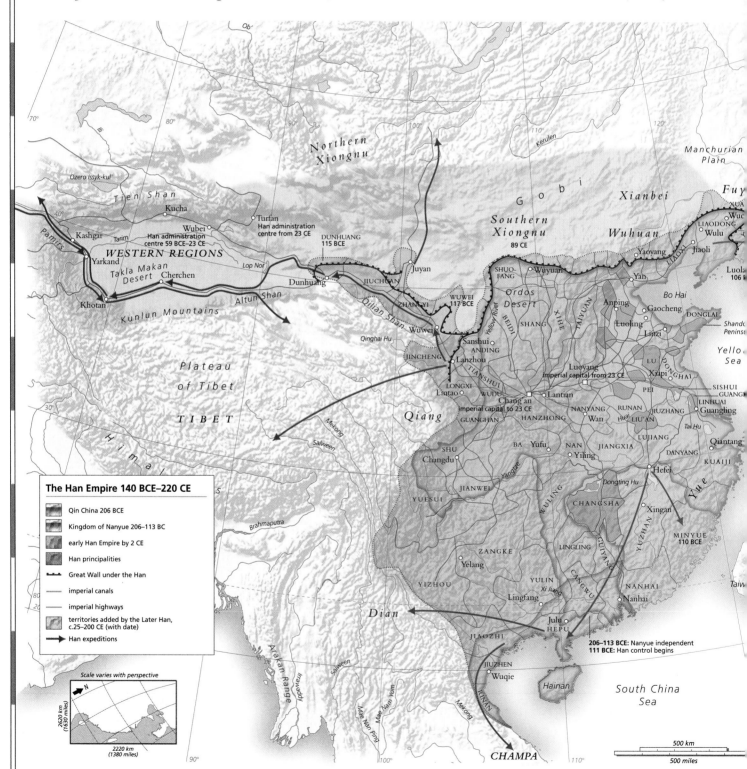

The Han Empire 140 BCE–220 CE

- Qin China 206 BCE
- Kingdom of Nanyue 206–113 BC
- early Han Empire by 2 CE
- Han principalities
- Great Wall under the Han
- imperial canals
- imperial highways
- territories added by the Later Han, c.25–200 CE (with date)
- Han expeditions

Scale varies with perspective

2620 km (1630 miles)

2220 km (1380 miles)

500 km

500 miles

44

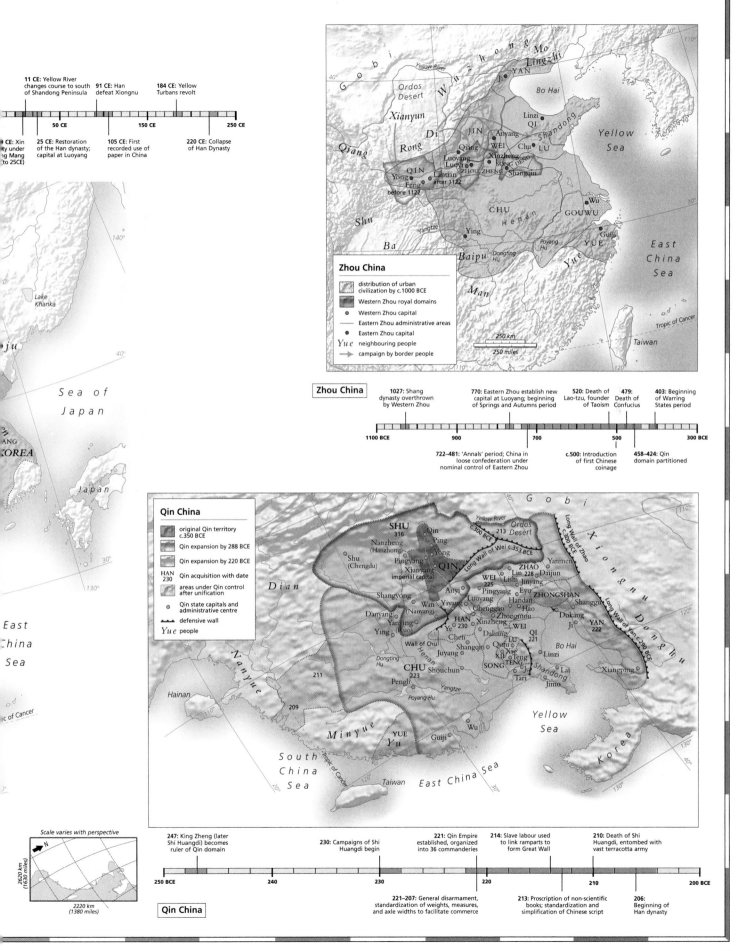

11 CE: Yellow River changes course to south of Shandong Peninsula

91 CE: Han defeat Xiongnu

184 CE: Yellow Turbans revolt

50 CE	150 CE	250 CE

CE: Xin ty under g Mang (to 25CE)

25 CE: Restoration of the Han dynasty; capital at Luoyang

105 CE: First recorded use of paper in China

220 CE: Collapse of Han Dynasty

Zhou China

- distribution of urban civilization by c.1000 BCE
- Western Zhou royal domains
- ● Western Zhou capital
- Eastern Zhou administrative areas
- ● Eastern Zhou capital
- *Yue* neighbouring people
- → campaign by border people

250 km
250 miles

Zhou China

1027: Shang dynasty overthrown by Western Zhou

770: Eastern Zhou establish new capital at Luoyang; beginning of Springs and Autumns period

520: Death of Lao-tzu, founder of Taoism

479: Death of Confucius

403: Beginning of Warring States period

1100 BCE	900	700	500	300 BCE

722–481: 'Annals' period; China in loose confederation under nominal control of Eastern Zhou

c.500: Introduction of first Chinese coinage

458–424: Qin domain partitioned

Qin China

- original Qin territory c.350 BCE
- Qin expansion by 288 BCE
- Qin expansion by 220 BCE
- HAN 230 Qin acquisition with date
- areas under Qin control after unification
- ● Qin state capitals and administrative centre
- defensive wall
- *Yue* people

Scale varies with perspective

2620 km (1630 miles)

2220 km (1380 miles)

247: King Zheng (later Shi Huangdi) becomes ruler of Qin domain

230: Campaigns of Shi Huangdi begin

221: Qin Empire established, organized into 36 commanderies

214: Slave labour used to link ramparts to form Great Wall

210: Death of Shi Huangdi, entombed with vast terracotta army

250 BCE	240	230	220	210	200 BCE

221–207: General disarmament, standardization of weights, measures, and axle widths to facilitate commerce

213: Proscription of non-scientific books; standardization and simplification of Chinese script

206: Beginning of Han dynasty

Qin China

RELIGIONS OF THE WORLD AFTER 400 CE

BETWEEN 400 CE and the advent of Islam in the mid-7th century, the disintegration of the Old World political order was balanced by the spread and diversification of world religions. Christianity became firmly established throughout the Roman Empire and its successor states. In South Asia, Hinduism became deeply rooted. Meanwhile, Buddhism spread overland to Central Asia and China. Between 400 and 650 CE, the political order disintegrated, but Buddhism spread into maritime Southeast Asia. In the west, Christianity spawned many sects, including Africa's Coptic church.

The growth of early Christianity

46–57: Journeys of St. Paul

132: Suppression of Jewish revolt in Palestine; beginning of diaspora

304: Persecution of Christians by Diocletian (284–305)

325: Council of Nicaea assembled by Constantine

404: Vulgate (Latin version of Bible) completed

0	100	200	300	400	500

c.32CE: Crucifixion of Christ

64: Probable martyrdom of St. Paul by Nero (37–68)

274: Mithras admitted into pantheon of Roman Empire

313: Edict of Milan under Constantine (306–337) confirms Christianity as official imperial creed

Compare this map with the map on pages 40–41. What are the connections between the movement of goods and the movement of ideas?

Religions of the Old World after 400 CE

- area largely embracing Christianity by 600
- spread of Gnosticism 200–400
- spread of Arianism 300–500
- spread of Manichaeism 300–500
- Coptic missions by 350
- Nestorian/Jacobite missions 600–1000
- area largely embracing Zoroastrianism by 500
- extent of Hinduism by 400
- spread of Hinduism 400–600
- extent of Jainism by 700
- extent of Buddhism by 400
- spread of Mahayana Buddhism 400–1000
- spread of Buddhism 400–1000
- heartland of Tibetan (Tantric) Buddhism by 800
- spread of Tibetan (Tantric) Buddhism 800–1100
- Shinto

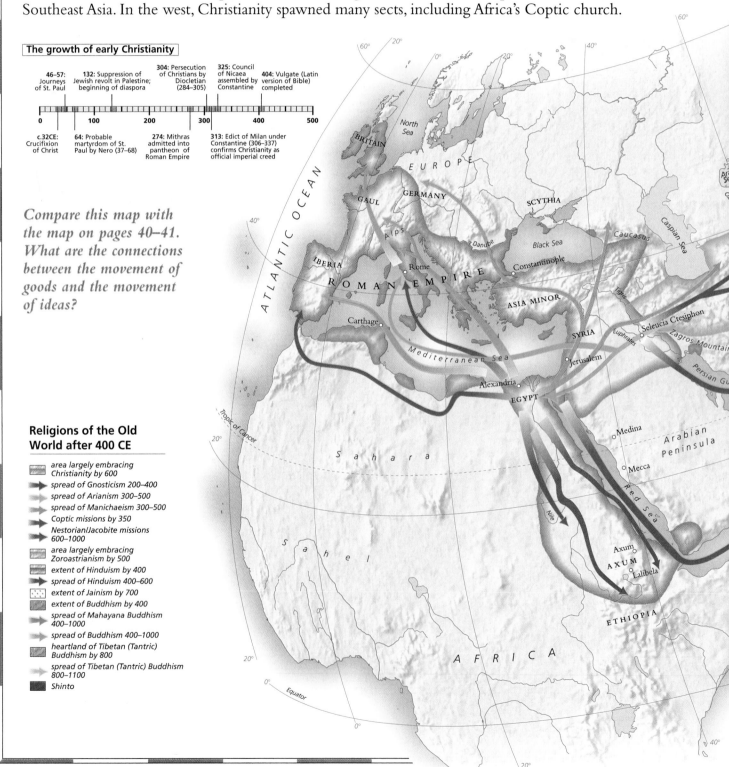

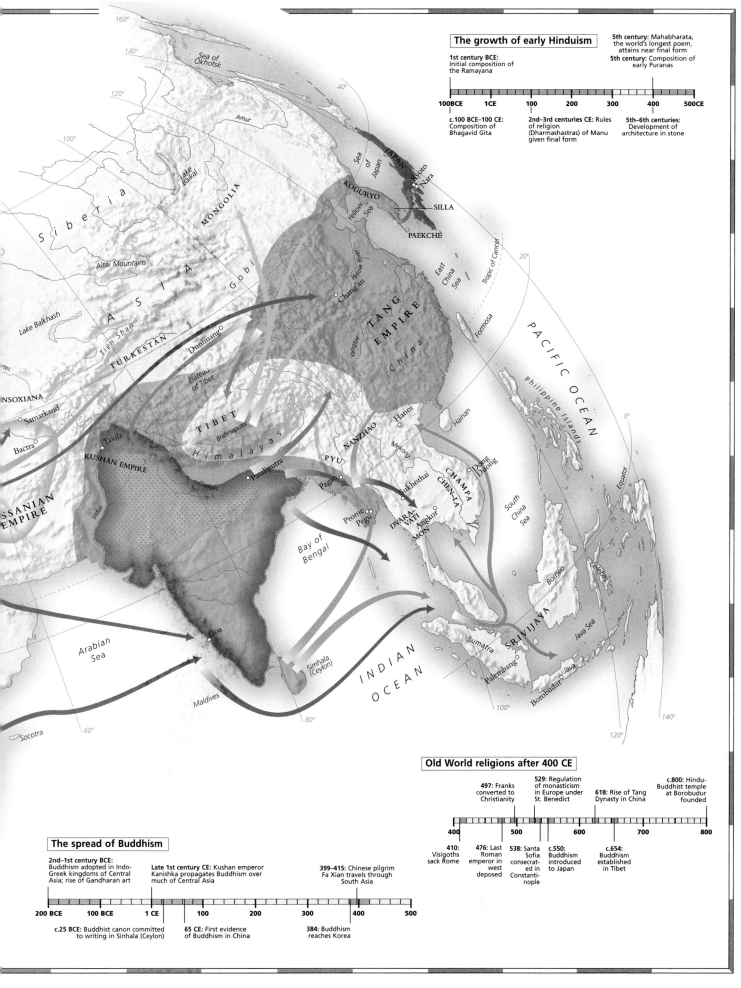

The growth of early Hinduism

1st century BCE:
Initial composition of
the Ramayana

5th century: Mahabharata,
the world's longest poem,
attains near final form

5th century: Composition of
early Puranas

100BCE | 1CE | 100 | 200 | 300 | 400 | 500CE

c.100 BCE–100 CE:
Composition of
Bhagavid Gita

2nd–3rd centuries CE: Rules
of religion (Dharmashastras) of Manu
given final form

5th–6th centuries:
Development of
architecture in stone

Old World religions after 400 CE

497: Franks
converted to
Christianity

529: Regulation
of monasticism
in Europe under
St. Benedict

618: Rise of Tang
Dynasty in China

c.800: Hindu-
Buddhist temple
at Borobudur
founded

400 | 500 | 600 | 700 | 800

410:
Visigoths
sack Rome

476: Last
Roman
emperor in
west
deposed

538: Santa
Sofia
consecrat-
ed in
Constanti-
nople

c.550:
Buddhism
introduced
to Japan

c.654:
Buddhism
established
in Tibet

The spread of Buddhism

2nd–1st century BCE:
Buddhism adopted in Indo-
Greek kingdoms of Central
Asia; rise of Gandharan art

Late 1st century CE: Kushan emperor
Kanishka propagates Buddhism over
much of Central Asia

399–415: Chinese pilgrim
Fa Xian travels through
South Asia

200 BCE | 100 BCE | 1 CE | 100 | 200 | 300 | 400 | 500

c.25 BCE: Buddhist canon committed
to writing in Sinhala (Ceylon)

65 CE: First evidence
of Buddhism in China

384: Buddhism
reaches Korea

THE WORLD: 500–750 CE

THE RAPID RECOVERY of the ancient world from the onslaught of invading nomads is evident in the rise of two great empires in Eurasia: the Umayyads in the Middle East and the Tang in China. In the Americas, the Maya remained the most advanced civilization. In Southeast Asia, the maritime empire of Srivijaya dominated an international trade network.

How did the cultural landscape change in the post-classical world?

The World in 750

- Tang Empire
- Byzantine Empire
- Umayyad Caliphate
- Kök Türk Empire 551–572
- East Roman Empire 554–565
- Horsha's Empire c.640
- Avar Empire c.595

The Americas

c.600: Maya civilization in Central America reaches its height

c.700: Beginnings of Puebloan culture

750: Devastation of city of Teotihuacán

500 — 550 — 600 — 650 — 700 — 750

c.500: Teotihuacán thriving as a major trading centre

c.600: Rise of closely-related Tiahuanaco and Huari civilizations in South America

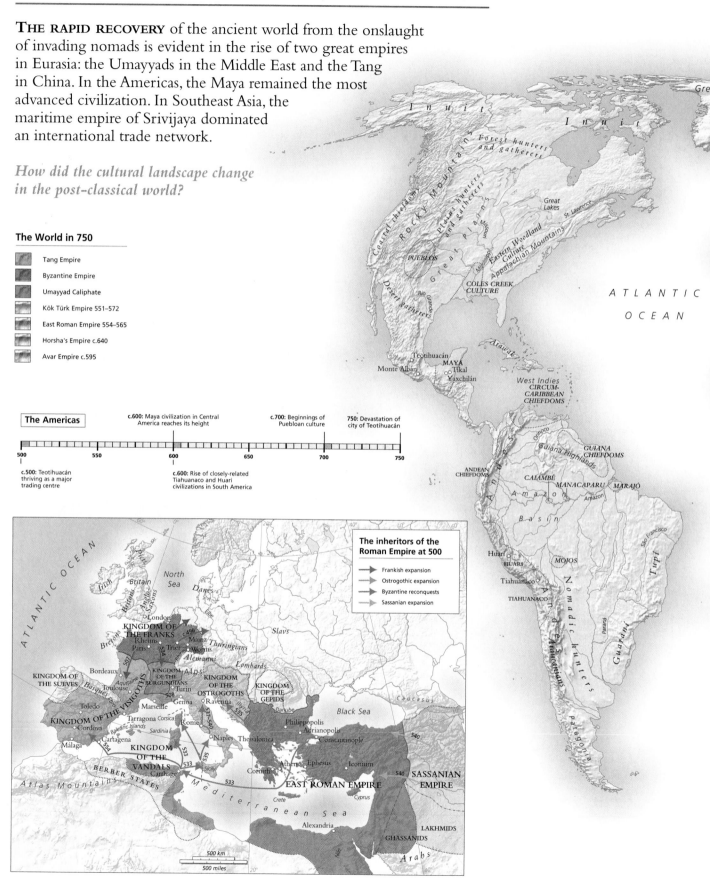

The inheritors of the
Roman Empire at 500
- Frankish expansion
- Ostrogothic expansion
- Byzantine reconquests
- Sassanian expansion

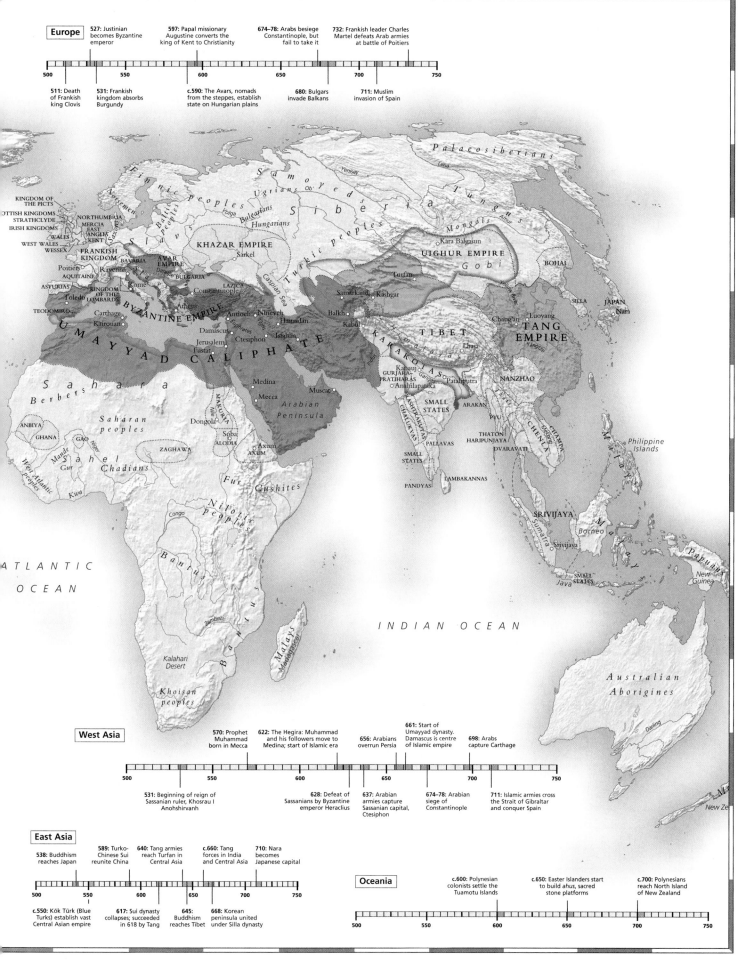

527: Justinian becomes Byzantine emperor

597: Papal missionary Augustine converts the king of Kent to Christianity

674–78: Arabs besiege Constantinople, but fail to take it

732: Frankish leader Charles Martel defeats Arab armies at battle of Poitiers

500   550   600   650   700   750

511: Death of Frankish king Clovis

531: Frankish kingdom absorbs Burgundy

c.590: The Avars, nomads from the steppes, establish state on Hungarian plains

680: Bulgars invade Balkans

711: Muslim invasion of Spain

West Asia

570: Prophet Muhammad born in Mecca

622: The Hegira: Muhammad and his followers move to Medina; start of Islamic era

656: Arabians overrun Persia

661: Start of Umayyad dynasty. Damascus is centre of Islamic empire

698: Arabs capture Carthage

500   550   600   650   700   750

531: Beginning of reign of Sassanian ruler, Khosrau I Anohshirvanh

628: Defeat of Sassanians by Byzantine emperor Heraclius

637: Arabian armies capture Sassanian capital, Ctesiphon

674–78: Arabian siege of Constantinople

711: Islamic armies cross the Strait of Gibraltar and conquer Spain

East Asia

538: Buddhism reaches Japan

589: Turko-Chinese Sui reunite China

640: Tang armies reach Turfan in Central Asia

c.660: Tang forces in India and Central Asia

710: Nara becomes Japanese capital

500   550   600   650   700   750

c.550: Kök Türk (Blue Turks) establish vast Central Asian empire

617: Sui dynasty collapses; succeeded in 618 by Tang

645: Buddhism reaches Tibet

668: Korean peninsula united under Silla dynasty

Oceania

c.600: Polynesian colonists settle the Tuamotu Islands

c.650: Easter Islanders start to build *ahus*, sacred stone platforms

c.700: Polynesians reach North Island of New Zealand

500   550   600   650   700   750

THE EMPIRE OF CHARLEMAGNE

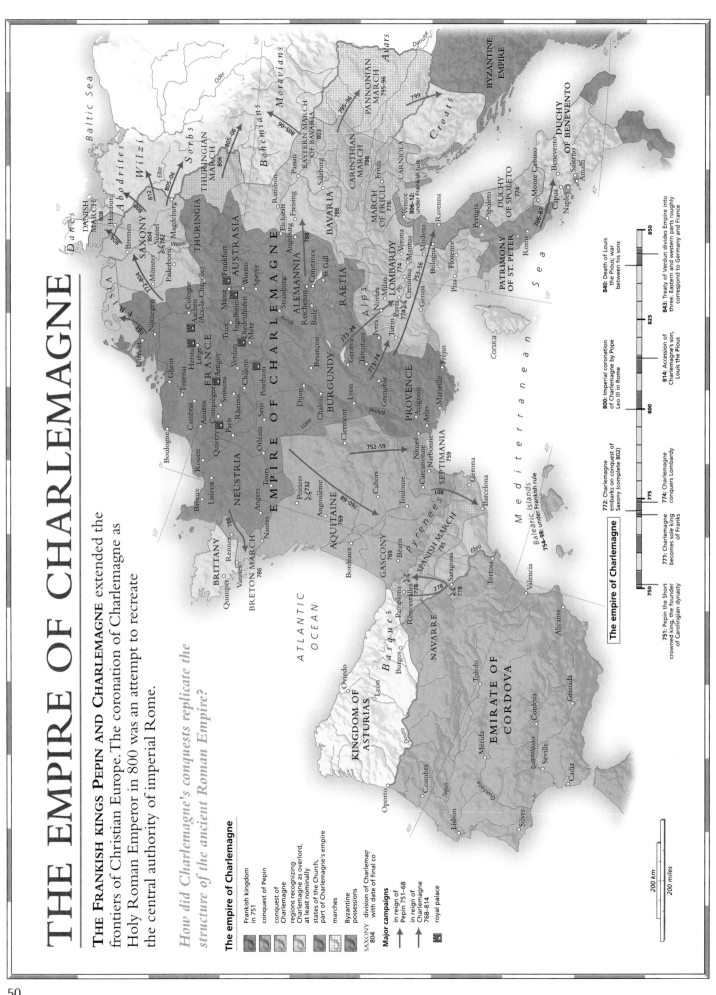

THE FRANKISH KINGS PEPIN AND CHARLEMAGNE extended the frontiers of Christian Europe. The coronation of Charlemagne as Holy Roman Emperor in 800 was an attempt to recreate the central authority of imperial Rome.

How did Charlemagne's conquests replicate the structure of the ancient Roman Empire?

The empire of Charlemagne

- Frankish kingdom in 751
- conquest of Pepin
- conquest of Charlemagne
- regions recognizing Charlemagne as overlord, at least nominally
- states of the Church, part of Charlemagne's empire
- marches
- Byzantine possessions

SAXONY division of Charlemagne with date of final co
804

Major campaigns
- in reign of Pepin 751–68
- in reign of Charlemagne 768–814
- royal palace

751: Pepin the Short crowned king, the founder of Carolingian dynasty

771: Charlemagne becomes sole king of Franks

772: Charlemagne embarks on conquest of Saxony (complete 802)

774: Charlemagne conquers Lombardy

800: Imperial coronation of Charlemagne by Pope Leo III in Rome

814: Accession of Charlemagne's son, Louis the Pious

840: Death of Louis the Pious; war between his sons

843: Treaty of Verdun divides Empire into three. Eastern and western parts roughly correspond to Germany and France

The empire of Charlemagne

THE ABBASID CALIPHATE

By 750 CE, Arab armies had carried Islam west to the Iberian peninsula and east to Central Asia. The Abbasid Caliphate, with its capital at Baghdad, was founded in 750. It was an era of great prosperity, especially in the reign of Harun al-Rashid.

What were the geographical advantages of the Abbasid Caliphate?

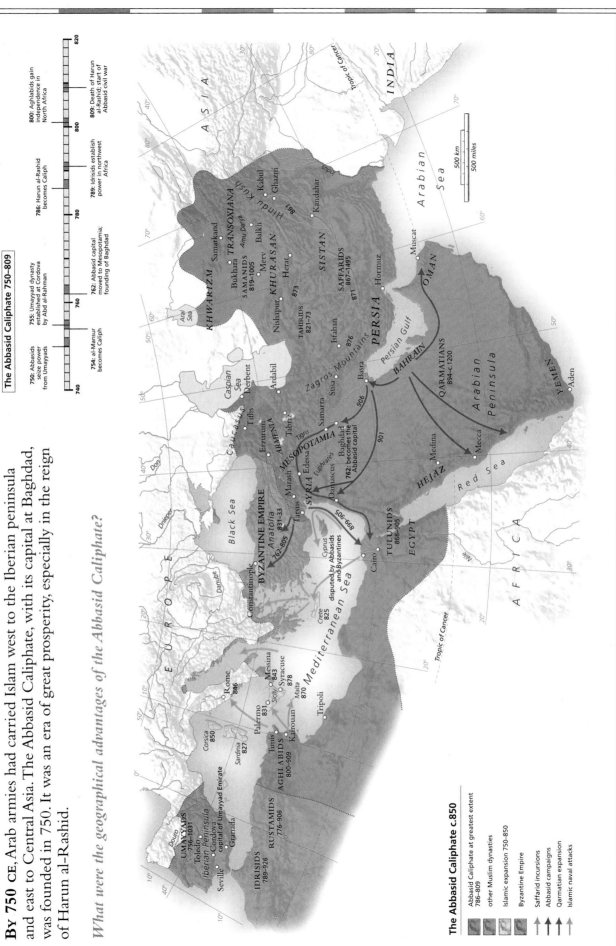

The Abbasid Caliphate 750–809

740	
750: Abbasids seize power from Umayyads	
754: al-Mansur becomes Caliph	
760	
755: Umayyad dynasty established at Cordova by Abd al-Rahman	
762: Abbasid capital moved to Mesopotamia; founding of Baghdad	
780	
786: Harun al-Rashid becomes Caliph	
789: Idrisids establish power in northwest Africa	
800	
800: Aghlabids gain independence in North Africa	
809: Death of Harun al-Rashid; start of Abbasid civil war	
820	

The Abbasid Caliphate c.850

- Abbasid Caliphate at greatest extent 786–809
- other Muslim dynasties
- Islamic expansion 750–850
- Byzantine Empire
- Saffarid incursions
- Abbasid campaigns
- Qarmatian expansion
- Islamic naval attacks

THE ISLAMIC IMPRINT

THE RAPID SPREAD OF ISLAM was one of the most decisive developments of the medieval period. Muslims controlled Eurasian trade on land and by sea – trade which would spread the faith further afield, deep into Africa, across the Indian Ocean, and north into Central Asia, over the subsequent centuries.

What role did merchants play in the spread of Islam?

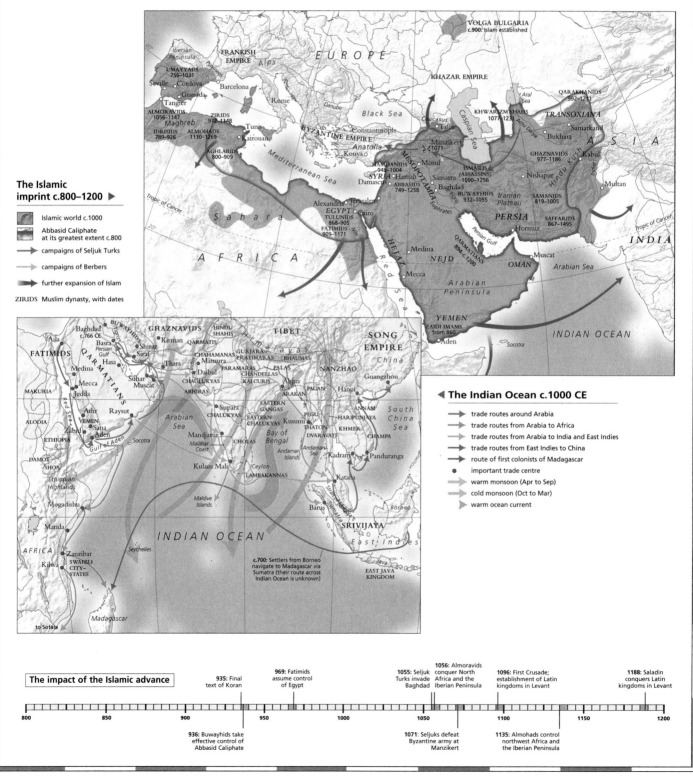

The Islamic imprint c.800–1200 ▶

- Islamic world c.1000
- Abbasid Caliphate at its greatest extent c.800
- → campaigns of Seljuk Turks
- → campaigns of Berbers
- → further expansion of Islam
- ZIRIDS Muslim dynasty, with dates

◀ The Indian Ocean c.1000 CE

- → trade routes around Arabia
- → trade routes from Arabia to Africa
- → trade routes from Arabia to India and East Indies
- → trade routes from East Indies to China
- → route of first colonists of Madagascar
- ● important trade centre
- → warm monsoon (Apr to Sep)
- → cold monsoon (Oct to Mar)
- → warm ocean current

c.700: Settlers from Borneo navigate to Madagascar via Sumatra (their route across Indian Ocean is unknown)

The impact of the Islamic advance

- **935:** Final text of Koran
- **936:** Buwayhids take effective control of Abbasid Caliphate
- **969:** Fatimids assume control of Egypt
- **1055:** Seljuk Turks invade Baghdad
- **1056:** Almoravids conquer North Africa and the Iberian Peninsula
- **1071:** Seljuks defeat Byzantine army at Manzikert
- **1096:** First Crusade; establishment of Latin kingdoms in Levant
- **1135:** Almohads control northwest Africa and the Iberian Peninsula
- **1188:** Saladin conquers Latin kingdoms in Levant

800 | 850 | 900 | 950 | 1000 | 1050 | 1100 | 1150 | 1200

AFRICAN EMPIRES AND CITY-STATES

THE PERIOD BETWEEN 800 AND 1500 witnessed the growth of several powerful African states, some of which – for example, Mali and Songhay – were centered on trans-Saharan trade routes.

Why did empires and city-states develop in only certain regions of Africa?

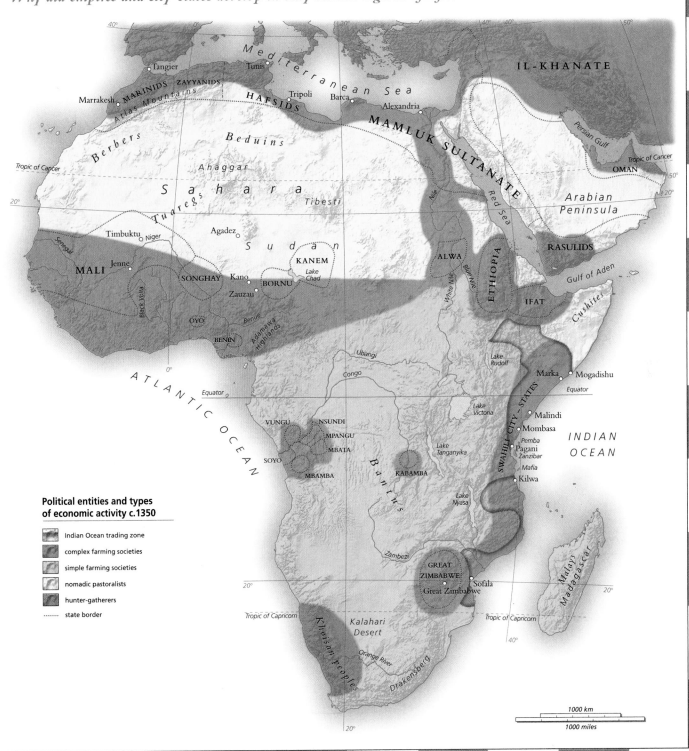

Political entities and types of economic activity c.1350

- Indian Ocean trading zone
- complex farming societies
- simple farming societies
- nomadic pastoralists
- hunter-gatherers
- .... state border

STATES AND EMPIRES IN SOUTH ASIA 300–1550

SOUTH ASIA WAS RULED by a great diversity of regional powers for much of this period. In the 4th century CE, the Gupta dynasty succeeded in uniting much of the Indian subcontinent. In the 13th century, much of India again came under the control of a single state, the Delhi Sultanate. In the East Indies, dominance passed from Srivijaya to Majapahit, which in the 14th century established the most extensive commercial empire that the area was to see in precolonial times.

What were the challenges to state-building in South and Southeast Asia at this time?

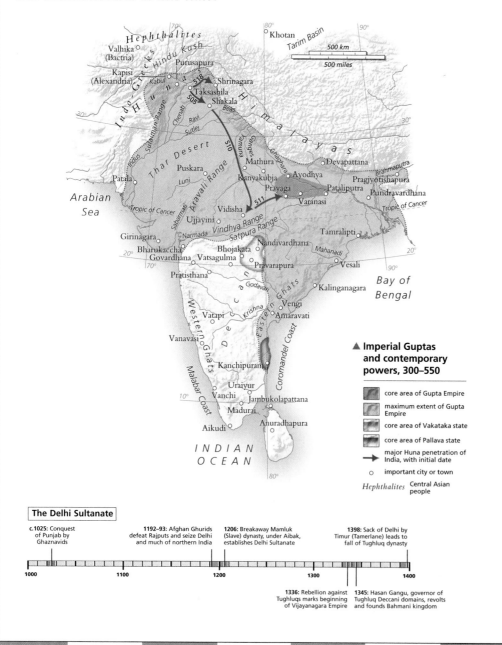

▲ Imperial Guptas and contemporary powers, 300–550

- core area of Gupta Empire
- maximum extent of Gupta Empire
- core area of Vakataka state
- core area of Pallava state
- → major Huna penetration of India, with initial date
- ○ important city or town
- *Hephthalites* Central Asian people

▲ The Delhi Sultanate, 1206–1526

- area of Sultanate at accession of Jalal ud-din Khalji, 1290
- additional territory at some time under direct Khalji administration
- limit of nominal Khalji vassals
- → possible route of Khalji raids against Mongols
- extent of Sultanate at accession of Ghiyas ud-din Tughluq, 1320
- maximum extent of Sultanate under direct Tughluq administration
- limit of nominal Tughluq vassals
- *Ahoms* peoples and dynasties
- *SIND* cultural region

The Delhi Sultanate

c.1025: Conquest of Punjab by Ghaznavids

1192–93: Afghan Ghurids defeat Rajputs and seize Delhi and much of northern India

1206: Breakaway Mamluk (Slave) dynasty, under Aibak, establishes Delhi Sultanate

1398: Sack of Delhi by Timur (Tamerlane) leads to fall of Tughluq dynasty

1336: Rebellion against Tughluqs marks beginning of Vijayanagara Empire

1345: Hasan Gangu, governor of Tughluq Deccani domains, revolts and founds Bahmani kingdom

1000 — 1100 — 1200 — 1300 — 1400

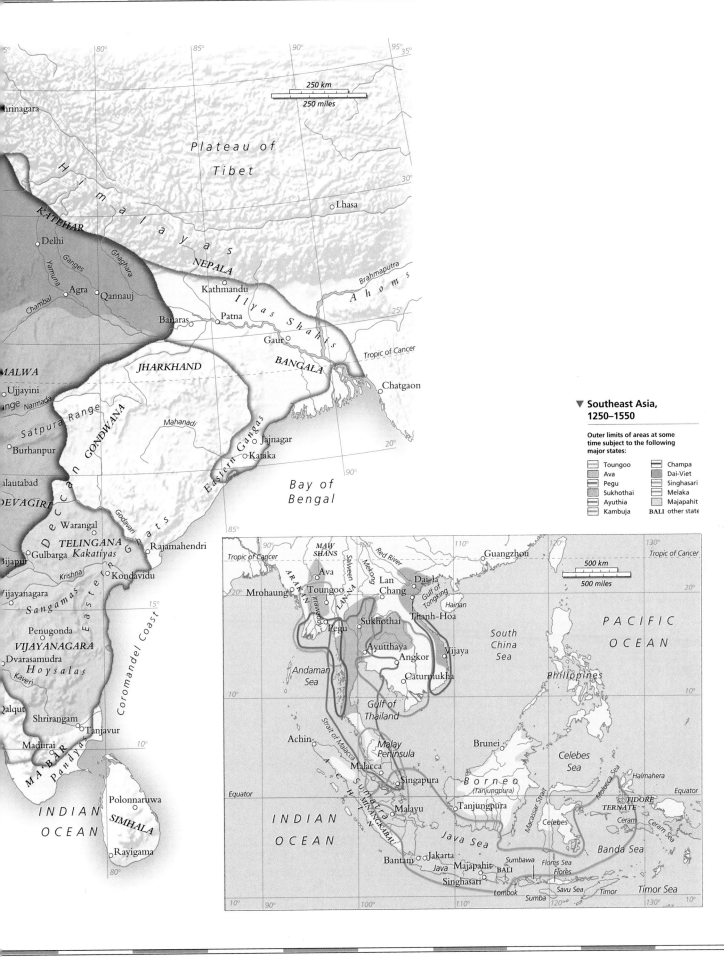

250 km
250 miles

Plateau of
Tibet

Shrinagara

KATEHAR

Delhi

Ghaghara

Yamuna
Ganges

Agra
Qannauj

Chambal

MALWA

Ujjayini

Narmada

Satpura Range

Burhanpur

GONDWANA

Mahanadi

JHARKHAND

Banaras

Patna

Ilyas Shahis

Kathmandu

NEPALA

Ahoms

Brahmaputra

Lhasa

Gaur

BANGALA

Tropic of Cancer

Chatgaon

Jajnagar
Kataka

Eastern Gangas

Bay of
Bengal

DEVAGIRI

Daulatabad

TELINGANA *Kakatiyas*

Warangal

Gulbarga

Bijapur

Krishna

Kondavidu

Godavari

Rajamahendri

Eastern Ghats

Vijayanagara

Sangamas

Penugonda

VIJAYANAGARA

Dvarasamudra

Hoysalas

Kaveri

Qalqut

Shrirangam

Tanjavur

Madurai

MABAR

Pandyas

Coromandel Coast

Polonnaruwa

SIMHALA

INDIAN
OCEAN

Rayigama

▼ Southeast Asia, 1250–1550

Outer limits of areas at some time subject to the following major states:

▢ Toungoo	▢ Champa		
▢ Ava	▢ Dai-Viet		
▢ Pegu	▢ Singhasari		
▢ Sukhothai	▢ Melaka		
▢ Ayuthia	▢ Majapahit		
▢ Kambuja	**BALI** other state		

500 km
500 miles

Tropic of Cancer

MAW
SHANS

Guangzhou

Tropic of Cancer

Red River

Salween

Mekong

Ava

ARAKAN

Mrohaung

Toungoo

LANNA

Irrawaddy

Lan
Chang

Dai-la

Gulf of
Tongking

Hainan

Sukhothai

Thanh-Hoa

Pegu

Ayutthaya

Angkor

Vijaya

PACIFIC
OCEAN

Andaman
Sea

Caturmukha

South
China
Sea

Philippines

Gulf of
Thailand

Achin

Strait of Malacca

Malay
Peninsula

Brunei

Celebes
Sea

Molucca Sea

Halmahera

Malacca

Singapura

B o r n e o
(Tanjungpura)

ACEH

SUMATRA

Malayu

Tanjungpura

Celebes

Macassar Strait

TIDORE
TERNATE

Ceram

Ceram Sea

MINANGKABAU

Equator

INDIAN
OCEAN

Java Sea

Banda Sea

Bantam

Jakarta

Java

Majapahit

BALI

Sumbawa

Flores Sea

Flores

Timor

Timor Sea

Singhasari

Lombok

Sumba

Savu Sea

Equator

THE AGE OF THE CRUSADES

HOLY WAR WAS NEVER PART of the doctrine of the early Church. This changed in 1095 when Pope Urban II urged French barons and knights to liberate the Holy Land from Muslim 'infidels.' In 1099, the Crusaders captured Jerusalem. The crusading ideal became firmly established in European consciousness, and there were many subsequent expeditions to defend or recapture Jerusalem, but none was as successful as the first.

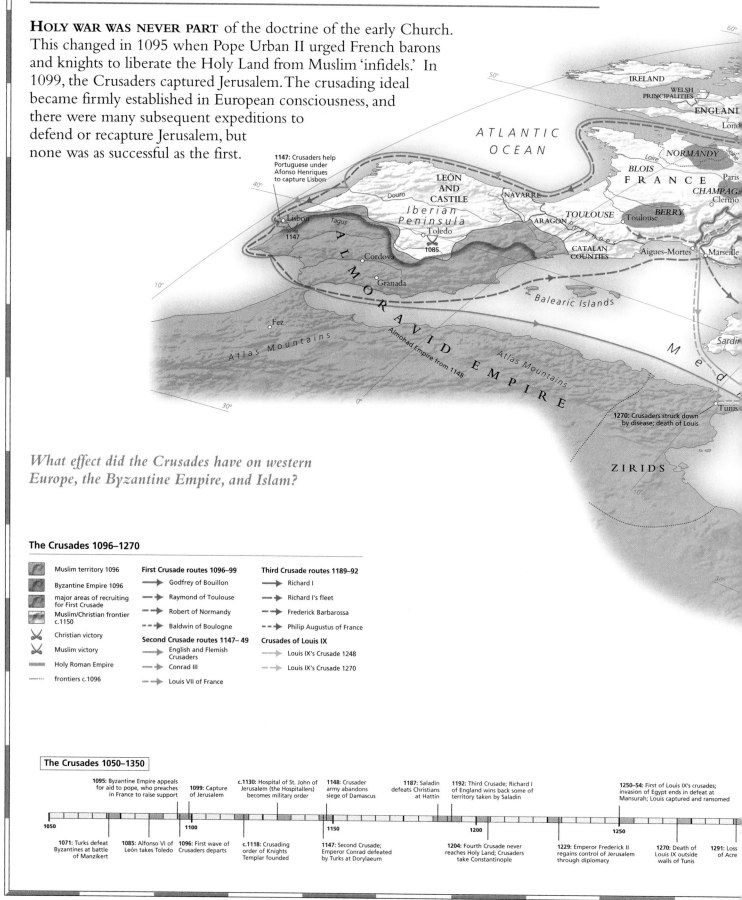

1147: Crusaders help Portuguese under Afonso Henriques to capture Lisbon

1270: Crusaders struck down by disease; death of Louis

What effect did the Crusades have on western Europe, the Byzantine Empire, and Islam?

The Crusades 1096–1270

Muslim territory 1096	
Byzantine Empire 1096	
major areas of recruiting for First Crusade	
Muslim/Christian frontier c.1150	
Christian victory	
Muslim victory	
Holy Roman Empire	
frontiers c.1096	

First Crusade routes 1096–99
→ Godfrey of Bouillon
→ Raymond of Toulouse
→ Robert of Normandy
→ Baldwin of Boulogne

Second Crusade routes 1147–49
→ English and Flemish Crusaders
→ Conrad III
→ Louis VII of France

Third Crusade routes 1189–92
→ Richard I
→ Richard I's fleet
→ Frederick Barbarossa
→ Philip Augustus of France

Crusades of Louis IX
→ Louis IX's Crusade 1248
→ Louis IX's Crusade 1270

The Crusades 1050–1350

1095: Byzantine Empire appeals for aid to pope, who preaches in France to raise support

1099: Capture of Jerusalem

c.1130: Hospital of St. John of Jerusalem (the Hospitallers) becomes military order

1148: Crusader army abandons siege of Damascus

1187: Saladin defeats Christians at Hattin

1192: Third Crusade; Richard I of England wins back some of territory taken by Saladin

1250–54: First of Louis IX's crusades; invasion of Egypt ends in defeat at Mansurah; Louis captured and ransomed

1050 — 1100 — 1150 — 1200 — 1250

1071: Turks defeat Byzantines at battle of Manzikert

1085: Alfonso VI of León takes Toledo

1096: First wave of Crusaders departs

c.1118: Crusading order of Knights Templar founded

1147: Second Crusade; Emperor Conrad defeated by Turks at Dorylaeum

1204: Fourth Crusade never reaches Holy Land; Crusaders take Constantinople

1229: Emperor Frederick II regains control of Jerusalem through diplomacy

1270: Death of Louis IX outside walls of Tunis

1291: Loss of Acre

Scale varies with perspective

4450 km (2760 miles)

4820 km (3000 miles)

TLAND

North Sea

FLANDERS

Soissons

Bruges

Bouillon

LORRAINE

NORWAY

DENMARK

SWEDEN

SAXONY

SWABIA

A l p s

Rhine

LOMBARDY

Genoa

Po

Venice

VENETIAN
REPUBLIC

Corsica

Rome
PAPAL
STATES

ITALY

Regensburg

Danube

BAVARIA

BOHEMIA

Elbe

Wends

Pomeranians

Vistula

POLAND

N o r t h   E u r o p e a n   P l a i n

Prussians

Lithuanians

Danube

HUNGARY

Carpathian Mountains

RUSSIAN
PRINCIPALITIES

Adriatic Sea

BYZANTINE EMPIRE

Belgrade

Nish

Dniester

Kiev

Dnieper

Bari

Taranto

Durazzo

Sofia

Balkan Mountains

Danube

Pechenegs

Tyrrhenian Sea

Sicily

Messina

Thessalonica

Adrianople

1147: Emperor Conrad
falls ill and returns
to Constantinople.

Aegean
Sea

Constantinople

Nicomedia

Nicaea

1096

SELJUKS
OF RUM

Dorylaeum

1097 1147

Black
Sea

Sinope

Ephesus

Crete

Rhodes

Adalia

Anatolia

Danishmends

1190: Frederick Barbarossa
drowned while crossing
River Göksu

Taurus Mountains

Armenians

M e d i t e r r a n e a n   S e a

Nicosia   *Cyprus*

Famagusta

1192: Richard I
twice fails to
reach Jerusalem

Antioch

1098

Edessa

1144

GREAT SELJUK
EMPIRE

1250: After taking Damietta,
Louis advances towards Cairo.
Vanguard destroyed in town
of Mansurah

FATIMID CALIPHATE

Ayyubid Sultanate from 1171

Damietta

Mansurah

1250

Tyre

Acre

Damascus

Hattin

1148: Siege of Damascus
ends in ignominious retreat
through poor organization
and lack of supplies and water

302: Last Christian
rritory in Levant
ls to Mamluks

Ascalon

1099

1187

Cairo

EGYPT

Jerusalem

1099 1187

1099: Jerusalem
falls to Crusaders
after five-week siege

20°

30°

1350

1310: Hospitallers, having
taken Rhodes, make it
their headquarters

Sinai

THE AGE OF THE MONGOLS

By the 13th century, the Chinese empire had become weak and fragmented. Into this power vacuum burst the Mongols, a fierce race of skilled horsemen united under the inspired leadership of Genghis Khan. Genghis's successors extended his conquests across Asia and deep into Europe, but the empire then split into four khanates (see p. 64).

How did Mongol expansion alter the politics, economics, and societies of Eurasia?

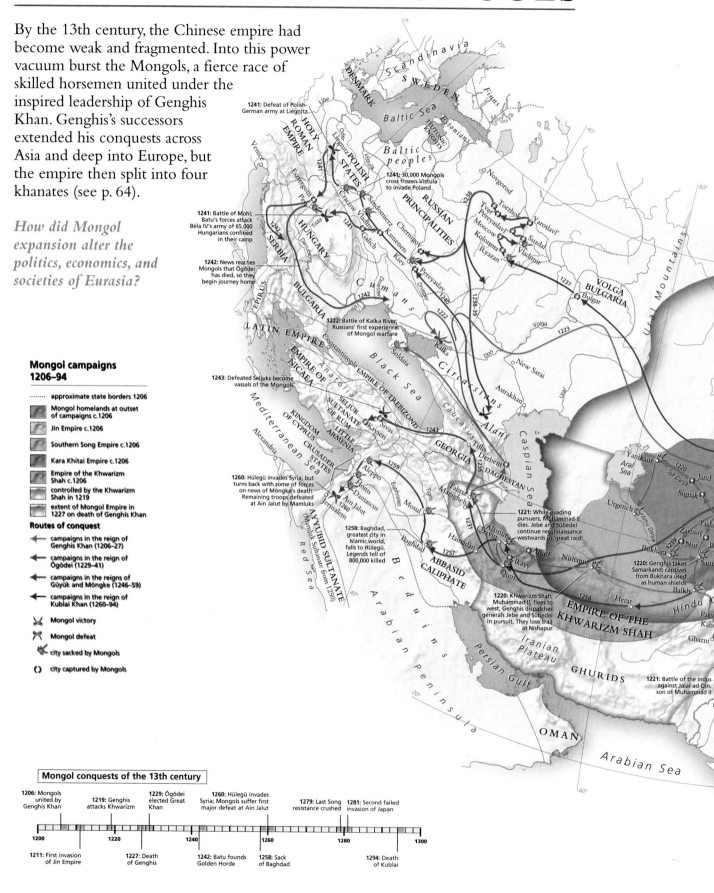

Mongol campaigns 1206–94

.... approximate state borders 1206

▨ Mongol homelands at outset of campaigns c.1206

▨ Jin Empire c.1206

▨ Southern Song Empire c.1206

▨ Kara Khitai Empire c.1206

▨ Empire of the Khwarizm Shah c.1206

▨ controlled by the Khwarizm Shah in 1219

▨ extent of Mongol Empire in 1227 on death of Genghis Khan

Routes of conquest

← campaigns in the reign of Genghis Khan (1206–27)

← campaigns in the reign of Ögödei (1229–41)

← campaigns in the reigns of Güyük and Möngke (1246–59)

← campaigns in the reign of Kublai Khan (1260–94)

✕ Mongol victory

✕ Mongol defeat

⚘ city sacked by Mongols

() city captured by Mongols

Map labels:

1241: Defeat of Polish-German army at Liegnitz

1241: 30,000 Mongols cross frozen Vistula to invade Poland

1241: Battle of Mohi; Batu's forces attack Béla IV's army of 65,000 Hungarians confined in their camp

1242: News reaches Mongols that Ögödei has died, so they begin journey home

1222: Battle of Kalka River; Russians' first experience of Mongol warfare

1243: Defeated Seljuks become vassals of the Mongols

1260: Hülegü invades Syria, but turns back with some of forces on news of Möngke's death. Remaining troops defeated at Ain Jalut by Mamluks

1258: Baghdad, greatest city in Islamic world, falls to Hülegü. Legends tell of 800,000 killed

1221: While evading pursuers, Muhammad II dies. Jebe and Sübedei continue reconnaissance westwards in 'great raid'

1221: Battle of the Indus against Jalal-ad-Din, son of Muhammad II

1220: Khwarizm Shah, Muhammad II, flees to west; Genghis dispatches generals Jebe and Sübedei in pursuit. They lose trail at Nishapur

1220: Genghis takes Samarkand; captives from Bukhara used as human shields

Mongol conquests of the 13th century

1206: Mongols united by Genghis Khan
1211: First invasion of Jin Empire
1219: Genghis attacks Khwarizm
1227: Death of Genghis
1229: Ögödei elected Great Khan
1242: Batu founds Golden Horde
1260: Hülegü invades Syria; Mongols suffer first major defeat at Ain Jalut
1258: Sack of Baghdad
1279: Last Song resistance crushed
1281: Second failed invasion of Japan
1294: Death of Kublai

1200   1220   1240   1260   1280   1300

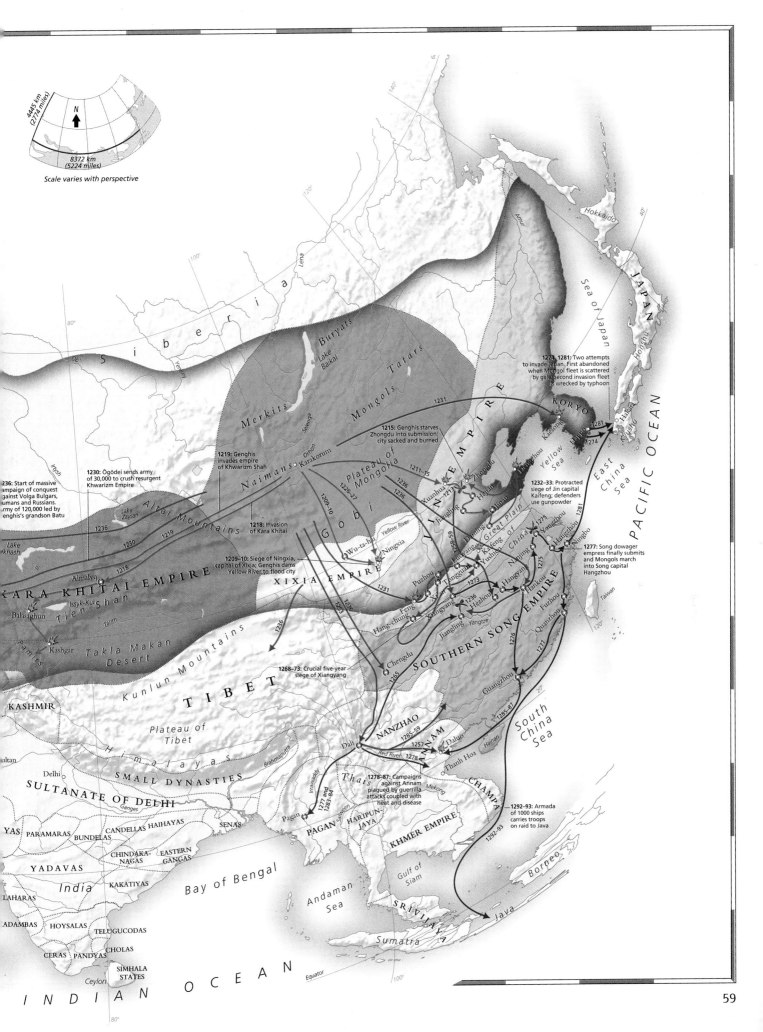

Scale varies with perspective

4445 km (2774 miles)

8372 km (5224 miles)

N

1236: Start of massive campaign of conquest against Volga Bulgars, Cumans and Russians. Army of 120,000 led by Genghis's grandson Batu

1230: Ögödei sends army of 30,000 to crush resurgent Khwarizm Empire

1219: Genghis invades empire of Khwarizm Shah

1218: Invasion of Kara Khitai

1209–10: Siege of Ningxia, capital of Xixia; Genghis dams Yellow River to flood city

1215: Genghis starves Zhongdu into submission; city sacked and burned

1274, 1281: Two attempts to invade Japan. First abandoned when Mongol fleet is scattered by gale; second invasion fleet is wrecked by typhoon

1232–33: Protracted siege of Jin capital Kaifeng; defenders use gunpowder

1277: Song dowager empress finally submits and Mongols march into Song capital Hangzhou

1268–73: Crucial five-year siege of Xiangyang

1278–87: Campaigns against Annam plagued by guerrilla attacks coupled with heat and disease

1292–93: Armada of 1000 ships carries troops on raid to Java

Siberia

Buryats

Lake Baikal

Merkits

Mongols

Tatars

Naimans

Plateau of Mongolia

Karakorum

Orhon

Selenga

Yenisey

Lena

Altai Mountains

Lake Zaysan

Gobi

KARA KHITAI EMPIRE

Lake Balkhash

Almalyq

Tien Shan

Issyk-Kul

Balasaghun

Kashgar

Pamirs

Takla Makan Desert

Kunlun Mountains

XIXIA EMPIRE

Wu-ta-hu

Ningxia

Yellow River

JIN EMPIRE

KORYO

Hokkaido

JAPAN

Honshu

Hakata

Kyushu

Sea of Japan

Yellow Sea

East China Sea

PACIFIC OCEAN

Zhongdu

Kuanhua

Fengxiang

Jinan

Daming

Great Plain of China

Kaifeng

Yushou

Puzhou

Tongguan

Xi'an

Feng

Hang-chung

Xiangyang

Hezhou

Hangyang

Nanjing

Yangzhou

Hangzhou

Hankou

Ningbo

Taiwan

Dengzhou

Kaesong

KASHMIR

TIBET

Plateau of Tibet

Himalayas

SMALL DYNASTIES

Delhi

SULTANATE OF DELHI

Ganges

...YAS

PARAMARAS

CANDELLAS HAIHAYAS

BUNDELAS

CHINDAKA-NAGAS

EASTERN GANGAS

YADAVAS

KAKATIYAS

India

...LAHARAS

...ADAMBAS

HOYSALAS

TELUGUCODAS

CERAS

PANDYAS

CHOLAS

SIMHALA STATES

Ceylon

Brahmaputra

SOUTHERN SONG EMPIRE

Chengdu

Jiangling

Yangtze

Fuzhou

Quanzhou

Guangzhou

Hainan

South China Sea

NANZHAO

Dali

Daluo

ANNAM

Red River

Thanh Hoa

CHAMPA

Irrawaddy

Pagan

PAGAN

Salween

Mekong

HARIPUN-JAYA

Thais

KHMER EMPIRE

Gulf of Siam

SRIVIJAYA

Andaman Sea

Bay of Bengal

Sumatra

Java

Borneo

INDIAN OCEAN

Equator

1231

1209–10

1226–27

1236

1211–15

1236

1273

1236

1255

1231

1238

1277 and 1283–84

1285–59

1257

1278–87

1285–87

1292–93

1274

1281

1275

1276

1277

59

TRADE IN MEDIEVAL EUROPE

THE EXPLOSION IN EUROPE'S POPULATION, which nearly doubled between the 10th and 14th centuries, was caused by greatly increased agricultural productivity and large land-clearance projects which brought marginal land, such as marshes and forests, under cultivation. This demographic surge led to increased trading activity; trade and commerce went hand in hand with urban development. As cities prospered, a new class, the bourgeoisie, emerged.

How did trade and commerce affect the growth of European states and cities in the Middle Ages?

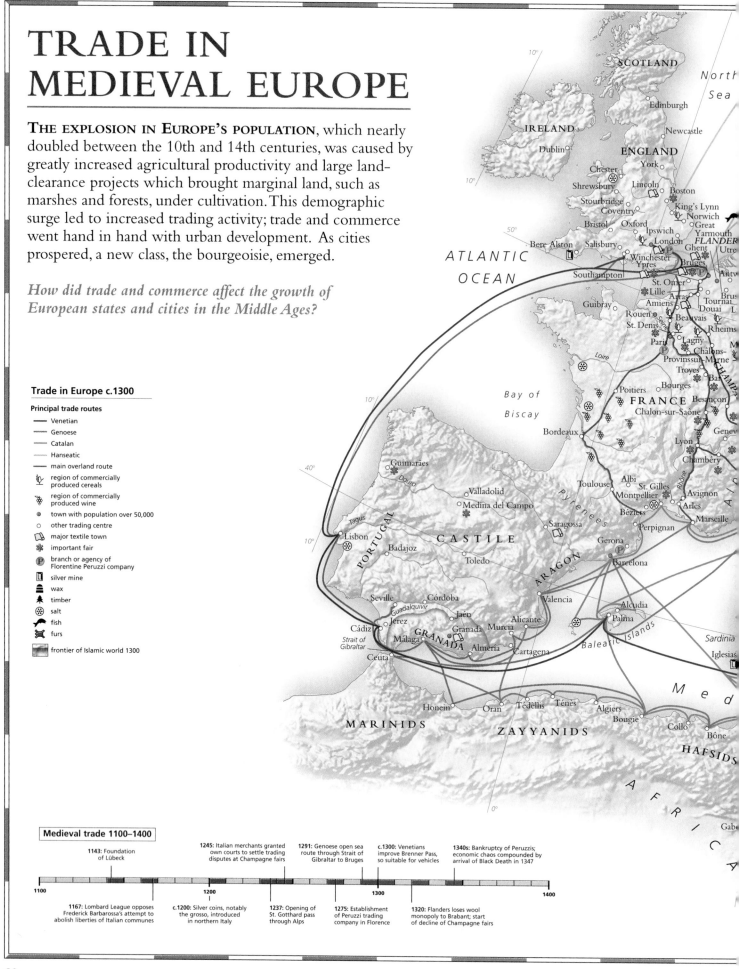

Trade in Europe c.1300

Principal trade routes

— Venetian
— Genoese
— Catalan
— Hanseatic
— main overland route

🌿 region of commercially produced cereals
🍇 region of commercially produced wine
● town with population over 50,000
○ other trading centre
📜 major textile town
✳️ important fair
Ⓟ branch or agency of Florentine Peruzzi company
silver mine
wax
🌲 timber
salt
🐟 fish
furs

frontier of Islamic world 1300

Medieval trade 1100–1400

1143: Foundation of Lübeck

1245: Italian merchants granted own courts to settle trading disputes at Champagne fairs

1291: Genoese open sea route through Strait of Gibraltar to Bruges

c.1300: Venetians improve Brenner Pass, so suitable for vehicles

1340s: Bankruptcy of Peruzzis; economic chaos compounded by arrival of Black Death in 1347

1167: Lombard League opposes Frederick Barbarossa's attempt to abolish liberties of Italian communes

c.1200: Silver coins, notably the grosso, introduced in northern Italy

1237: Opening of St. Gotthard pass through Alps

1275: Establishment of Peruzzi trading company in Florence

1320: Flanders loses wool monopoly to Brabant; start of decline of Champagne fairs

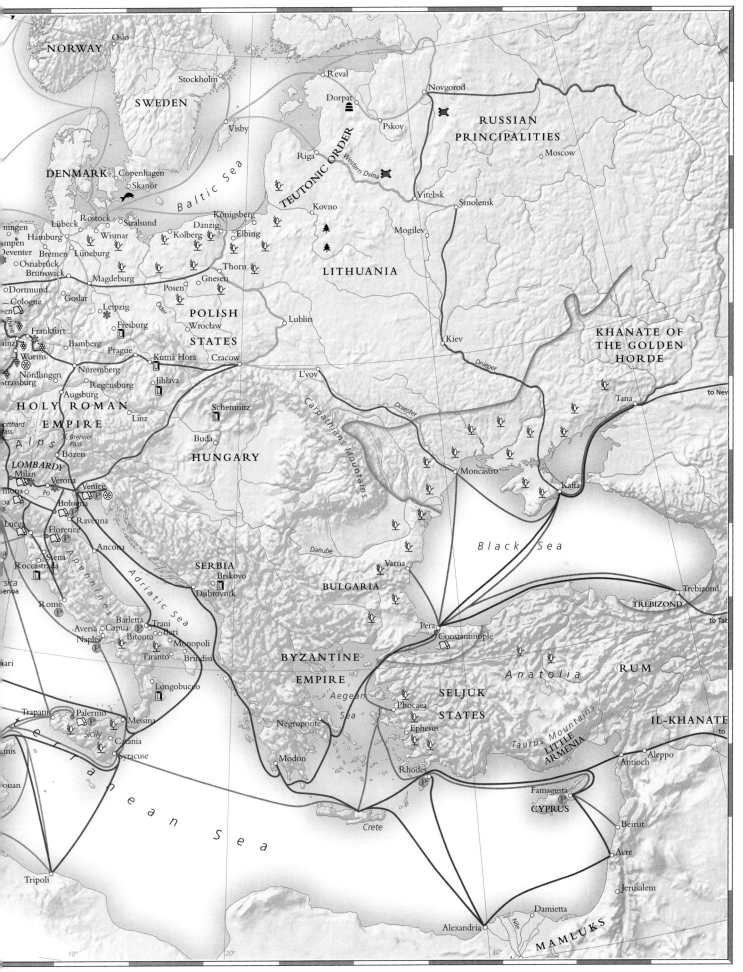

NORWAY

Oslo

Stockholm

SWEDEN

Reval

Novgorod

RUSSIAN
PRINCIPALITIES

Visby

Dorpat

Pskov

Moscow

DENMARK

Copenhagen

Skanör

Baltic Sea

Riga

TEUTONIC ORDER

Western Dvina

Vitebsk

Smolensk

Lübeck

Rostock

Stralsund

Königsberg

Kovno

Mogilev

Hamburg

Wismar

Danzig

Kolberg

Elbing

Bremen

Lüneburg

Osnabrück

Brunswick

Magdeburg

Posen

Thorn

Gnesen

LITHUANIA

Dortmund

Cologne

Goslar

Leipzig

Freiburg

POLISH

Wrocław

Lublin

Kiev

KHANATE OF
THE GOLDEN
HORDE

Frankfurt

Bamberg

Prague

STATES

to New

Worms

Nördlingen

Strassburg

Nuremberg

Regensburg

Kutná Hora

Jihlava

Cracow

L'vov

Dnieper

Tana

Augsburg

Linz

Schemnitz

Dniester

Moncastro

Kaffa

HOLY ROMAN

EMPIRE

Gotthard
Pass

Brenner
Pass

Bozen

Buda

HUNGARY

Carpathians Mountains

Alps

LOMBARDY

Milan

Verona

Venice

Bologna

Ravenna

Florence

Ancona

Danube

Varna

Black Sea

Trebizond

TREBIZOND

Lucca

Siena

Roccastrada

SERBIA

Brskovo

Adriatic Sea

Rome

Barletta

Trani

Aversa

Capua

Bari

Naples

Bitonto

Monopoli

Taranto

Brindisi

Dubrovnik

BULGARIA

Pera

Constantinople

to Tab

Apennines

Genoa

Longobucco

BYZANTINE

EMPIRE

*Aegean
Sea*

SELJUK

STATES

Anatolia

RUM

IL-KHANATE

Trapani

Palermo

Messina

Sicily

Catania

Syracuse

Negroponte

Modon

Phocaea

Ephesus

Taurus Mountains

LITTLE
ARMENIA

Aleppo

Antioch

Tunis

Rhodes

Famagusta

CYPRUS

Beirut

Crete

Acre

Mediterranean Sea

Tripoli

Jerusalem

Damietta

Alexandria

Nile

MAMLUKS

10°

20°

30°

THE BLACK DEATH

FROM 500 TO 1500 CE, imperial expansion, mass migration, cross-cultural trade, and long-distance travel all facilitated the spread of crops, domesticated animals, and diseases throughout much of the Old World. In the early 14th century, Mongol armies helped infected fleas spread from Yunnan to the rest of China. From China, bubonic plague spread rapidly west along the Silk Road. By 1346 it had reached the Black Sea. Muslim merchants carried it south and west, while Italian merchants carried it to western Europe, where it became known as the Black Death. Up to one third of Europe's population is thought to have died from the plague.

How did the Black Death affect the societies of the Old World?

The spread of the Black Death

- Arab trade route
- Chinese trade route
- Genoese trade route
- main Hanseatic trade routes
- Silk Road } routes opened during the 'Mongol Peace' c.1250–1350
- other route
- Venetian trade route
- other trade route
- principal route of Hajj pilgrimage to Mecca
- progress of bubonic plague
- area of earliest outbreak of bubonic plague
- area of outbreak of bubonic plague
- recorded outbreak of bubonic plague

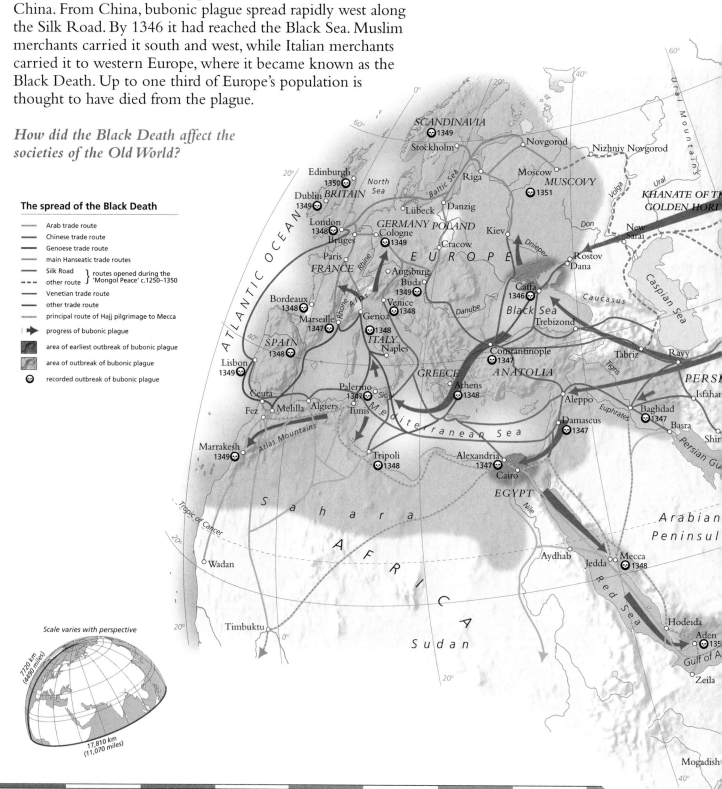

Scale varies with perspective

7720 km (4490 miles)

17,810 km (11,070 miles)

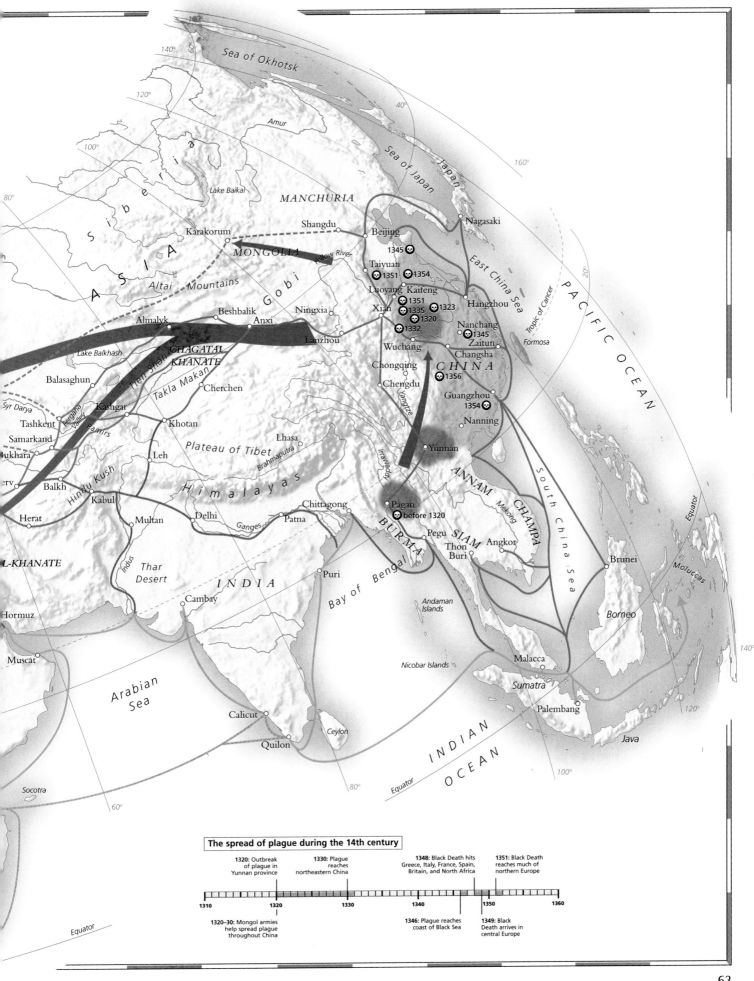

Sea of Okhotsk

Sea of Japan

PACIFIC OCEAN

MANCHURIA

Lake Baikal

Karakorum   Shangdu   Beijing   Nagasaki

MONGOLIA   *Yellow River*   1345 ☠

Altai Mountains   Taiyuan ☠ 1351   ☠ 1354

Gobi   Luoyang   Kaifeng

Ningxia   Xian ☠ 1335   ☠ 1323   Hangzhou

Beshbalik   Anxi   ☠ 1320   East China Sea

Almalyk   Lanzhou   ☠ 1332   Nanchang   Zaitun

Tien Shan   CHAGATAL   Wuchang   ☠ 1345

Lake Balkash   KHANATE   Chongqing   Changsha   *Formosa*

Balasaghun   Takla Makan   Chengdu   C H I N A   ☠ 1356

Syr Darya   Cherchen   *Yangtze*   Guangzhou

Tashkent   Kashgar   Khotan   Nanning   ☠ 1354

Samarkand   Leh   Lhasa

Bukhara   Plateau of Tibet   *Brahmaputra*   Yunnan   South China Sea

Merv   H i m a l a y a s   *Irrawaddy*

Balkh   Hindu Kush   Kabul   ANNAM   CHAMPA

Herat   Multan   Delhi   Chittagong   Pagan   ☠ before 1320

Ganges   Patna   BURMA   Pegu   SIAM   Brunei   Moluccas

IL-KHANATE   *Indus*   Thon   Angkor   Equator

Hormuz   Thar   Desert   I N D I A   Buri

Cambay   Puri   *Bay of Bengal*   Andaman   Islands   Borneo

Muscat   Calicut   *Ceylon*   Nicobar Islands   Malacca   *140°*

Arabian   Sea   Quilon   Sumatra

Socotra   I N D I A N   O C E A N   Palembang   *Java*

Equator   *100°*

The spread of plague during the 14th century

1320: Outbreak of plague in Yunnan province	**1330:** Plague reaches northeastern China	**1348:** Black Death hits Greece, Italy, France, Spain, Britain, and North Africa	**1351:** Black Death reaches much of northern Europe	

1310   1320   1330   1340   1350   1360

1320–30: Mongol armies help spread plague throughout China   **1346:** Plague reaches coast of Black Sea   **1349:** Black Death arrives in central Europe

THE WORLD: 1300–1400

DURING THE 14TH CENTURY, dramatic demographic decline led to economic and social disruption that weakened states throughout Eurasia and North Africa. The Mongol Empire, which had dominated Eurasia for over a century, began to disintegrate. In China, a new dynasty, the Ming, emerged, while in west Asia, the Ottoman Turks seized Anatolia and encroached on Byzantine holdings in southeastern Europe. The Islamic Mali Empire controlled the trans-Saharan caravan trade, using the profits to maintain a powerful army and dominate West Africa.

What factors contributed to political change in Europe and new empires in Asia?

Europe

1312: Order of Knights Templar suppressed by pope	**1337:** Beginning of the Hundred Years' War	**1346:** English defeat French at Battle of Crécy	**1378:** Beginning of Great Schism in Catholic church	**1381:** Peasants' Revolt in England	

1300 — 1320 — 1340 — 1360 — 1380 — 1400

1309: Pope takes up residence at Avignon

1347: Arrival of bubonic plague in Italy

1358: The Jacquerie, uprising against nobility in France

1397: Union of Kalmar; Norway, Denmark, and Sweden united under a single monarch

The Mongol peace

1235: Walled city built at Karakorum as fixed Mongol capital

1275: Marco Polo reaches Kublai's summer palace at Shangdu (Xanadu)

1325: Ibn Battuta's first pilgrimage to Mecca

1345–46: Ibn Battuta visits Southeast Asia and China

1225 — 1250 — 1275 — 1300 — 1325 — 1350

1264: Kublai defeats rival for title of Great Khan, ending civil war

1266: Kublai founds new capital at Khanbaliq (Beijing)

1334–41: Ibn Battuta serves as *qadi* (judge) in Delhi

▲ **Eurasia and Africa c.1300**

route of Marco Polo 1271 ——— 1295

route of Ibn Battuta 1325 ➤➤➤ 1345

┆┆┆ disputed journeys of Ibn Battuta

——— Silk Road

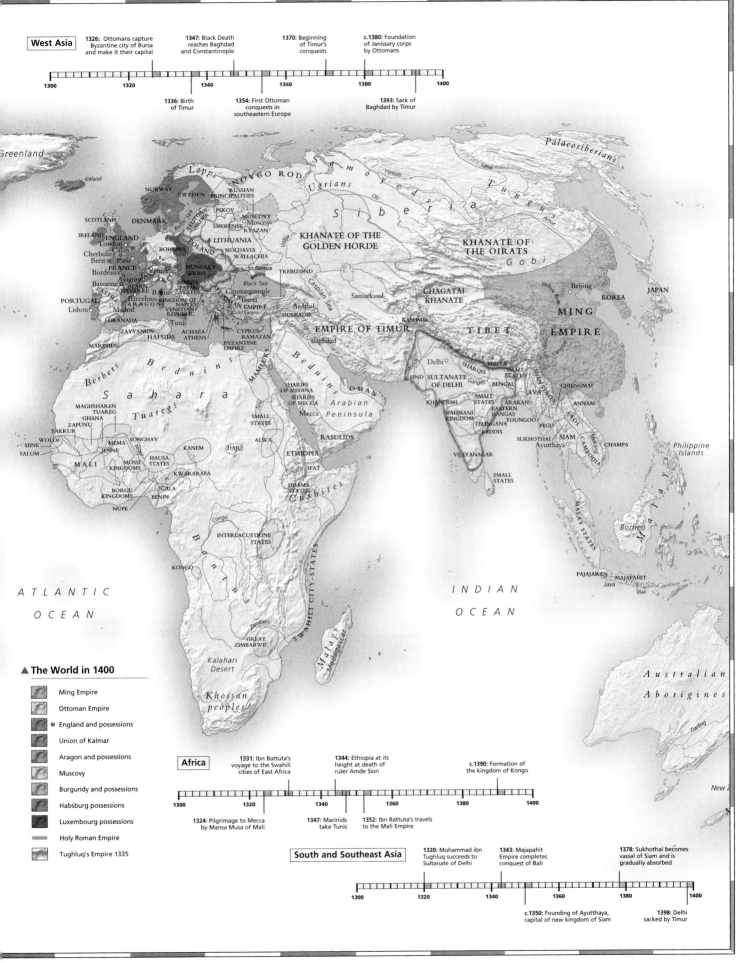

THE AZTEC EMPIRE

THE AZTECS ENTERED THE VALLEY OF MEXICO around 1200, establishing their island capital of Tenochtitlan on Lake Texcoco in 1325. By 1519 the Aztec Empire controlled most of central Mexico as well as Maya areas further east. The Aztecs maintained a state of constant military activity which served to provide a flow of tribute from neighboring states.

How was tribute collection central to the Aztec Empire?

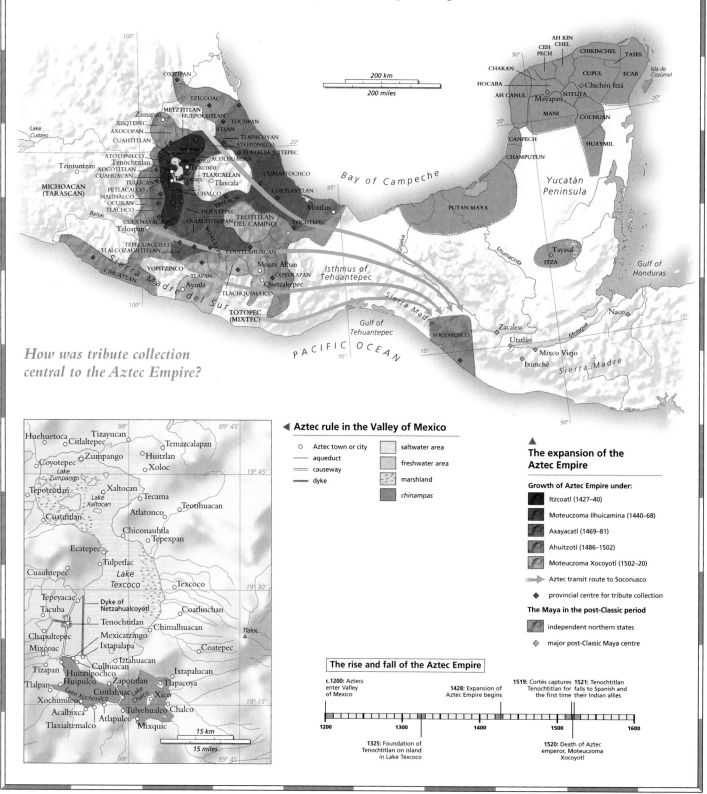

◄ Aztec rule in the Valley of Mexico

- ○ Aztec town or city
- —— aqueduct
- ═══ causeway
- ━━ dyke

- saltwater area
- freshwater area
- marshland
- *chinampas*

▲ The expansion of the Aztec Empire

Growth of Aztec Empire under:

- Itzcoatl (1427–40)
- Moteuczoma Ilhuicamina (1440–68)
- Axayacatl (1469–81)
- Ahuitzotl (1486–1502)
- Moteuczoma Xocoyotl (1502–20)
- → Aztec transit route to Soconusco
- ◆ provincial centre for tribute collection

The Maya in the post-Classic period

- independent northern states
- ◇ major post-Classic Maya centre

The rise and fall of the Aztec Empire

c.1200: Aztecs enter Valley of Mexico

1325: Foundation of Tenochtitlan on island in Lake Texcoco

1428: Expansion of Aztec Empire begins

1519: Cortés captures Tenochtitlan for the first time

1520: Death of Aztec emperor, Moteuczoma Xocoyotl

1521: Tenochtitlan falls to Spanish and their Indian allies

| 1200 | 1300 | 1400 | 1500 | 1600 |

THE INCA EMPIRE

THE INCA EMERGED, in less than a century, as the preeminent state in South America; from 1470 they ruled vast territories from their capital, Cuzco. An extensive road network bound the empire together.

How did the Andes contribute to the development of Inca civilization?

The Inca Empire 1525

Expansion of the Inca Empire

- by 1400
- in reign of Pachacutec 1438–71
- in reign of Tupac Yupanqui 1471–93
- in reign of Huayna Capac 1493–1525
- border of Inca Empire 1525
- Inca road

South America c.1500

- border of Inca Empire
- high civilization
- chiefdoms
- tropical forest farming villages
- other farming villages
- nomadic hunter-gatherers

Ona indigenous people

The Inca Empire

1440s: Pachacutec Inca begins a series of conquests, from Lake Titicaca to Quito

1438: Incas rise to power; attack Lake Titicaca basin, and establish upland empire

1475: Chimú conquered by Inca

1500: Protracted military campaigns at northern and southern extremes of empire lead to establishment of second capital at Tomebamba

1525: Huayna Capac dies leaving two rival claimants to the throne; civil war ensues

1532: Francisco Pizarro defeats the Sapa Inca

1400 · 1425 · 1450 · 1475 · 1500 · 1525 · 1550

EUROPEAN EXPANSION

THE 16TH CENTURY SAW THE EXPANSION of several European nations far beyond their continental limits. The Spanish and the Portuguese led the way, followed by the French and English. Travelers transported numerous species of fruits, vegetables, and animals from the Americas to Europe. At the same time, settlers introduced European species to the Americas and Oceania. European expansion also led to a spread of European diseases. Vast numbers of indigenous American peoples died from measles and smallpox, which broke out in massive epidemics.

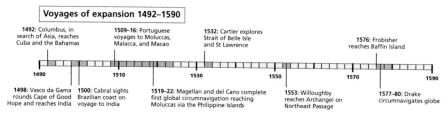

Voyages of expansion 1492–1590

1492: Columbus, in search of Asia, reaches Cuba and the Bahamas

1509–16: Portuguese voyages to Moluccas, Malacca, and Macao

1532: Cartier explores Strait of Belle Isle and St Lawrence

1576: Frobisher reaches Baffin Island

1490 — 1510 — 1530 — 1550 — 1570 — 1590

1498: Vasco da Gama rounds Cape of Good Hope and reaches India

1500: Cabral sights Brazilian coast on voyage to India

1519–22: Magellan and del Cano complete first global circumnavigation reaching Moluccas via the Philippine Islands

1553: Willoughby reaches Archangel on Northeast Passage

1577–80: Drake circumnavigates globe

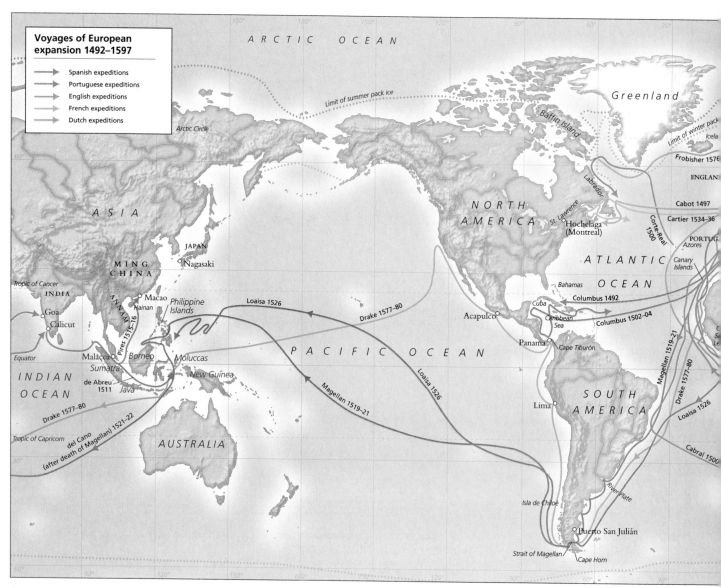

Voyages of European expansion 1492–1597

- Spanish expeditions
- Portuguese expeditions
- English expeditions
- French expeditions
- Dutch expeditions

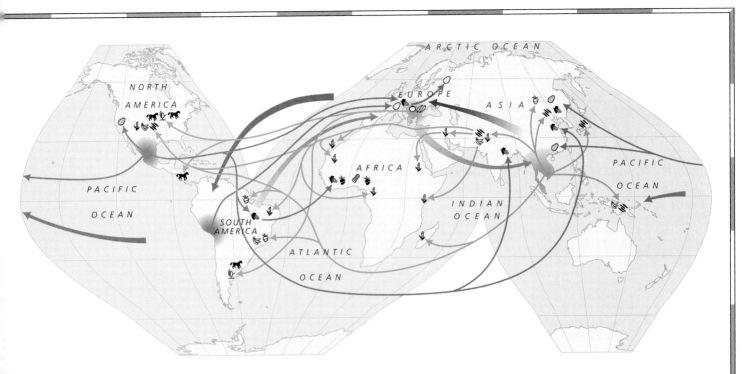

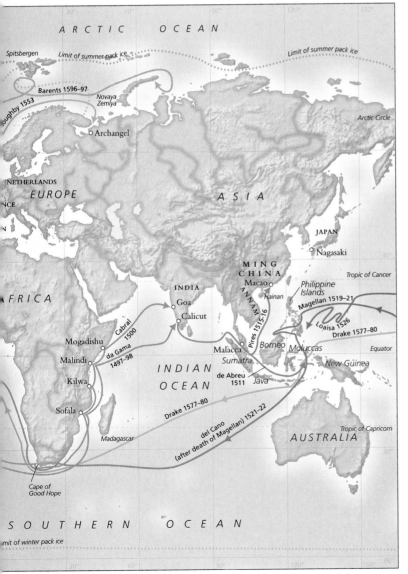

Biological exchanges ▲

Origin and movement of plants and animals

- ➙ from Europe
- ➙ from America
- ➙ from Asia

Plants and animals

- ⤳ bananas
- ⬭ chilli peppers
- 🐎 horses
- 🌾 maize
- ⚇ manioc
- ⬮ peanuts
- ◯ potatoes
- ⫴ rice
- ⬇ sugar cane
- ⬭ sweet potatoes
- ◯ tomatoes
- ⚘ wheat
- ⚇ yams

Diseases

- ➤ bubonic plague
- ➤ diptheria, influenza, measles, smallpox, and whooping cough
- ➤ syphilis

How did European expansion transform societies, economies, and biota around the world?

THE WORLD: 1500–1600

IN THE 16TH CENTURY Spain seized a vast land empire that encompassed much of the Americas and the Philippines. Meanwhile, Portugal acquired a large maritime empire stretching from Brazil to Macao. Ferdinand Magellan demonstrated that all of the world's oceans were linked and sea lanes were established through the Indian, Atlantic, and Pacific oceans.

Europe

1500 — 1520 — 1540 — 1560 — 1580 — 1600

1519: Charles V elected Holy Roman Emperor
1545: Council of Trent called to counter threat of Protestantism
1580: Philip II of Spain seizes Portuguese crown
1598: Edict of Nantes ends over 30 years of religious wars in France

1517: Martin Luther's *95 Theses* attack abuses of Catholic church
1534: Act of Supremacy; Henry VIII of England breaks with Rome
1565: Dutch Revolt starts long series of wars to gain independence from Spain
1588: English defeat Spanish Armada

Why is this period considered the beginnng of the modern world?

The Americas

1500 — 1520 — 1540 — 1560 — 1580 — 1600

1502: Start of reign of last Aztec emperor, Montezuma II
1519: Cortés reaches Tenochtitlán (now México), capital of the Aztec Empire
1545: Opening of vast silver mine at Potosí
1580: Philip II of Spain becomes king of Portugal and its Brazilian empire

1510: First African slaves brought to Americas
1527: Death of Inca emperor Huayna Capac ignites civil war
1533: Pizarro captures Inca capital Cuzco
1549: Portuguese royal government established in Brazil
c.1575: Brazil becomes world's largest sugar producer

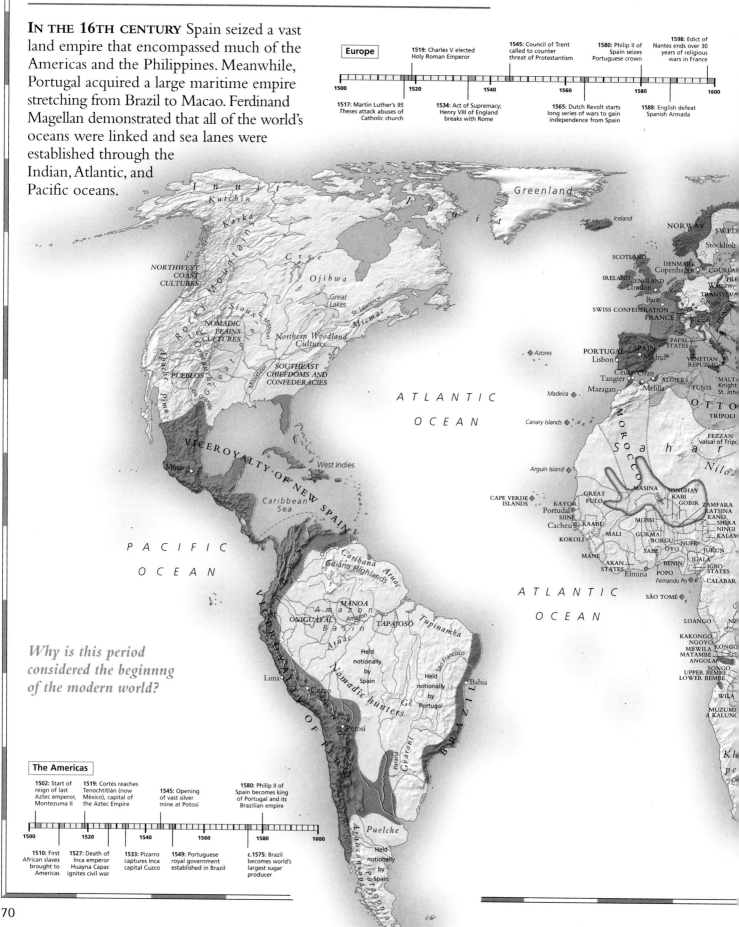

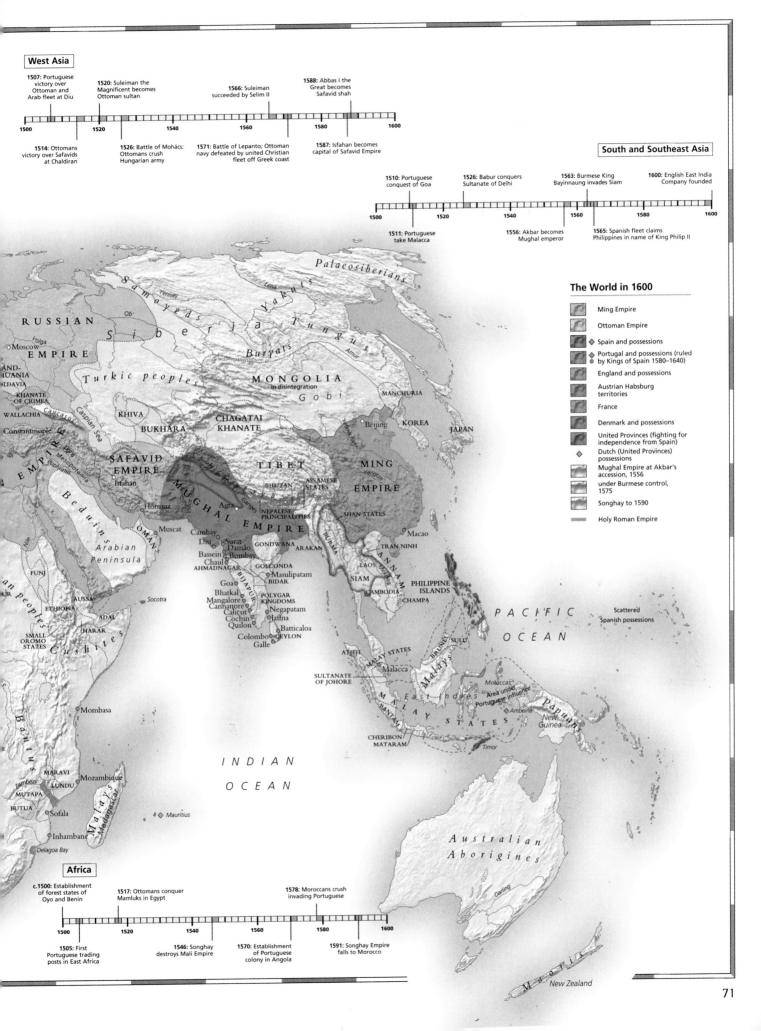

West Asia

1507: Portuguese
victory over
Ottoman and
Arab fleet at Diu

1520: Suleiman the
Magnificent becomes
Ottoman sultan

1566: Suleiman
succeeded by Selim II

1588: Abbas I the
Great becomes
Safavid shah

1500   1520   1540   1560   1580   1600

1514: Ottomans
victory over Safavids
at Chaldiran

1526: Battle of Mohács:
Ottomans crush
Hungarian army

1571: Battle of Lepanto; Ottoman
navy defeated by united Christian
fleet off Greek coast

1587: Isfahan becomes
capital of Safavid Empire

South and Southeast Asia

1510: Portuguese
conquest of Goa

1526: Babur conquers
Sultanate of Delhi

1563: Burmese King
Bayinnaung invades Siam

1600: English East India
Company founded

1500   1520   1540   1560   1580   1600

1511: Portuguese
take Malacca

1556: Akbar becomes
Mughal emperor

1565: Spanish fleet claims
Philippines in name of King Philip II

The World in 1600

- Ming Empire
- Ottoman Empire
- ◇ Spain and possessions
- ◇ Portugal and possessions (ruled by Kings of Spain 1580–1640)
- England and possessions
- Austrian Habsburg territories
- France
- Denmark and possessions
- United Provinces (fighting for independence from Spain)
- ◇ Dutch (United Provinces) possessions
- Mughal Empire at Akbar's accession, 1556
- under Burmese control, 1575
- Songhay to 1590
- Holy Roman Empire

Africa

c.1500: Establishment
of forest states of
Oyo and Benin

1517: Ottomans conquer
Mamluks in Egypt

1578: Moroccans crush
invading Portuguese

1500   1520   1540   1560   1580   1600

1505: First
Portuguese trading
posts in East Africa

1546: Songhay
destroys Mali Empire

1570: Establishment
of Portuguese
colony in Angola

1591: Songhay Empire
falls to Morocco

THE MING AND THE OUTSIDE WORLD

WITH THE ESTABLISHMENT of the Ming Empire in 1368, China came under the control of a native dynasty for the first time in 400 years. Despite its isolationism, in the 16th century Ming China's sheer wealth and productivity made it a great magnet for global trade.

How did Ming China drive the global economy of the early–modern world?

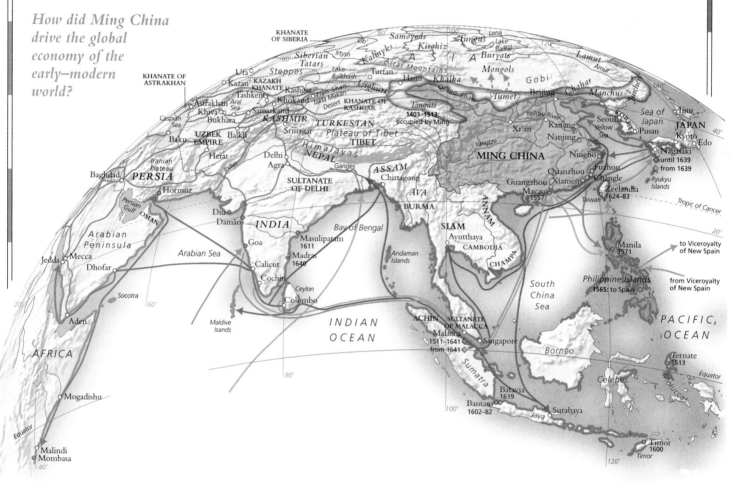

The Ming and the outside world

- Ming Empire
- Ming tributary peoples
- Spanish area of control in the Philippines
- transcontinental trade route
- coastline known to Chinese sailors

- → Portuguese trade routes
- → Dutch trade routes
- → Spanish trade routes
- → Chinese Manila trade routes
- → voyages of Zheng He
- → Japanese raids
- ⇢ campaigns against the Mongols

- ◆◇ Dutch territory/trading station with date
- ◆◆ Portuguese territory/trading station with date
- ● English territory/trading station with date
- ● Spanish trading station with date
- ○ major Chinese port

Scale varies with perspective

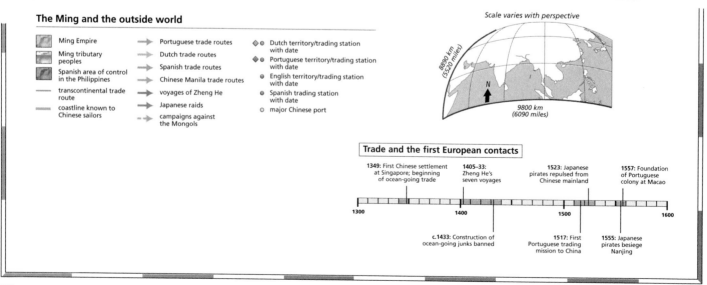

Trade and the first European contacts

- **1349:** First Chinese settlement at Singapore; beginning of ocean-going trade
- **1405–33:** Zheng He's seven voyages
- **1523:** Japanese pirates repulsed from Chinese mainland
- **1557:** Foundation of Portuguese colony at Macao

- **c.1433:** Construction of ocean-going junks banned
- **1517:** First Portuguese trading mission to China
- **1555:** Japanese pirates besiege Nanjing

1300 — 1400 — 1500 — 1600

THE REUNIFICATION OF JAPAN

THE STRUGGLE FOR SUPREMACY between *bushido* warlords in 16th-century Japan led to the emergence of two shoguns: Oda Nobunaga, who enforced national unfication under a virtual dictatorship, and his succesor Toyotmi Hideyoshi, whose imperial ambitions led to repeated campaigns in Korea. This period was accompanied by the first contacts with European trade and Christian missions.

What were the challenges to unity in Japan?

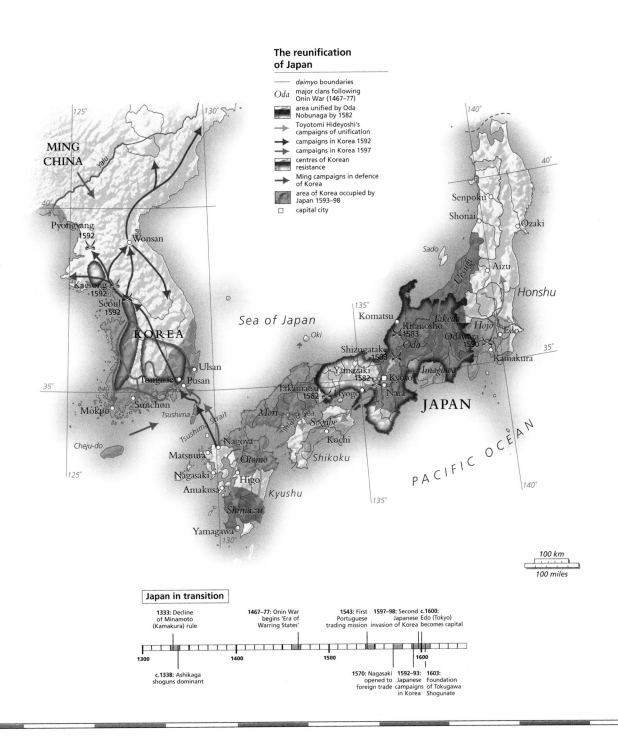

The reunification of Japan

——— *daimyo* boundaries

Oda major clans following Onin War (1467–77)

■ area unified by Oda Nobunaga by 1582

→ Toyotomi Hideyoshi's campaigns of unification

→ campaigns in Korea 1592

→ campaigns in Korea 1597

▨ centres of Korean resistance

→ Ming campaigns in defence of Korea

▨ area of Korea occupied by Japan 1593–98

□ capital city

Japan in transition

1333: Decline of Minamoto (Kamakura) rule	**1467–77:** Onin War begins 'Era of Warring States'	**1543:** First Portuguese trading mission	**1597–98:** Second Japanese invasion of Korea	**c.1600:** Edo (Tokyo) becomes capital		

1300   1400   1500   1600

c.1338: Ashikaga shoguns dominant

1570: Nagasaki opened to foreign trade

1592–93: Japanese campaigns in Korea

1603: Foundation of Tokugawa Shogunate

THE RELIGIOUS MAP
OF EUROPE IN 1590

A SERIES OF PROFOUND CHANGES in theological doctrine and
practice caused violent political upheavals in 16th century Europe.
The Reformation, spearheaded by Martin Luther, divided much of
the continent along religious lines.

*How did Protestantism
spread throughout
northern Europe?*

The religious map of Europe 1590

- almost exclusively Catholic, with just minimal Protestant presence in northern areas
- overwhelmingly Catholic, with appreciable Protestant minority
- Catholic majority, but with very strong Protestant minority
- exclusively or overwhelmingly Protestant, with only slight Catholic presence in places
- Protestant majority, with some Catholic presence
- mainly Catholic, with strong Greek Orthodox presence
- Greek Orthodox, with significant Muslim presence in some areas of the Balkans
- Muslim majority
- - - - - frontiers 1590
- frontier of Holy Roman Empire 1590

Calvinist locally dominant Protestant denomination

The Reformation in Europe 1517–55

1529: At Diet of Speyer, Charles V attempts to reach compromise with Lutheran princes

1535: John Calvin formulates doctrine of predestination in Geneva

1545: Start of Council of Trent, which defines modern Catholicism

| 1510 | 1520 | 1530 | 1540 | 1550 | 1560 |

1517: Martin Luther posts 95 Theses condemning abuses of Catholic church at Wittenberg

1532: Henry VIII of England declares himself head of Church of England

1555: At Peace of Augsburg; Lutheran princes win right to choose their religion

THE HEIGHT OF OTTOMAN POWER

THE OTTOMAN EMPIRE was one of the great world powers of the early modern era. At its height, the empire stretched from the Persian Gulf to Algiers, Hungary, and the Crimea.

Was the geographical position of the Ottoman Empire a source of strength or weakness?

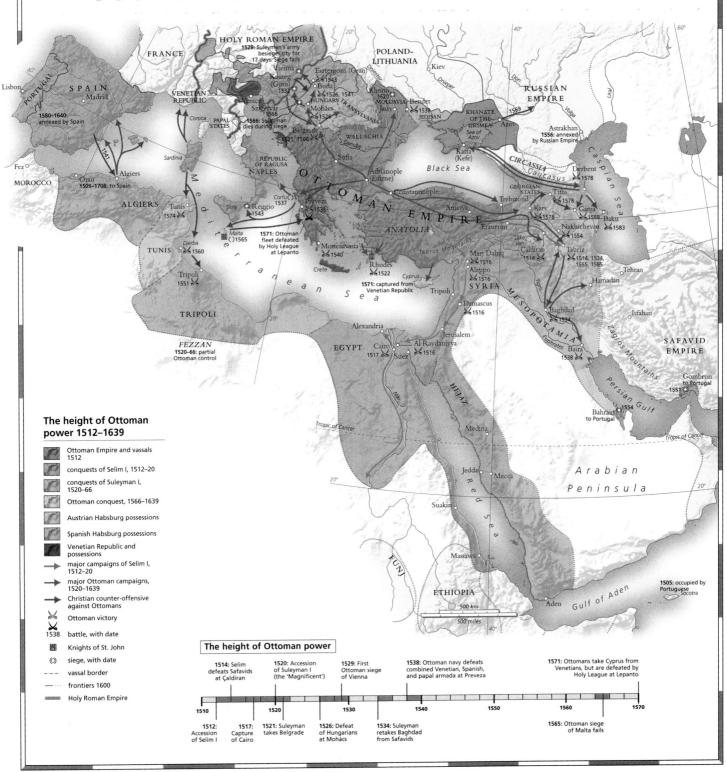

The height of Ottoman power 1512–1639

- Ottoman Empire and vassals 1512
- conquests of Selim I, 1512–20
- conquests of Suleyman I, 1520–66
- Ottoman conquest, 1566–1639
- Austrian Habsburg possessions
- Spanish Habsburg possessions
- Venetian Republic and possessions
- → major campaigns of Selim I, 1512–20
- → major Ottoman campaigns, 1520–1639
- → Christian counter-offensive against Ottomans
- ✕ Ottoman victory
- 1538 battle, with date
- Knights of St. John
- ⊚ siege, with date
- --- vassal border
- ···· frontiers 1600
- ▬ Holy Roman Empire

The height of Ottoman power

1510	1520	1530	1540	1550	1560	1570

- **1514:** Selim defeats Safavids at Çaldiran
- **1520:** Accession of Suleyman I (the 'Magnificent')
- **1529:** First Ottoman siege of Vienna
- **1538:** Ottoman navy defeats combined Venetian, Spanish, and papal armada at Preveza
- **1571:** Ottomans take Cyprus from Venetians, but are defeated by Holy League at Lepanto

- **1512:** Accession of Selim I
- **1517:** Capture of Cairo
- **1521:** Suleyman takes Belgrade
- **1526:** Defeat of Hungarians at Mohács
- **1534:** Suleyman retakes Baghdad from Safavids
- **1565:** Ottoman siege of Malta fails

THE MUGHAL EMPIRE

THE CONQUEST OF NORTHERN INDIA in 1526 by the Muslim Mughal chief, Babur, ushered in a new era, marked by orderly government, economic prosperity, and great achievements in the arts. Vasco da Gama's voyage to India in 1498 opened up new trade routes, enabling European powers to establish commercial toeholds.

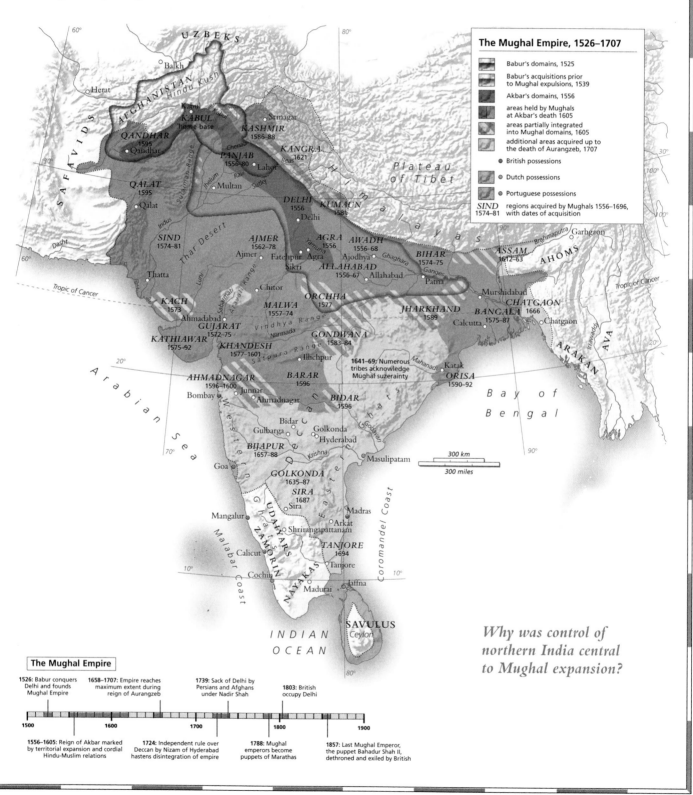

The Mughal Empire, 1526–1707

- Babur's domains, 1525
- Babur's acquisitions prior to Mughal expulsions, 1539
- Akbar's domains, 1556
- areas held by Mughals at Akbar's death 1605
- areas partially integrated into Mughal domains, 1605
- additional areas acquired up to the death of Aurangzeb, 1707
- ● British possessions
- ● Dutch possessions
- ● Portuguese possessions
- *SIND 1574–81* regions acquired by Mughals 1556–1696, with dates of acquisition

Why was control of northern India central to Mughal expansion?

The Mughal Empire

- **1526:** Babur conquers Delhi and founds Mughal Empire
- **1658–1707:** Empire reaches maximum extent during reign of Aurangzeb
- **1739:** Sack of Delhi by Persians and Afghans under Nadir Shah
- **1803:** British occupy Delhi

1500 — 1600 — 1700 — 1800 — 1900

- **1556–1605:** Reign of Akbar marked by territorial expansion and cordial Hindu-Muslim relations
- **1724:** Independent rule over Deccan by Nizam of Hyderabad hastens disintegration of empire
- **1788:** Mughal emperors become puppets of Marathas
- **1857:** Last Mughal Emperor, the puppet Bahadur Shah II, dethroned and exiled by British

STATES OF WEST AND CENTRAL AFRICA 1625

IN THE 17TH CENTURY, much of Sub-Saharan Africa consisted of small, self-governing units. In West Africa, 70% of the population lived in these "ministates." Boundaries remained stable for long periods, the people choosing their leaders on the basis of heredity, election, or other local customs.

Why did African ministates remain stable for long periods of time?

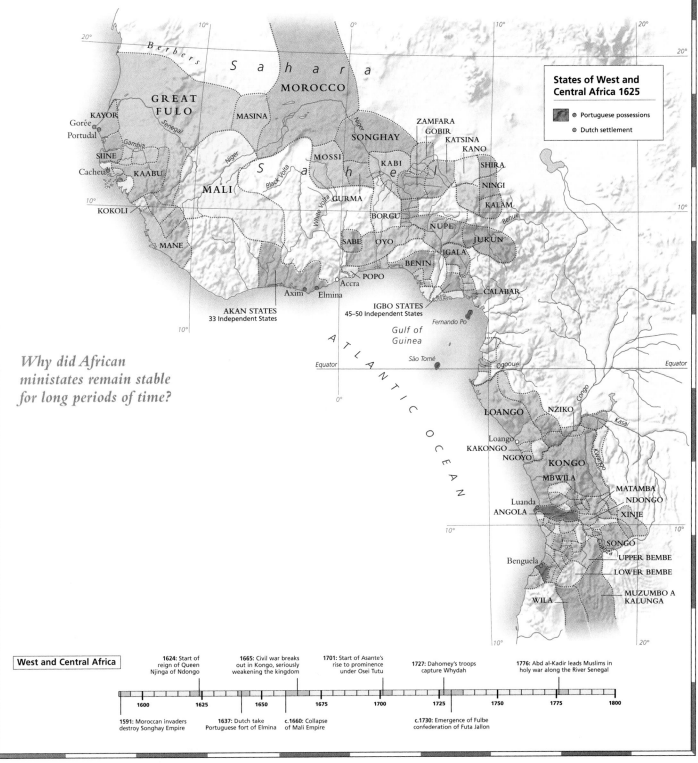

States of West and Central Africa 1625

- Portuguese possessions
- Dutch settlement

AKAN STATES
33 Independent States

IGBO STATES
45–50 Independent States

West and Central Africa

1624: Start of reign of Queen Njinga of Ndongo

1665: Civil war breaks out in Kongo, seriously weakening the kingdom

1701: Start of Asante's rise to prominence under Osei Tutu

1727: Dahomey's troops capture Whydah

1776: Abd al-Kadir leads Muslims in holy war along the River Senegal

1600 1625 1650 1675 1700 1725 1750 1775 1800

1591: Moroccan invaders destroy Songhay Empire

1637: Dutch take Portuguese fort of Elmina

c.1660: Collapse of Mali Empire

c.1730: Emergence of Fulbe confederation of Futa Jallon

77

THE WORLD: 1600–1700

DURING THE 17TH CENTURY, Dutch, British, and French mariners followed the Iberians into the world's seas, establishing colonies in North America. Trade between Europe, Africa, and the Americas knitted the Atlantic Ocean basin, while trade in the Indian Ocean linked European and Asian markets.

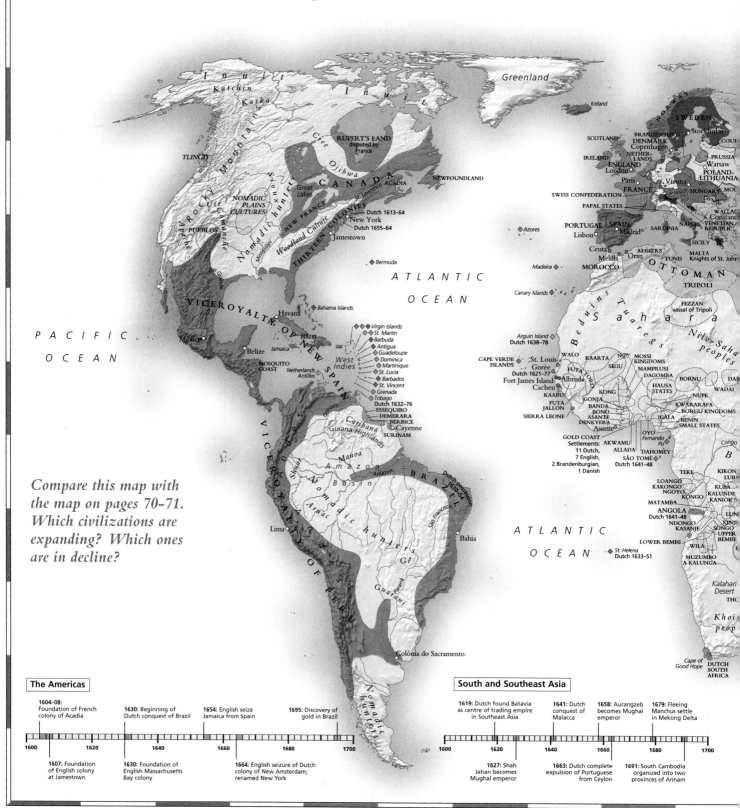

Compare this map with the map on pages 70–71. Which civilizations are expanding? Which ones are in decline?

The Americas

1604–08: Foundation of French colony of Acadia

1630: Beginning of Dutch conquest of Brazil

1654: English seize Jamaica from Spain

1695: Discovery of gold in Brazil

1600   1620   1640   1660   1680   1700

1607: Foundation of English colony at Jamestown

1630: Foundation of English Massachusetts Bay colony

1664: English seizure of Dutch colony of New Amsterdam; renamed New York

South and Southeast Asia

1619: Dutch found Batavia as centre of trading empire in Southeast Asia

1641: Dutch conquest of Malacca

1658: Aurangzeb becomes Mughal emperor

1679: Fleeing Manchus settle in Mekong Delta

1600   1620   1640   1660   1680   1700

1627: Shah Jahan becomes Mughal emperor

1663: Dutch complete expulsion of Portuguese from Ceylon

1691: South Cambodia organized into two provinces of Annam

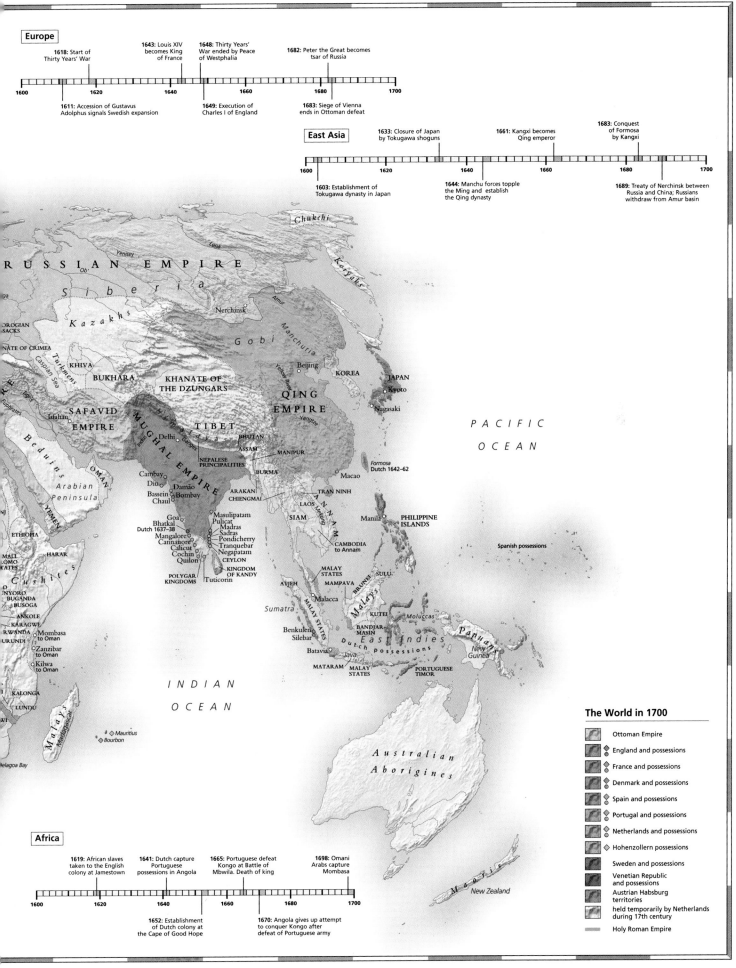

Europe

1618: Start of
Thirty Years' War

1643: Louis XIV
becomes King
of France

1648: Thirty Years'
War ended by Peace
of Westphalia

1682: Peter the Great becomes
tsar of Russia

1600   1620   1640   1660   1680   1700

1611: Accession of Gustavus
Adolphus signals Swedish expansion

1649: Execution of
Charles I of England

1683: Siege of Vienna
ends in Ottoman defeat

East Asia

1633: Closure of Japan
by Tokugawa shoguns

1661: Kangxi becomes
Qing emperor

1683: Conquest
of Formosa
by Kangxi

1600   1620   1640   1660   1680   1700

1603: Establishment of
Tokugawa dynasty in Japan

1644: Manchu forces topple
the Ming and establish
the Qing dynasty

1689: Treaty of Nerchinsk between
Russia and China; Russians
withdraw from Amur basin

Africa

1619: African slaves
taken to the English
colony at Jamestown

1641: Dutch capture
Portuguese
possessions in Angola

1665: Portuguese defeat
Kongo at Battle of
Mbwila. Death of king

1698: Omani
Arabs capture
Mombasa

1600   1620   1640   1660   1680   1700

1652: Establishment
of Dutch colony at
the Cape of Good Hope

1670: Angola gives up attempt
to conquer Kongo after
defeat of Portuguese army

The World in 1700

- Ottoman Empire
- England and possessions
- France and possessions
- Denmark and possessions
- Spain and possessions
- Portugal and possessions
- Netherlands and possessions
- Hohenzollern possessions
- Sweden and possessions
- Venetian Republic and possessions
- Austrian Habsburg territories
- held temporarily by Netherlands during 17th century
- Holy Roman Empire

SAFAVID PERSIA

OTTOMAN EXPANSION TO THE EAST (see p. 75) was checked by the sudden rise to power in 1500 of a new Persian dynasty, the Safavids. The first Safavid ruler, Shah Ismail I, rapidly united Persia, converting it from Sunni to Shi'ite Islam.

What were the geographical and political constraints on Safavid expansion?

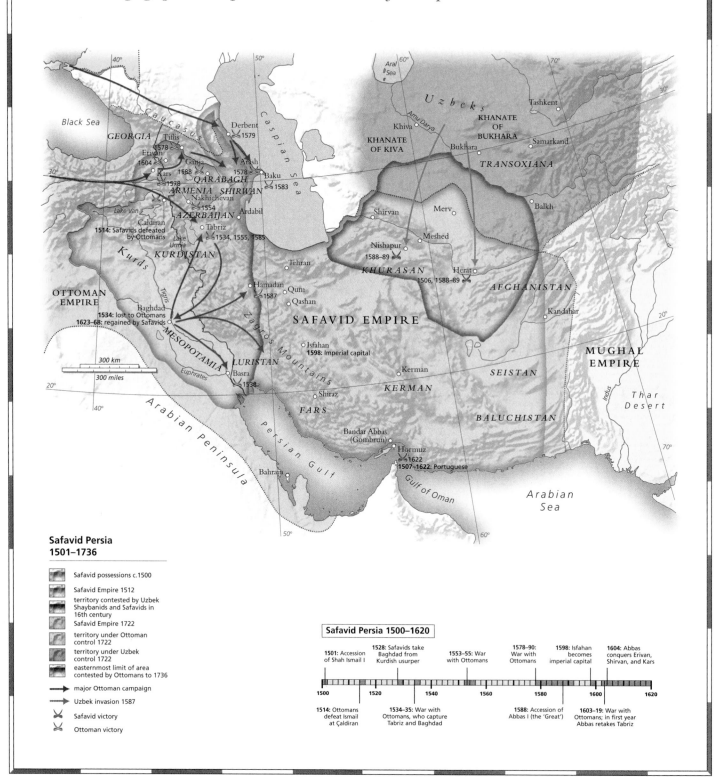

Safavid Persia
1501–1736

- Safavid possessions c.1500
- Safavid Empire 1512
- territory contested by Uzbek Shaybanids and Safavids in 16th century
- Safavid Empire 1722
- territory under Ottoman control 1722
- territory under Uzbek control 1722
- easternmost limit of area contested by Ottomans to 1736
- ⟶ major Ottoman campaign
- ⟶ Uzbek invasion 1587
- ⚔ Safavid victory
- ⚔ Ottoman victory

Safavid Persia 1500–1620

- **1501:** Accession of Shah Ismail I
- **1528:** Safavids take Baghdad from Kurdish usurper
- **1553–55:** War with Ottomans
- **1578–90:** War with Ottomans
- **1598:** Isfahan becomes imperial capital
- **1604:** Abbas conquers Erivan, Shirvan, and Kars

1500 — 1520 — 1540 — 1560 — 1580 — 1600 — 1620

- **1514:** Ottomans defeat Ismail at Çaldiran
- **1534–35:** War with Ottomans, who capture Tabriz and Baghdad
- **1588:** Accession of Abbas I (the 'Great')
- **1603–19:** War with Ottomans; in first year Abbas retakes Tabriz

THE COLONIZATION OF NORTH AMERICA

FROM THE EARLY 17TH CENTURY, British, French, and Dutch migrants settled along the Atlantic seaboard and in the Gulf of St. Lawrence. As they grew in numbers, they displaced Native American peoples from their lands.

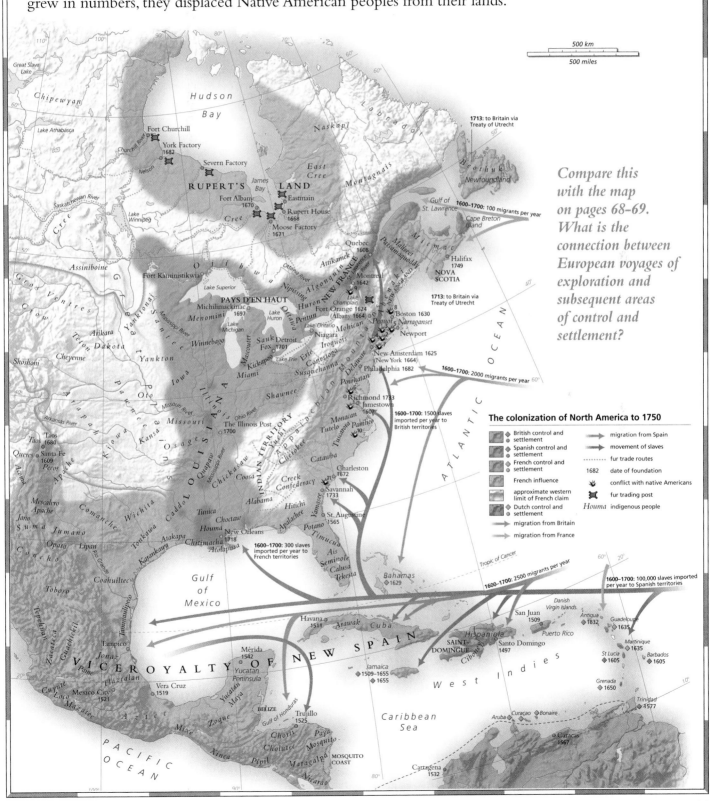

Compare this with the map on pages 68–69. What is the connection between European voyages of exploration and subsequent areas of control and settlement?

500 km
500 miles

1713: to Britain via Treaty of Utrecht

1600–1700: 100 migrants per year

1713: to Britain via Treaty of Utrecht

1600–1700: 2000 migrants per year

1600–1700: 1500 slaves imported per year to British territories

1600–1700: 300 slaves imported per year to French territories

1600–1700: 2500 migrants per year

1600–1700: 100,000 slaves imported per year to Spanish territories

The colonization of North America to 1750

- British control and settlement
- Spanish control and settlement
- French control and settlement
- French influence
- approximate western limit of French claim
- Dutch control and settlement
- migration from Britain
- migration from France
- migration from Spain
- movement of slaves
- - - - fur trade routes
- 1682 date of foundation
- ⚔ conflict with native Americans
- ⚒ fur trading post
- *Houma* indigenous people

Great Slave Lake
Chipewyan
Lake Athabasca
Hudson Bay
Naskapi
Labrador
Fort Churchill
York Factory 1682
Severn Factory
Nelson
East Cree
James Bay
Beothuk
Newfoundland
RUPERT'S LAND
Fort Albany 1670
Eastmain
Rupert House 1668
Moose Factory 1671
Cree
Montagnais
Gulf of St. Lawrence
Cape Breton Island
Assiniboine
Ojibwa
Ottawa River
Attikamek
Quebec 1608
Maliseet
Passamaquoddy
Micmac
Halifax 1749
NOVA SCOTIA
Cree
Saskatchewan River
Lake Winnipeg
Fort Kaministikwia
Lake Superior
PAYS D'EN HAUT
Nipissing
Algonquin
NEW FRANCE
Montreal 1642
St. Lawrence River
NEW ENGLAND
Boston 1630
Gros Ventres
Crow
Yanktonai
Santee
Sisseton
Menomini 1697
Michilimackinac
Lake Michigan
Lake Huron
Huron
Ottawa
Pentun
Lake Ontario
Fort Orange 1624 (Albany 1664)
Lake Champlain
Mohican
Pequot
Narraganset
Newport
Teton Dakota
Arikara
Yankton
Winnebago
Sauk Fox
Mascouten
Detroit 1701
Niagara
Erie
Iroquois
Conestoga
Susquehanna
Delaware
New Amsterdam 1625 (New York 1664)
Shoshoni
Cheyenne
Iowa
Kickapoo
Lake Erie
Miami
Philadelphia 1682
ATLANTIC OCEAN
Arapaho
Oto
Pawnee
Missouri River
Illinois
Shawnee
Powhatan
Kiowa
Kansa
Osage
Missouri
The Illinois Post 1700
Ohio River
Appalachian Mountains
Richmond 1733
Jamestown 1607
Taos 1680
Queres
Santa Fe 1609
Pecos
Apache
Acoma
Arkansas River
Wichita
Caddo
Quapaw
LOUISIANA
Yuchi
Monacan
Tutelo
Tuscarora
Pamlico
INDIAN TERRITORY
Cherokee
Catawba
Mescalero Apache
Comanche
Tonkawa
Chickasaw
Coosa
Creek Confederacy
Charleston 1672
Jano
Suma
Jumano
Opata
Lipan
Atakapa
Karankawa
Tunica
Choctaw
Alabama
Hitichi
Apalachee
Savannah 1733
Yamasee
Cancho
Coahuiltec
Chitimacha
Atolapissa
Houma
New Orleans 1718
Potano
St. Augustine 1565
Toboso
Timucua
Ais
Seminole
Calusa
Tekesta
Bahamas 1629
Tropic of Cancer
Tepehuan
Guachichil
Rio Grande
Tamaulipeco
Mérida 1542
Yucatan Peninsula
Gulf of Mexico
Havana 1511
Arawak
Cuba
Danish Virgin Islands
San Juan 1509
Antigua 1632
Guadeloupe 1635
Zacatec
Cuyute
Caca
Mexico City 1521
Vera Cruz 1519
Tlazcalan
Yucatan
Maya
VICEROYALTY OF NEW SPAIN
Jamaica 1509–1655 1655
Hispaniola
SAINT-DOMINGUE
Santo Domingo 1497
Cibon
Puerto Rico
St Lucia 1605
Martinique 1635
Barbados 1605
Mazatec
Mixe
Zoque
BELIZE
Gulf of Honduras
Trujillo 1525
Chorti
Cholutec
Paya
Mosquito
West Indies
Grenada 1650
Trinidad 1577
PACIFIC OCEAN
Pipil
Matagalpa
MOSQUITO COAST
Vinca
Nicarao
Caribbean Sea
Aruba
Curaçao
Bonaire
Caracas 1567
Cartagena 1532

THE WORLD SLAVE TRADE

THE USE OF SLAVES is endemic in most human societies. Between the 9th and 19th centuries Muslim merchants may have transported as many as 14 million slaves across the Sahara to destinations in the Middle East and the Indian Ocean. The establishment of European colonies between the 16th and 19th centuries saw the creation of a slave trade on an industrial scale. From the 15th to 19th centuries European merchants carried on a massive trade in African slaves across the Atlantic.

What is the relationship between the trade in slaves and the trade in manufactured goods?

The world slave trade 1400–1860

	major slave trading nation
	export centre for African slaves
	export centre for Muslim slaves
	distribution of African slaves
	distribution of Muslim slaves
	African nations with active slave trade
⚖	number of slaves imported
➡	routes of European slave traders
➡	routes of Ottoman slave traders
➡	routes of Saharan slave traders
➡	routes of Arab slave traders
➡	exports of Muslim slaves from Southeast Asia
➡	goods exported in exchange for slaves
➡	goods exported for slaves
➡	European exports to Africa
●	slave factory

Goods produced using slaves

- ⦿ cacao
- ◖ coffee
- ⬦ cotton
- ▢ diamonds
- ▯ gold
- ▯ silver
- ⬇ sugar
- ⬂ tobacco

Other goods traded

- ⊛ dyestuffs
- ⬥ furs and hides
- ⋌ pepper
- ▨ silk and textiles
- ⋎ spices
- ▯ tin

Goods imported for slaves

- 🐟 salt cod

(map labels)

Greenland

CANADA — Hudson Bay — Rocky Mountains

UNITED STATES OF AMERICA ⚖ 500,000 — Quebec — Montreal — Newfoundland — New York — Richmond — Charleston — salt cod — Mississippi — New Orleans — Mobile — San Agustín — Gulf of Mexico

PACIFIC OCEAN — Tropic of Cancer — Equator — silver

Mexico City — Veracruz — Acapulco — Portobelo — Havana — Cuba — Bahama Islands

VICEROYALTY OF NEW SPAIN ⚖ c.1,000,000

Jamaica ⚖ 750,000 — HAITI — Hispaniola ⚖ 860,000 — Caribbean Sea — Cartagena — Tobago

Antigua — Guadeloupe ⚖ 290,000 — Dominica — Martinique ⚖ 360,000 — St Lucia — Barbados ⚖ 360,000 — St. Vincent — Grenada ⚖ 67,000 — Middle Passage — Cape Verde Islands

ATLANTIC OCEAN — silver, sugar, cacao, coffee — furs, tobacco, dyestuffs, sugar, cotton — silver, gold, sugar, tobacco, coffee, diamonds

VICEROYALTY OF NEW GRANADA ⚖ c.320,000

GUIANA — SURINAM ⚖ 500,000

VICEROYALTY OF PERU ⚖ 95,000 — Callao — Lima — Andes — Potosí

Amazon — BRAZIL ⚖ 3,600,000 — Pernambuco — Salvador (Bahia) — Rio de Janeiro — São Paulo

VICEROYALTY OF RÍO DE LA PLATA — Buenos Aires

82

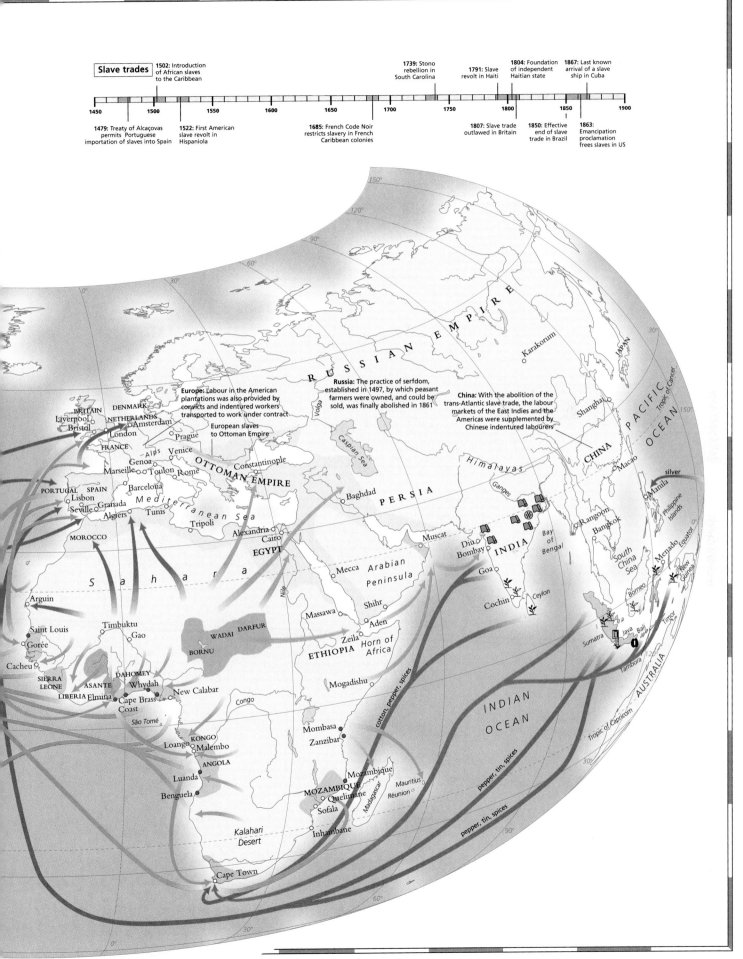

Slave trades

1502: Introduction of African slaves to the Caribbean

1739: Stono rebellion in South Carolina

1791: Slave revolt in Haiti

1804: Foundation of independent Haitian state

1867: Last known arrival of a slave ship in Cuba

1450 1500 1550 1600 1650 1700 1750 1800 1850 1900

1479: Treaty of Alcaçovas permits Portuguese importation of slaves into Spain

1522: First American slave revolt in Hispaniola

1685: French Code Noir restricts slavery in French Caribbean colonies

1807: Slave trade outlawed in Britain

1850: Effective end of slave trade in Brazil

1863: Emancipation proclamation frees slaves in US

Europe: Labour in the American plantations was also provided by convicts and indentured workers transported to work under contract

Russia: The practice of serfdom, established in 1497, by which peasant farmers were owned, and could be sold, was finally abolished in 1861

China: With the abolition of the trans-Atlantic slave trade, the labour markets of the East Indies and the Americas were supplemented by Chinese indentured labourers

European slaves to Ottoman Empire

RUSSIAN EMPIRE

BRITAIN
DENMARK
Liverpool
Bristol
NETHERLANDS
Amsterdam
London
Prague
FRANCE
Alps
Venice
Marseille
Genoa
Toulon
Rome
Constantinople
OTTOMAN EMPIRE
Baghdad
PERSIA
PORTUGAL SPAIN
Lisbon
Barcelona
Seville
Granada
Algiers
Tunis
Mediterranean Sea
Tripoli
Alexandria
Cairo
MOROCCO
EGYPT
Muscat

Karakorum

JAPAN

Shanghai

CHINA
PACIFIC OCEAN
Macao
silver
Manila
Philippine Islands

Himalayas
Ganges
INDIA
Bay of Bengal
Rangoon
Bangkok
Diu
Bombay
Goa
Cochin
Ceylon
South China Sea
Menado
New Guinea

Equator

Sahara
Arguin
Mecca
Arabian Peninsula
Shihr
Massawa
Aden
Borneo
Timbuktu
Gao
WADAI DARFUR
BORNU
Zeila
ETHIOPIA Horn of Africa
Sumatra
Java
Bali
Timor
Tambora
AUSTRALIA

Saint Louis
Gorée
Cacheu
SIERRA LEONE
ASANTE
DAHOMEY
Whydah
LIBERIA Elmina
Cape Brass
Coast
New Calabar
São Tomé
Mogadishu
Congo
cotton, pepper, spices

INDIAN OCEAN

KONGO
Loango
Malembo
ANGOLA
Luanda
Benguela
Mombasa
Zanzibar
Mozambique
MOZAMBIQUE
Quelimane
Sofala
Madagascar
Mauritius
Réunion
pepper, tin, spices

Kalahari
Desert
Inhambane

Cape Town

pepper, tin, spices

Nile
Volga
Caspian Sea

150°
120°
90°
60°
30°
30°
150°
Tropic of Cancer
Tropic of Capricorn
0°
60°
30°
90°

PORTUGUESE SOUTH AMERICA

BRAZIL WAS FORMALLY CLAIMED for Portugal in 1500. There were no conspicuous mineral resources until a gold boom in the 18th century, so colonization depended on agriculture, especially labor-intensive sugar cultivation. Apart from slave-raiders hunting for natives and prospectors searching for gold and diamonds, penetration of the interior was limited.

Consider this map and the map on the following page. What factors influenced the extent to which Portugal and Spain were able to expand and settle their territories?

Portuguese South America

- Portuguese territory by 1600
- Portuguese territory by 1750
- Portuguese frontier territory
- region disputed by Spain and Portugal up to 1777
- PARÁ 1616 captaincy and date of foundation
- ☐ capital city
- 🏛 gold
- ⬡ diamonds
- ⊕ dyes
- ✖ hides
- ⬇ sugar

1502: First expedition sent from Lisbon to exploit new-found coastline

1549: Direct royal rule imposed from new capital at Bahia

1580: Portugal and her empire come under rule of Spanish kings

1663: Brazil becomes viceroyalty

1674: Foundation of Manaus, 1,600 km from mouth of Amazon

1750: Portugal renounces claim to Colônia do Sacramento

| 1500 | 1525 | 1550 | 1575 | 1600 | 1625 | 1650 | 1675 | 1700 | 1725 | 1750 | 1775 | 1800 |

1532: First captaincies granted for purposes of settlement

1562–63: War and disease kill much of Indian population

1621: Formation of separate Estado do Maranhão with its own governor-general

1680s: Portuguese found Colônia do Sacramento

1695: Gold discovered in Minas Gerais region

1763: Rio de Janeiro becomes Brazilian capital

SPANISH SOUTH AMERICA

IN THEIR CONQUEST of South America, it took less than 10 years for Spanish conquistadores to take over the rich, organized states of the Andes. Wherever Europeans settled, the native population declined rapidly, mainly though lack of resistance to alien diseases. To make up for labor shortages, the Spanish imported African slaves. Catholic missionaries were active throughout the colonial era, often defending the rights of Indians.

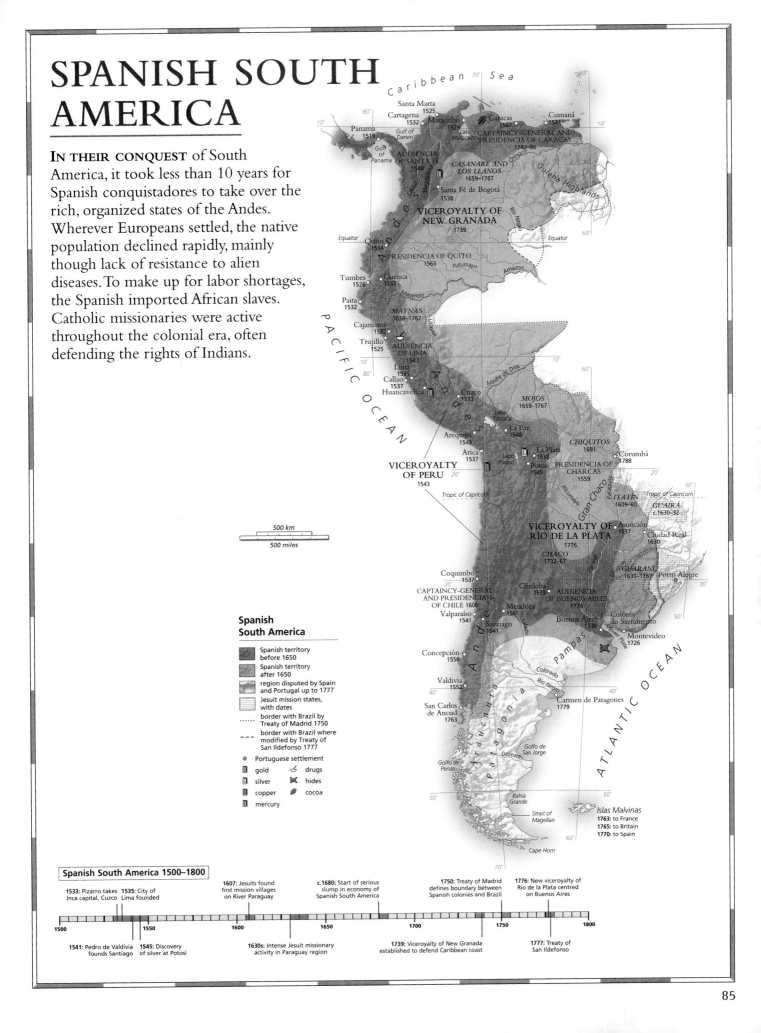

Caribbean Sea

Santa Marta 1525
Cartagena 1532
Maracaibo 1529
Caracas 1567
Cumaná 1521
Panama 1519
Gulf of Darien
Gulf of Panama
Lake Maracaibo
CAPTAINCY-GENERAL AND PRESIDENCIA OF CARACAS 1742–86
AUDIENCIA OF SANTA FÉ 1548
CASANARE AND LOS LLANOS 1659–1767
Santa Fé de Bogotá 1538
Guiana Highlands
Orinoco
Rio Negro
VICEROYALTY OF NEW GRANADA 1739
Equator
Quito 1534
PRESIDENCIA OF QUITO 1563
Putumayo
Amazon
Equator
Tumbes 1526
Cuenca 1557
Marañon
Paita 1532
MAYNAS 1638–1767
Ucayali
Cajamarca 1532
Trujillo 1525
AUDIENCIA OF LIMA 1543
Lima 1535
Callao 1537
Huancavelica
Madre de Dios
Cuzco 1533
MOJOS 1659–1767
Lake Titicaca
PACIFIC OCEAN
Arequipa 1540
La Paz 1548
CHIQUITOS 1691
Corumbá 1788
Arica 1537
Lago Poopó
La Plata 1538
Potosí 1545
PRESIDENCIA OF CHARCAS 1559
VICEROYALTY OF PERU 1543
Gran Chaco
Pilcomayo
ITATÍN 1609–60
GUAIRÁ c.1630–32
Tropic of Capricorn
Tropic of Capricorn
VICEROYALTY OF RÍO DE LA PLATA 1776
Asunción 1537
Ciudad Real 1630
CHACO 1732–67
Paraguay
GUARANÍ 1630–1767
Porto Alegre
Coquimbo 1537
Córdoba 1573
AUDIENCIA OF BUENOS AIRES 1776
Colónia do Sacramento
CAPTAINCY-GENERAL AND PRESIDENCIA OF CHILE 1606
Mendoza 1561
Buenos Aires 1536
Valparaíso 1541
Santiago 1541
Uruguay
Rio de la Plata
Montevideo 1726
Pampas
Concepción 1550
Colorado
ATLANTIC OCEAN
Valdivia 1552
Rio Negro
Carmen de Patagones 1779
San Carlos de Ancud 1763
Araucania
Patagonia
Deseado
Golfo de San Jorge
Golfo de Penas
Bahía Grande
Strait of Magellan
Cape Horn

Islas Malvinas
1763: to France
1765: to Britain
1770: to Spain

500 km
500 miles

Spanish South America

- Spanish territory before 1650
- Spanish territory after 1650
- region disputed by Spain and Portugal up to 1777
- Jesuit mission states, with dates
- ······· border with Brazil by Treaty of Madrid 1750
- − − − border with Brazil where modified by Treaty of San Ildefonso 1777
- ● Portuguese settlement
- gold
- silver
- copper
- mercury
- drugs
- hides
- cocoa

Spanish South America 1500–1800

1533: Pizarro takes Inca capital, Cuzco
1535: City of Lima founded
1607: Jesuits found first mission villages on River Paraguay
c.1680: Start of serious slump in economy of Spanish South America
1750: Treaty of Madrid defines boundary between Spanish colonies and Brazil
1776: New viceroyalty of Río de la Plata centred on Buenos Aires

1500 1550 1600 1650 1700 1750 1800

1541: Pedro de Valdivia founds Santiago
1545: Discovery of silver at Potosí
1630s: Intense Jesuit missionary activity in Paraguay region
1739: Viceroyalty of New Granada established to defend Caribbean coast
1777: Treaty of San Ildefonso

17TH-CENTURY EUROPE

IN THE 17TH CENTURY, following years of destructive warfare, the modern European state system began to evolve. European states were transformed in a process of internal political centralization and external consolidation. The legitimacy of these developments was often questioned, leading to civil wars and popular resistance.

What factors were critical to the development of the early modern European state?

Political consolidation and resistance in 17th-century Europe

- Austrian Habsburg possessions 1683
- Spanish Habsburg possessions 1683
- civil war or widespread disturbance
- local revolt or unrest
- civic autonomy suppressed by territorial rulers
- frontiers 1683
- Holy Roman empire 1683

Expansionist tendencies

- Sweden
- Russia
- England
- Ottoman Empire
- Austrian Habsburgs
- France
- United Provinces

Civil wars and revolts 1625–65

- 1628–29: Siege of Protestant stronghold of La Rochelle
- 1640: Portugal declares independence from Spain
- 1640: Catalan Revolt
- 1649: Execution of Charles I of England
- 1660: Restoration of English monarchy
- 1640: Civil War breaks out in England
- 1648–53: The Fronde: resistance to royal authority throughout France

1625   1635   1645   1655   1665

INDUSTRIAL DEVELOPMENT IN EUROPE 1850–1914

IN THE 18TH AND 19TH CENTURIES, technological, social, and economic changes transformed Europe into an urban, industrial society.

By 1914, which regions of Europe were the most industrialized? Which regions were the least industrialized?

Scale varies with perspective
6220 km (3870 miles)
5980 km (3710 miles)

The industrialization of Europe by 1914

Land use 1914
- ☐ mountain/wasteland
- ☐ agriculture and stock rearing
- ☐ forest
- ☐ industrial area

Resources
- coalfield
- lignite (brown coal)
- iron ore
- oil
- △ potash

Manufacturing industry
- cotton
- linen
- silk
- wool
- iron smelting
- machinery
- shipbuilding

Population growth
- ● city with population over 500,000 in 1850
- ◕ city with population over 500,000 in 1890
- ◐ city with population over 500,000 in 1914
- ○ city with population under 500,000 in 1914
- ◎ major port
- principal railways 1914
- frontiers 1914

Industrial developments in Europe from 1840

1847: Siemens lays first telegraph line between Berlin and Frankfurt

1851: Great Exhibition of Industry at Crystal Palace, London

1870: Industrial expansion begins in Germany

1878: Gilchrist-Thomas method for steel production; internal-combustion engine constructed by Nikolaus Otto

1891: Construction of Trans-Siberian railway begun

1840 — 1850 — 1860 — 1870 — 1880 — 1890 — 1900 — 1910

1844: Engels' *The Condition of the Working Class in England* is published

1867: Publication of Marx's *Das Kapital*, an analysis of the economic injustices of the Capitalist system

1868: First British Congress of Trade Unions meet in Manchester

1889: Eiffel Tower completed for centennial exhibition

1908: First radio transmitter built by Marconi

AN ERA OF REVOLUTION

RAPID POPULATION GROWTH, the creation of the first industrial societies, the maturing of Europe's American colonies, and new ideas about statehood and freedom of the individual, combined to create an overwhelming demand for political change in the 18th century, most notably exemplified by the French Revolution of 1789. Uprisings and revolutions continued into the middle of the 19th century.

What connections does this map reveal between revolution and empire?

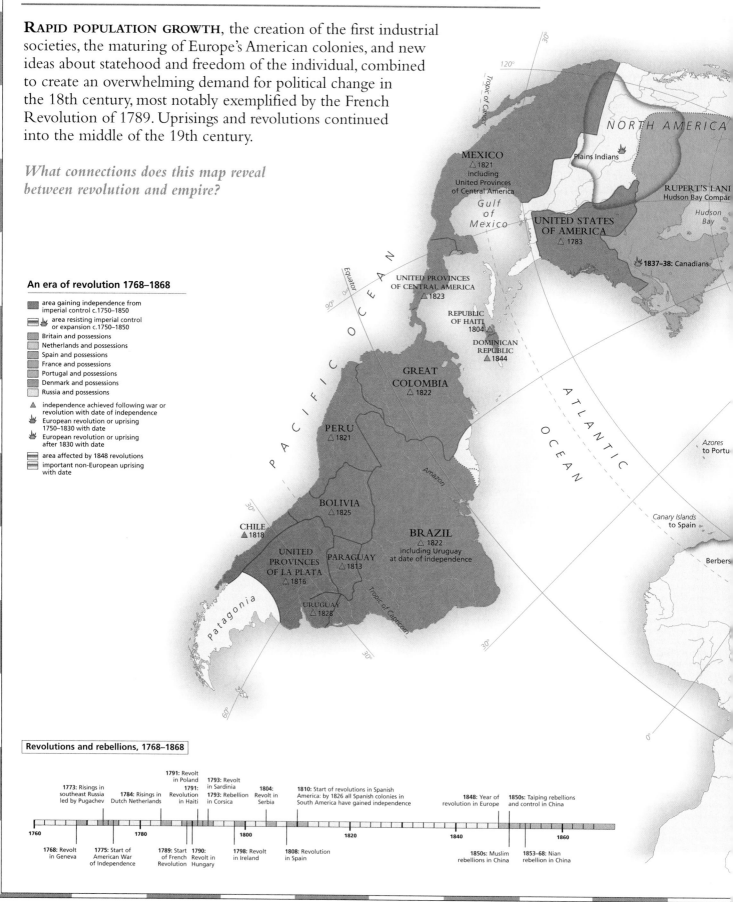

An era of revolution 1768–1868

- area gaining independence from imperial control c.1750–1850
- area resisting imperial control or expansion c.1750–1850
- Britain and possessions
- Netherlands and possessions
- Spain and possessions
- France and possessions
- Portugal and possessions
- Denmark and possessions
- Russia and possessions
- △ independence achieved following war or revolution with date of independence
- European revolution or uprising 1750–1830 with date
- European revolution or uprising after 1830 with date
- area affected by 1848 revolutions
- important non-European uprising with date

NORTH AMERICA

MEXICO
△ 1821
including
United Provinces
of Central America

Plains Indians

Gulf of Mexico

RUPERT'S LAND
Hudson Bay Company

Hudson Bay

UNITED STATES
OF AMERICA
△ 1783

1837–38: Canadians

UNITED PROVINCES
OF CENTRAL AMERICA
△ 1823

REPUBLIC
OF HAITI
1804

DOMINICAN
REPUBLIC
△ 1844

GREAT
COLOMBIA
△ 1822

PERU
△ 1821

BOLIVIA
△ 1825

CHILE
▲ 1818

UNITED
PROVINCES
OF LA PLATA
△ 1816

PARAGUAY
△ 1813

BRAZIL
△ 1822
including Uruguay
at date of independence

URUGUAY
△ 1828

Amazon

Patagonia

Equator

Tropic of Cancer

Tropic of Capricorn

PACIFIC OCEAN

ATLANTIC OCEAN

Azores to Portu

Canary Islands to Spain

Berbers

Revolutions and rebellions, 1768–1868

- **1773:** Risings in southeast Russia led by Pugachev
- **1784:** Risings in Dutch Netherlands
- **1791:** Revolt in Poland
- **1791:** Revolution in Haiti
- **1793:** Revolt in Sardinia
- **1793:** Rebellion in Corsica
- **1804:** Revolt in Serbia
- **1810:** Start of revolutions in Spanish America: by 1826 all Spanish colonies in South America have gained independence
- **1848:** Year of revolution in Europe
- **1850s:** Taiping rebellions and control in China

- **1768:** Revolt in Geneva
- **1775:** Start of American War of Independence
- **1789:** Start of French Revolution
- **1790:** Revolt in Hungary
- **1798:** Revolt in Ireland
- **1808:** Revolution in Spain
- **1850s:** Muslim rebellions in China
- **1853–68:** Nian rebellion in China

1760   1780   1800   1820   1840   1860

ARCTIC OCEAN

Alaska

Arctic Circle

60°

120°

150°

180°

30°

JAPAN

KOREA

Yellow
Sea

Tropic of Cancer

Greenland

60°

Iceland

30°

DUTCH
NETHERLANDS

RUSSIAN EMPIRE

Siberia

90°

60°

30°

QING EMPIRE

1853–68:
Nian rebellion

1853–63:
Taiping
rebellion

1863–73: Northwest
Muslim revolts

1850–53:
Taiping advance

HONG KONG
1842: to Britain

Macao

Philippine
Islands

local
tribes

Equator

IRELAND
1798

BRITAIN

POLAND
1791,
1830–31

GIUM
'87
331

DENMARK

1784

HOLY
ROMAN
EMPIRE

1825: Decembrist
uprising

1831: Ostrolenka

Kazakhs and
Turkmen

1773–74: Pugachev's
and Cossack revolt

Jiantian
1850: Beginning of
Taiping rebellion

1855–73: Yunnan
Muslim rising

South
China
Sea

FRANCE
1789,
1830

1821

HUNGARY

1790

TUGAL
821

SPAIN
1808,
1820–23

Corsica
1793

1848–49

SERBIA
1804

1840–60:
Circassians

1834–59: Shamil

Celebes

1793, 1821

SARDINIA

SICILY
1820–21

ALGERIA
1832–47:
Abd el Kader

GREECE
1830

1844–50:
Babism

Pashtun

Nepal

Shan Tribes

Chandernagore

Borneo

Dayaks

PORTUGUESE
TIMOR

Timor

OTTOMAN EMPIRE

PERSIA

1857–59:
The Mutiny

Bay
of
Bengal

Gulf
of
Siam

Flores

INDIA

Wahhabis

Arabian
Peninsula

Diu

Damão

Yanaon

Arabian
Sea

DUTCH POSSESSIONS AND DEPENDENCIES

Sumba

AFRICA

Nile

Goa

Pondicherry
Karikal

Mahé

Ceylon

Nicobar Islands
to Denmark

Achin

Sumatra

120°

Equator

60°

INDIAN OCEAN

90°

0°

1825–30:
Dipo Negoro

Java

30°

Equator

89

THE NAPOLEONIC EMPIRE

THE BRILLIANT revolutionary general Napoleon Bonaparte in 1799 staged a coup d'etat which made him ruler of France. In 1804, just ten years after revolutionaries had executed Louis XVI, Napoleon took the title of emperor and began to create a dynasty. His imperial ambitions were ultimately thwarted by Britain: its navy blockaded France and overran French colonies, while a series of alliances completed an encirclement that contained and eventually defeated Napoleon.

What role did geography play in the downfall of Napoleon's empire?

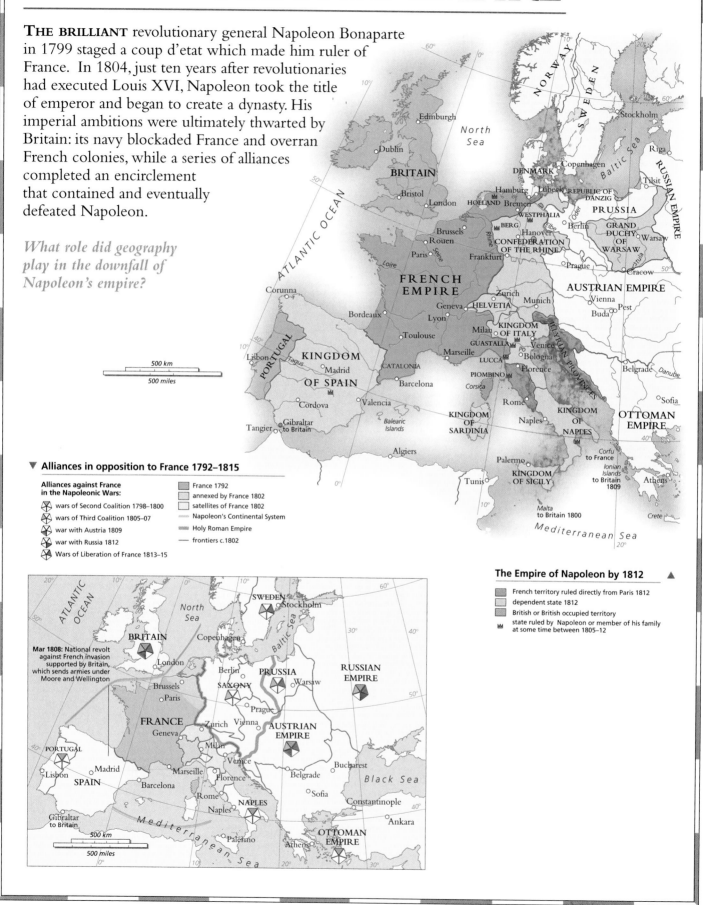

Alliances in opposition to France 1792–1815

Alliances against France in the Napoleonic Wars:

- wars of Second Coalition 1798–1800
- wars of Third Coalition 1805–07
- war with Austria 1809
- war with Russia 1812
- Wars of Liberation of France 1813–15

- France 1792
- annexed by France 1802
- satellites of France 1802
- Napoleon's Continental System
- Holy Roman Empire
- frontiers c.1802

The Empire of Napoleon by 1812

- French territory ruled directly from Paris 1812
- dependent state 1812
- British or British occupied territory
- state ruled by Napoleon or member of his family at some time between 1805–12

Mar 1808: National revolt against French invasion supported by Britain, which sends armies under Moore and Wellington

EUROPE AFTER THE CONGRESS OF VIENNA 1815–52

TO RESTORE STABLITY after the turmoil of the Napoleonic wars, the Congress of Vienna redrew the political map of Europe and restored many former ruling houses. The result was three decades of reactionary rule, during which nationalist and republican movements challenged the status quo.

Europe after the Congress of Vienna 1815–52

MAIN MAP

- small German states
- areas in revolt against Louis-Napoleon in 1851
- German Confederation
- threat to Vienna System 1817–39
- revolution in 1848–49
- frontiers 1815

NORWAY
1814: Denmark forced to cede Norway to Sweden

SWEDEN
Stockholm

Helsingfors

St. Petersburg

SCOTLAND
Edinburgh

IRELAND
1822–29: Catholic Emancipation campaign

BRITAIN
Dublin

North Sea

DENMARK
Copenhagen
Bornholm

Riga

Moscow

RUSSIAN EMPIRE

ENGLAND
1830–32: First Reform Act crisis
WALES
1840s: Chartist agitation
London
1831: Belgium gains independence from United Netherlands

SCHLESWIG-HOLSTEIN
Hamburg

HANOVER
in personal union 1817–31: with Britain
Hanover
1817–31: German student protests
Berlin

EAST PRUSSIA
Danzig

Baltic Sea

Amsterdam
UNITED NETHERLANDS
Brussels
PRUSSIA
Cologne

Posen

Vistula

ATLANTIC OCEAN

1830: Revolution
Paris
Jan–Mar 1848: fighting at the barricades

SAXONY
Prague

PRUSSIA

POLAND
Warsaw
Brest-Litovsk
1830–31: national revolt
Cracow

Kiev

Dnieper

1831: Vendean uprising
Loire
FRANCE

BAVARIA
Stuttgart
WÜRTTEMBERG
BADEN
BAVARIA
Munich

Vienna
AUSTRIAN EMPIRE

REP. OF CRACOW
1847: to Austria
1847: Peasant uprising
GALICIA

Dniester

Odessa

Bay of Biscay

Bordeaux

PR. OF NEUCHÂTEL
Geneva
SWITZERLAND
1847–48: Swiss Civil War
Lyon

SARDINIA

Milan
1821: Piedmontese revolution
LOMBARDY-VENETIA
Venice
PARMA
MODENA
MONACO
MASSA AND CARRARA
LUCCA

HUNGARY
Buda Pest

ILLYRIAN KINGDOM
DALMATIA

TRANSYLVANIA

MOLDAVIA

1829: to Russia
Sebastopol

Marseille

Barcelona

1820: Revolution in Portugal against British control of country
Oporto

1833–39: First Carlist War
ANDORRA

1820: Revolution
Madrid

SPAIN
1846–48: Second Carlist War

GIBRALTAR to Britain

Balearic Islands

Corsica

TUSCANY
PAPAL STATES

Rome

1820: Revolution
Naples

SAN MARINO

MILITARY FRONTIER
1807–33: Serbian revolts
Belgrade

BOSNIA
SERBIA
MONTENEGRO

WALLACHIA
Bucharest
1821: Revolts in Wallachia and Moldavia

Danube

BULGARIA
RUMELIA

Black Sea

SARDINIA

Mediterranean Sea

Palermo
1821: Revolution

KINGDOM OF THE TWO SICILIES

Malta
1800: to Britain

Corfu
1815: to Britain

ALBANIA
GREECE
1821–33: War of Independence
Athens

Ionian Islands
1815: to Britain

OTTOMAN EMPIRE
THRACE
Salonica

Constantinople

ANATOLIA
Smyrna

Crete

Cyprus

How did the Congress of Vienna alter the borders of European states?

400 km

400 miles

SOUTH AND SOUTHEAST ASIA 1765

EVEN AFTER THE COLLAPSE of the Mughal Empire in 1761, significant states stood in the path of Western colonial expansion in both India and Southeast Asia. In India, the foremost power was the Maratha Confederacy, while in Southeast Asia, Burma, Siam, and Vietnam expanded in size and strength.

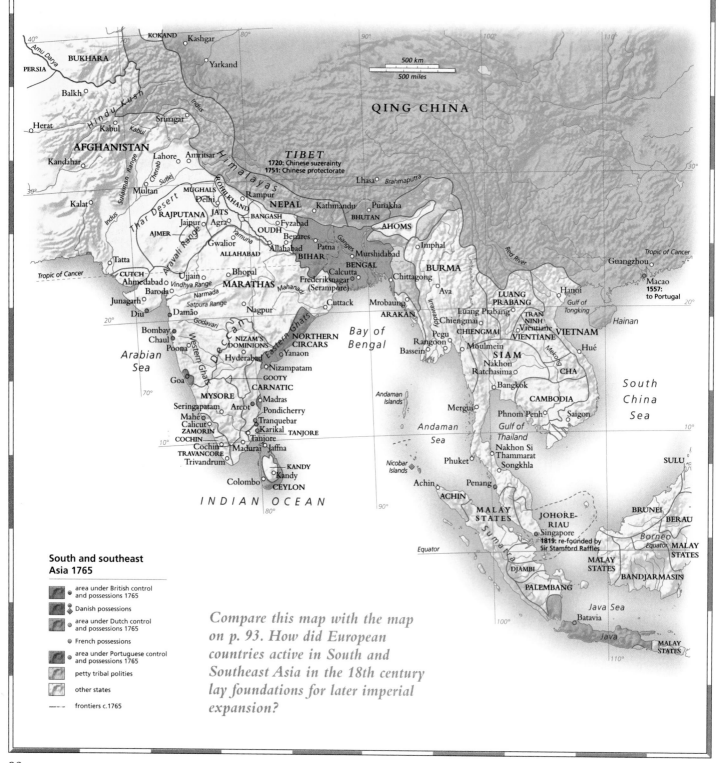

South and southeast Asia 1765

- area under British control and possessions 1765
- Danish possessions
- area under Dutch control and possessions 1765
- French possessions
- area under Portuguese control and possessions 1765
- petty tribal polities
- other states
- frontiers c.1765

Compare this map with the map on p. 93. How did European countries active in South and Southeast Asia in the 18th century lay foundations for later imperial expansion?

FOREIGN IMPERIALISM IN EAST ASIA

THE RAPIDLY EXPANDING Qing economy of the 18th century made it prey to foreign ambitions. The dynasty's failure in the Opium War of 1839-42 revealed its weaknesses. Hong Kong was the first of many territorial and trading concessions which gave not only the Europeans but the Russians and Japanese valuable toeholds.

In what ways did foreign influence in Qing China weaken its stability?

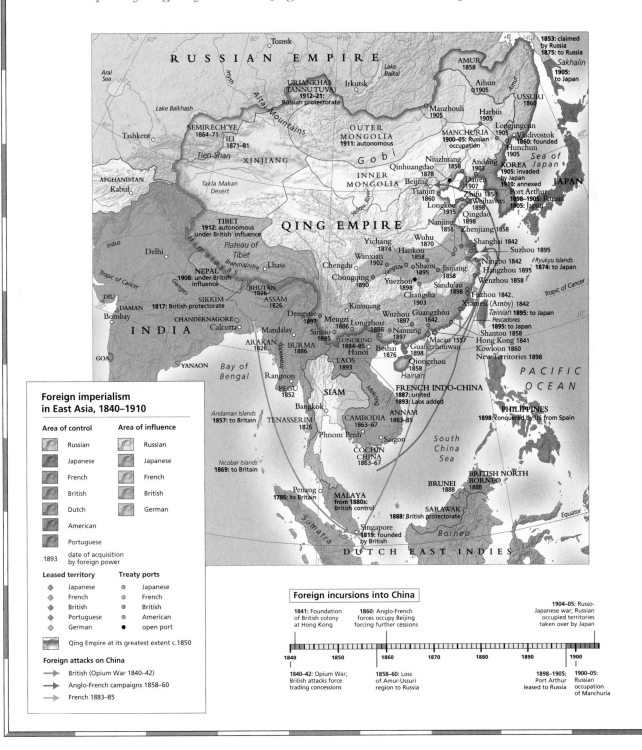

Foreign imperialism in East Asia, 1840–1910

Area of control	Area of influence
Russian	Russian
Japanese	Japanese
French	French
British	British
Dutch	German
American	
Portuguese	
1893 date of acquisition by foreign power	

Leased territory
◆ Japanese
◆ French
◆ British
◆ Portuguese
◆ German

Treaty ports
◉ Japanese
◉ French
◉ British
◉ American
● open port

Qing Empire at its greatest extent c.1850

Foreign attacks on China
→ British (Opium War 1840–42)
→ Anglo-French campaigns 1858–60
→ French 1883–85

Foreign incursions into China

1841: Foundation of British colony at Hong Kong

1860: Anglo-French forces occupy Beijing forcing further cessions

1904–05: Russo-Japanese war; Russian occupied territories taken over by Japan

| 1840 | 1850 | 1860 | 1870 | 1880 | 1890 | 1900 |

1840–42: Opium War; British attacks force trading concessions

1858–60: Loss of Amur-Ussuri region to Russia

1898–1905: Port Arthur leased to Russia

1900–05: Russian occupation of Manchuria

IMPERIALISM IN THE PACIFIC

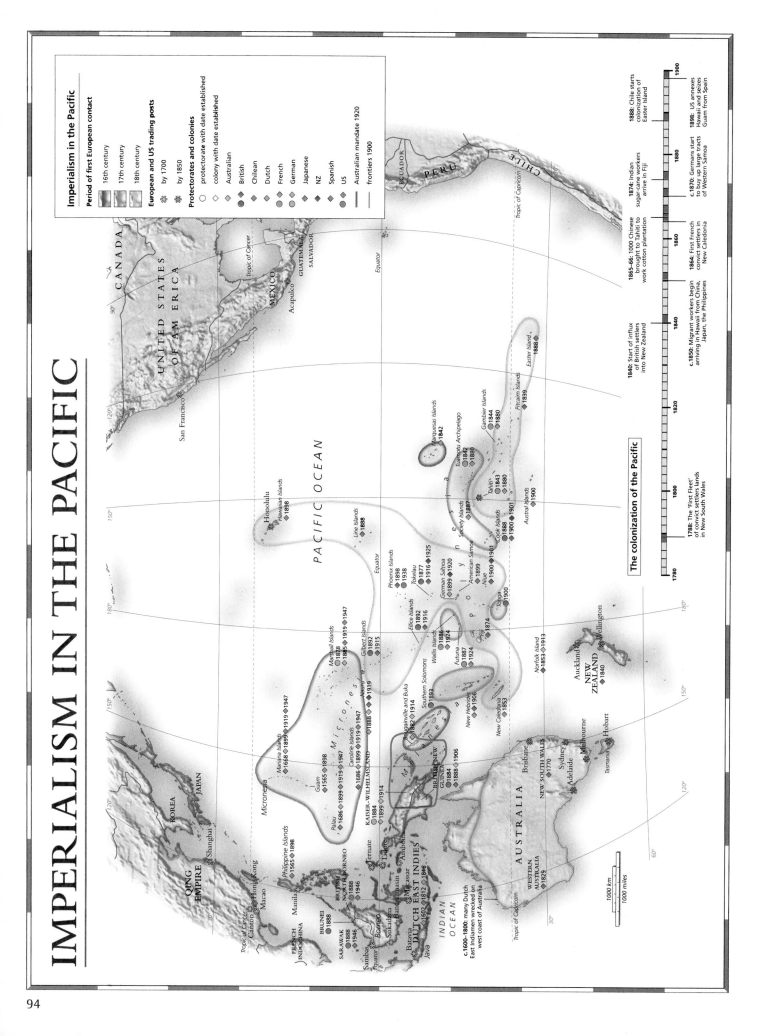

Imperialism in the Pacific

Period of first European contact

- 16th century
- 17th century
- 18th century

European and US trading posts

- by 1700
- by 1850

Protectorates and colonies

	protectorate with date established	colony with date established
Australian		
British		
Chilean		
Dutch		
French		
German		
Japanese		
NZ		
Spanish		
US		

— Australian mandate 1920

— frontiers 1900

The colonization of the Pacific

1780 — 1788 — 1800 — 1820 — 1840 — 1860 — 1880 — 1900

1788: The 'First Fleet' of convict settlers lands in New South Wales

1840: Start of influx of British settlers into New Zealand

c.1850: Migrant workers begin arriving in Hawaii from China, Japan, the Philippines

1864: First French convict settlers in New Caledonia

1865–66: 1000 Chinese brought to Tahiti to work cotton plantation

c.1870: Germans start to buy up large tracts of Western Samoa

1874: Indian sugar-cane workers arrive in Fiji

1888: Chile starts colonization of Easter Island

1898: US annexes Hawaii and seizes Guam from Spain

CANADA

UNITED STATES OF AMERICA

San Francisco

MEXICO

Acapulco

GUATEMALA

SALVADOR

ECUADOR

PERU

CHILE

Tropic of Cancer

Equator

Tropic of Capricorn

PACIFIC OCEAN

QING EMPIRE

Canton ◆ Hong Kong

Macao

Shanghai

KOREA

JAPAN

FRENCH INDOCHINA

Manila

Philippine Islands ◆ 1565 ◆ 1898

BRUNEI ● 1888

Borneo

SARAWAK ◇ 1888 ◇ 1946

BRITISH NORTH BORNEO ◇ 1888 ◇ 1946

Sambas

Equator

Sukadana

Bandjarmasin ◇ 1602 ◆ 1812 ◇ 1846

Batavia

Java

DUTCH EAST INDIES

Makassar

Ternate

Tidore

Amboina

INDIAN OCEAN

Micronesia

Guam ◆ 1565 ● 1898

Palau ◇ 1686 ◇ 1899 ◇ 1919 ◇ 1947

Caroline Islands ◇ 1686 ◇ 1899 ◇ 1919 ◇ 1947

Mariana Islands ◇ 1668 ◇ 1899 ◇ 1919 ◇ 1947

Marshall Islands ◇ 1878 ◇ 1885 ◇ 1919 ◇ 1947

KAISER-WILHELMSLAND ◇ 1884 ◇ 1899 ◇ 1914

BRITISH NEW GUINEA ◇ 1884 ◇ 1888 ◇ 1906

Bougainville and Buka ◇ 1862 ◇ 1914

Southern Solomons ◇ 1893

Melanesia

Nauru ◇ 1888 ◇ 1919

Gilbert Islands ◇ 1892 ◇ 1915

Ellice Islands ◇ 1892 ◇ 1916

Line Islands ● 1888

Phoenix Islands ◇ 1898 ◇ 1938

Tokelau ◇ 1877 ◇ 1916 ◇ 1925

Wallis Islands ◇ 1886 ◇ 1924

Futuna ◇ 1887 ◇ 1924

Fiji ● 1874

German Samoa ◇ 1899 ◇ 1920

American Samoa ◆ 1899

Niue ◇ 1900 ◇ 1901

Tonga ◇ 1900

Polynesia

New Hebrides ◇ 1906

New Caledonia ◆ 1853

Honolulu

Hawaiian Islands ● 1898

Marquesas Islands ◆ 1842

Tuamotu Archipelago ◆ 1842 ◆ 1880

Tahiti ◆ 1843 ◆ 1880

Society Islands ◆ 1887

Cook Islands ◇ 1888 ◇ 1900 ◇ 1901

Austral Islands ◆ 1900

Gambier Islands ◆ 1844 ◆ 1880

Pitcairn Islands ◆ 1839

Easter Island ◆ 1888

Norfolk Island ◇ 1853 ◇ 1913

Auckland ◇ 1840

NEW ZEALAND

Wellington

AUSTRALIA

WESTERN AUSTRALIA ◇ 1829

NEW SOUTH WALES ◇ 1770

Brisbane

Sydney

Adelaide

Melbourne

Hobart

Tasmania

c.1600–1800: many Dutch East Indiamen wrecked on west coast of Australia

1000 km

1000 miles

120° 90°

150° 180° 150° 120° 60° 30°

EARLY EUROPEAN IMPACT IN AUSTRALIA

THE 19TH CENTURY WITNESSED the near annihilation of many Pacific island societies, as European and American powers extended their rule. The British colonies of Australia and New Zealand rank with the US as the most successful transplantations of European culture to another continent; however in doing so, the Aborigines of Australia and the Maori of New Zealand were brutally subjugated.

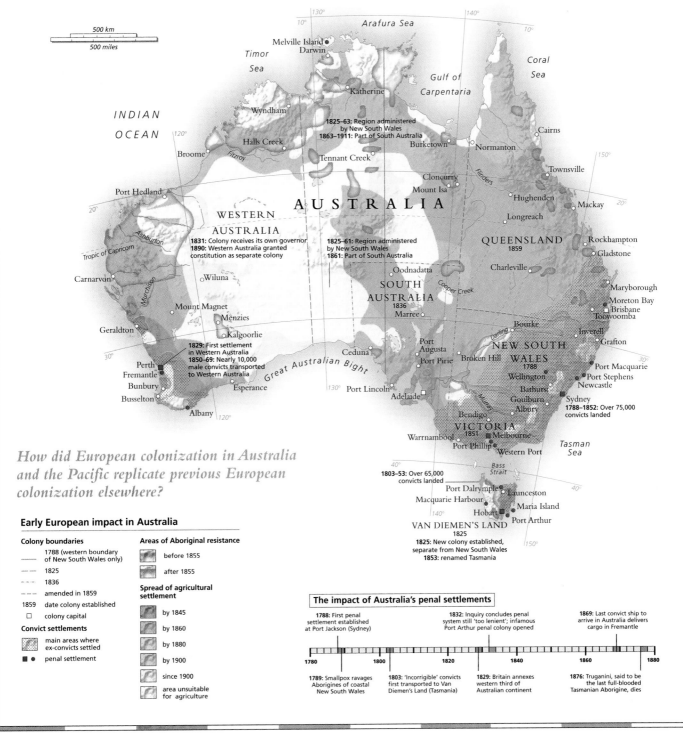

How did European colonization in Australia and the Pacific replicate previous European colonization elsewhere?

1825–63: Region administered by New South Wales
1863–1911: Part of South Australia

1831: Colony receives its own governor
1890: Western Australia granted constitution as separate colony

1825–61: Region administered by New South Wales
1861: Part of South Australia

1829: First settlement in Western Australia
1850–69: Nearly 10,000 male convicts transported to Western Australia

1788–1852: Over 75,000 convicts landed

1803–53: Over 65,000 convicts landed

1825: New colony established, separate from New South Wales
1853: renamed Tasmania

Early European impact in Australia

Colony boundaries

— 1788 (western boundary of New South Wales only)
– – 1825
–·– 1836
– – – amended in 1859
1859 date colony established
☐ colony capital

Convict settlements
▨ main areas where ex-convicts settled
■ ● penal settlement

Areas of Aboriginal resistance
▨ before 1855
▨ after 1855

Spread of agricultural settlement
▨ by 1845
▨ by 1860
▨ by 1880
▨ by 1900
▨ since 1900
▨ area unsuitable for agriculture

The impact of Australia's penal settlements

1788: First penal settlement established at Port Jackson (Sydney)

1832: Inquiry concludes penal system still 'too lenient'; infamous Port Arthur penal colony opened

1869: Last convict ship to arrive in Australia delivers cargo in Fremantle

1780 | 1800 | 1820 | 1840 | 1860 | 1880

1789: Smallpox ravages Aborigines of coastal New South Wales

1803: 'Incorrigible' convicts first transported to Van Diemen's Land (Tasmania)

1829: Britain annexes western third of Australian continent

1876: Truganini, said to be the last full-blooded Tasmanian Aborigine, dies

THE WORLD: 1800–1850

THE AFTERMATH of the French and American revolutions and the Napoleonic wars led to new nationalism and demands for democacy and freedom. There were mass movements of peoples to expanding cities or to new lives abroad. Hunger for raw materials to feed industry and the desire to dominate world markets soon led to unprecedented colonial expansion.

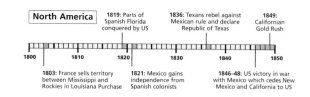

North America

1819: Parts of Spanish Florida conquered by US

1836: Texans rebel against Mexican rule and declare Republic of Texas

1849: Californian Gold Rush

1800 — 1810 — 1820 — 1830 — 1840 — 1850

1803: France sells territory between Mississippi and Rockies in Louisiana Purchase

1821: Mexico gains independence from Spanish colonists

1846–48: US victory in war with Mexico which cedes New Mexico and California to US

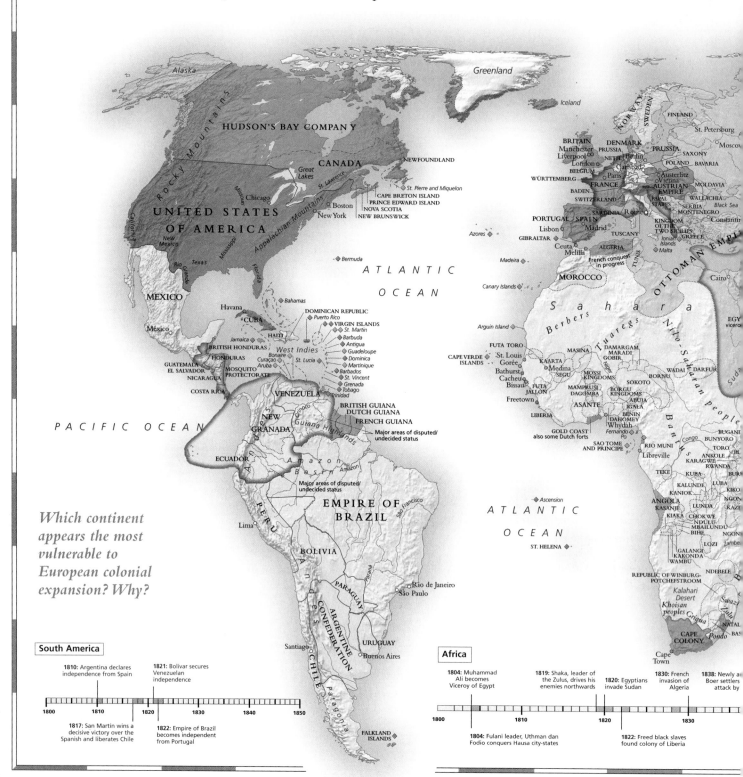

Which continent appears the most vulnerable to European colonial expansion? Why?

South America

1810: Argentina declares independence from Spain

1821: Bolivar secures Venezuelan independence

1800 — 1810 — 1820 — 1830 — 1840 — 1850

1817: San Martin wins a decisive victory over the Spanish and liberates Chile

1822: Empire of Brazil becomes independent from Portugal

Africa

1804: Muhammad Ali becomes Viceroy of Egypt

1819: Shaka, leader of the Zulus, drives his enemies northwards

1820: Egyptians invade Sudan

1830: French invasion of Algeria

1838: Newly arrived Boer settlers attack by

1800 — 1810 — 1820 — 1830

1804: Fulani leader, Uthman dan Fodio conquers Hausa city-states

1822: Freed black slaves found colony of Liberia

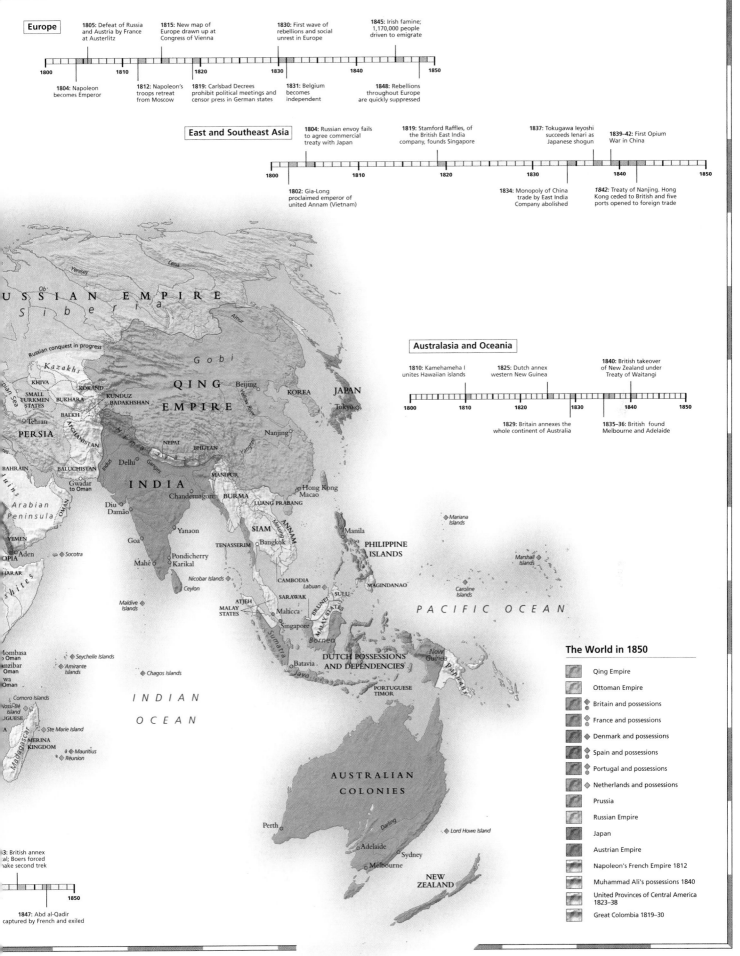

Europe

1805: Defeat of Russia and Austria by France at Austerlitz

1815: New map of Europe drawn up at Congress of Vienna

1830: First wave of rebellions and social unrest in Europe

1845: Irish famine; 1,170,000 people driven to emigrate

1800   1810   1820   1830   1840   1850

1804: Napoleon becomes Emperor

1812: Napoleon's troops retreat from Moscow

1819: Carlsbad Decrees prohibit political meetings and censor press in German states

1831: Belgium becomes independent

1848: Rebellions throughout Europe are quickly suppressed

East and Southeast Asia

1804: Russian envoy fails to agree commercial treaty with Japan

1819: Stamford Raffles, of the British East India company, founds Singapore

1837: Tokugawa Ieyoshi succeeds Ienari as Japanese shogun

1839–42: First Opium War in China

1800   1810   1820   1830   1840   1850

1802: Gia-Long proclaimed emperor of united Annam (Vietnam)

1834: Monopoly of China trade by East India Company abolished

1842: Treaty of Nanjing. Hong Kong ceded to British and five ports opened to foreign trade

Australasia and Oceania

1810: Kamehameha I unites Hawaiian islands

1825: Dutch annex western New Guinea

1840: British takeover of New Zealand under Treaty of Waitangi

1800   1810   1820   1830   1840   1850

1829: Britain annexes the whole continent of Australia

1835–36: British found Melbourne and Adelaide

3: British annex
al; Boers forced
ake second trek

1850

1847: Abd al-Qadir
captured by French and exiled

The World in 1850

- Qing Empire
- Ottoman Empire
- Britain and possessions
- France and possessions
- Denmark and possessions
- Spain and possessions
- Portugal and possessions
- Netherlands and possessions
- Prussia
- Russian Empire
- Japan
- Austrian Empire
- Napoleon's French Empire 1812
- Muhammad Ali's possessions 1840
- United Provinces of Central America 1823–38
- Great Colombia 1819–30

NORTH AMERICA 1783–1905

THE LOUISIANA PURCHASE of 1803 added to the US a huge swath of western lands formerly controlled by France. Settlers poured into the Great Plains, the Pacific Northwest, and the periphery of the Republic of Mexico, including California and Texas. The settlement of the West was met with serious armed resistance from Native Americans. Elsewhere, the nations of central America achieved independence beginning in the 1820s, though greatly weakened from their former colonial status.

What effect did US expansion have on the native peoples and ecosystems of the American West?

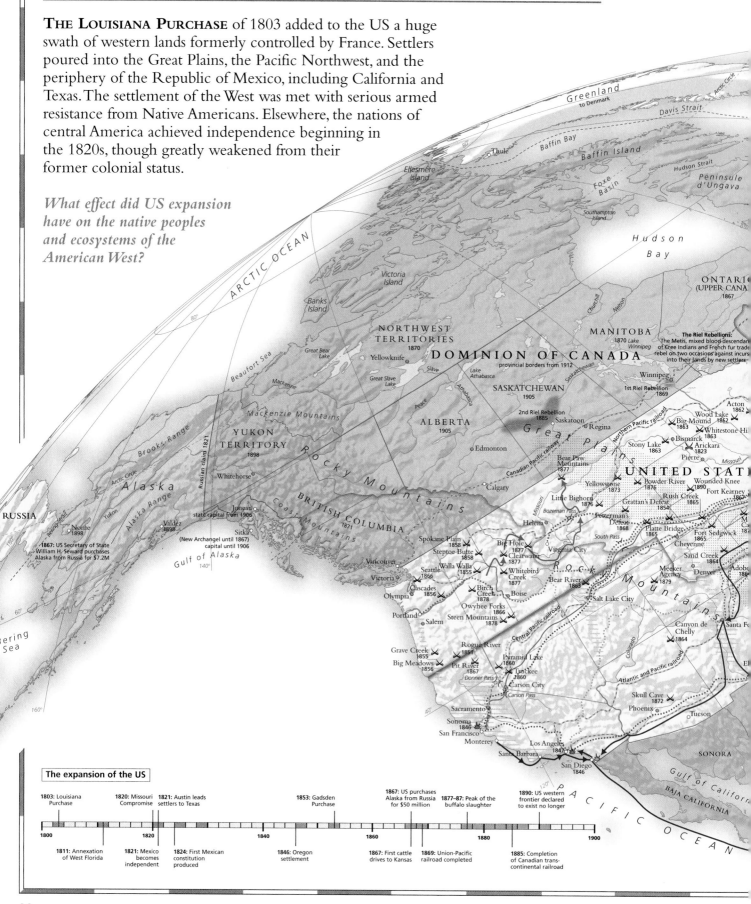

The expansion of the US

1803: Louisiana Purchase

1811: Annexation of West Florida

1820: Missouri Compromise

1821: Austin leads settlers to Texas

1821: Mexico becomes independent

1824: First Mexican constitution produced

1853: Gadsden Purchase

1846: Oregon settlement

1867: US purchases Alaska from Russia for $50 million

1867: First cattle drives to Kansas

1869: Union-Pacific railroad completed

1877–87: Peak of the buffalo slaughter

1885: Completion of Canadian trans-continental railroad

1890: US western frontier declared to exist no longer

1800   1820   1840   1860   1880   1900

North America 1783–1905: struggles for nationhood and the seizing of the West

European settlement in the US and Canada
- by c.1860
- extent of Russian claim 1821–24
- northern frontier of Mexico 1821
- Mexican territory 1821–23, United Provinces of Central America 1823–38
- Mexico after 1854
- Alaska Purchase 1867
- Canada at the creation of the Dominion, 1867
- Canadian territory 1880 with dates of provincial incorporation
- Canadian territory added in 1905

Conflicts between natives and settlers
- "Trail of Tears" removal of the southern tribes
- flight of the Nez Percé
- local wars 1783–1850
- Creek War 1813–14
- Seminole Wars 1816–58
- battles for the West 1850–1890

International conflicts
- War of 1812
- Texas Revolution 1835–36
- US victory: US-Mexican War 1846–48
- Mexican victory: US-Mexican War 1846–48
- Riel rebellions 1869–1885

Texas Revolution 1835–36
- routes of Santa Ana

The US-Mexican War 1846–48
- movement of US forces
- movement of Mexican forces

Wagon trails
- Oregon Trail
- Mormon Trail
- Central Overland Trail
- Southern Overland Trail
- Santa Fe Trail
- Old Spanish Trail
- California Trail
- Chisholm Trail
- Bozeman Trail

- country capital
- state/province capital
- 1804 date of independence
- railroad
- Pony Express route
- range of buffalo

Scale varies with perspective

8770 km (5450 miles)
12,230 km (7600 miles)

Texas Revolution 1835–36:
US settlers in Mexican province of Texas rebel, declaring independence from Mexico and driving out troops – led by General Santa Ana – sent in to quell the uprising

The US-Mexican War 1846–48:
Admission of Texas to the US in 1845 leads to war with Mexico. US quickly wins California and by 1848, Mexico has ceded 33% of its US territory for a fee of $15M

THE SCRAMBLE FOR AFRICA

THE RACE FOR EUROPEAN political control of Africa began in the early 1880s. In most cases, control was directly imposed by conquest. By 1914, Africa was fully partitioned along lines that bore little relations to cultural or linguistic traditions.

What factors made the African continent ideal for European colonial expansion?

Imperialism in Africa, 1880–1920

Territory controlled by European nations by 1914

- Belgium
- Britain
- France
- Germany
- Italy
- Portugal
- Spain
- nominally Ottoman, under British control
- 1882 date of taking control
- borders in 1914

Important mineral deposits

- coal
- copper
- diamonds
- gold

Scale varies with perspective

8200 km (5100 miles)

7000 km (4350 miles)

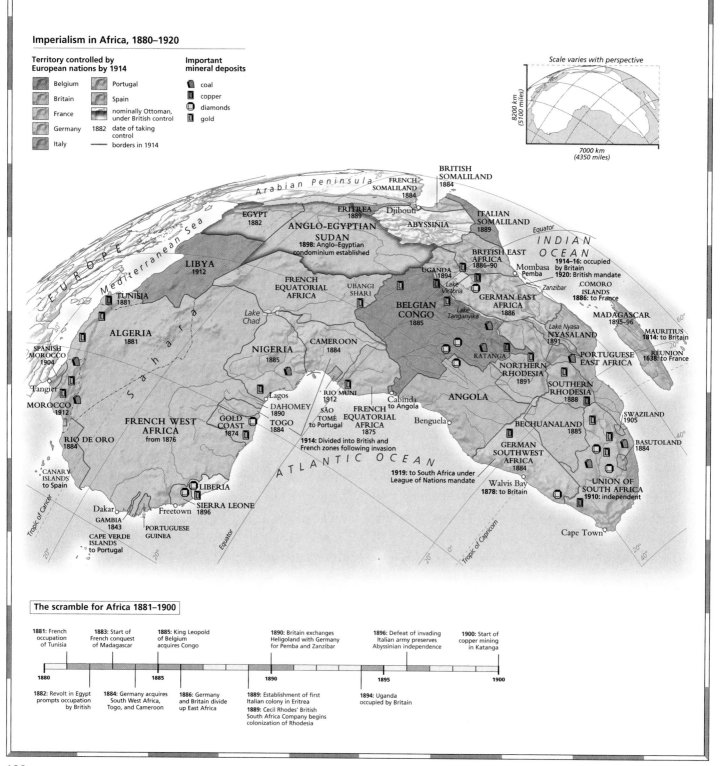

EUROPE

Arabian Peninsula

Mediterranean Sea

EGYPT 1882

FRENCH SOMALILAND 1884

BRITISH SOMALILAND 1884

ERITREA 1889

Djibouti

ITALIAN SOMALILAND 1889

Equator

INDIAN OCEAN

ANGLO-EGYPTIAN SUDAN
1898: Anglo-Egyptian condominium established

ABYSSINIA

LIBYA 1912

FRENCH EQUATORIAL AFRICA

UBANGI SHARI

UGANDA 1894

BRITISH EAST AFRICA 1886–90

Mombasa Pemba

1914–16: occupied by Britain
1920: British mandate

TUNISIA 1881

Lake Chad

BELGIAN CONGO 1885

Lake Victoria

GERMAN EAST AFRICA 1886

Zanzibar

COMORO ISLANDS
1886: to France

ALGERIA 1881

CAMEROON 1884

Lake Tanganyika

Lake Nyasa

MADAGASCAR 1895–96

MAURITIUS
1814: to Britain

SPANISH MOROCCO 1904

NIGERIA 1885

KATANGA

NYASALAND 1891

NORTHERN RHODESIA 1891

PORTUGUESE EAST AFRICA

RÉUNION
1638: to France

Tangier

RIO MUNI 1912

Cabinda to Angola

ANGOLA

SOUTHERN RHODESIA 1888

MOROCCO 1912

Lagos

DAHOMEY 1890

SÃO TOMÉ to Portugal

FRENCH EQUATORIAL AFRICA 1875

Benguela

SWAZILAND 1905

FRENCH WEST AFRICA from 1876

GOLD COAST 1874

TOGO 1884

1914: Divided into British and French zones following invasion

BECHUANALAND 1885

BASUTOLAND 1884

RIO DE ORO 1884

ATLANTIC OCEAN

GERMAN SOUTHWEST AFRICA 1884

1919: to South Africa under League of Nations mandate

Walvis Bay
1878: to Britain

UNION OF SOUTH AFRICA 1910: independent

CANARY ISLANDS to Spain

Tropic of Cancer

LIBERIA

SIERRA LEONE 1896

Dakar

Freetown

GAMBIA 1843

CAPE VERDE ISLANDS to Portugal

PORTUGUESE GUINEA

Equator

Tropic of Capricorn

Cape Town

The scramble for Africa 1881–1900

1881: French occupation of Tunisia

1883: Start of French conquest of Madagascar

1885: King Leopold of Belgium acquires Congo

1890: Britain exchanges Heligoland with Germany for Pemba and Zanzibar

1896: Defeat of invading Italian army preserves Abyssinian independence

1900: Start of copper mining in Katanga

1880   1885   1890   1895   1900

1882: Revolt in Egypt prompts occupation by British

1884: Germany acquires South West Africa, Togo, and Cameroon

1886: Germany and Britain divide up East Africa

1889: Establishment of first Italian colony in Eritrea

1889: Cecil Rhodes' British South Africa Company begins colonization of Rhodesia

1894: Uganda occupied by Britain

SOUTH AMERICA 1830-1920

IN THE AFTERMATH OF LIBERATION, many South American countries saw power seized by *caudillos*, military dictators. Economies depended on raw materials such as coffee, rubber, and beef for export.

How did economic dependency inhibit South American attempts at nation-building?

1904–14: Panama canal constructed

PANAMA
1830: Independent republic under US protection; 10-mile wide Canal Zone under complete American control

TRINIDAD 1797: to Britain

BRITISH GUIANA 1803: to Britain
Georgetown
Paramaribo
Cayenne
FRENCH GUIANA 1817: to France

SURINAM 1815: to Netherlands

VENEZUELA

1848: Civil war drives Páez, first president of the country, into exile

COLOMBIA
1851

1899–1901: War of a Thousand Days. Civil war is endemic in Colombia throughout 19th century, usually over question of federalism

ECUADOR 1853

1890–1920: Manáos flourishes as centre of rubber boom in Amazon region

B R A Z I L
1888
1889: Liberals overthrow Emperor and establish republic

Pernambuco (Recife)

Maceió

ACRE 1899–1903: Independent

1839: Chilean army invades Peru in protest at confederation of Peru and Bolivia

PERU 1854

Bahia (Salvador)

1828: Peru invades Bolivia
1836–39: Shortlived confederation of Peru and Bolivia

1865–66: Spain seizes guano-rich Islas de Chincha

BOLIVIA 1854

1878–83: War of the Pacific over valuable nitrate deposits (see map 4)

1864–70: The Paraguayan War; almost half population of Paraguay killed in disastrous war with Brazil, Argentina, and Uruguay

PARAGUAY 1870

Political and economic development in South America 1830–1930

▨ approximate international borders 1830	▽ nitrates
— international borders 1930	◊ rubber
⬓ region temporarily independent	⬇ sugar
	⬓ silver
Major export products	⬓ tin
⚘ bananas	⚥ tobacco
🐃 beef	⚘ wheat
▨ cacao	⊞ wool
◖ coffee	--- major railways by 1910
⬓ copper	⚡1853 date slavery abolished
▲ guano	✱ major port
⚥ hides	⚘ major international and civil wars 1830–1930

CHILE 1823

ARGENTINA 1853

URUGUAY 1853

1843–52: In one of many civil wars between Blanco and Colorado parties, the Blanco party besieges Montevideo

1852: Rosas defeated by Urquiza, rival caudillo
1852–59: Buenos Aires refuses to join new Argentine confederation

BUENOS AIRES

1860–63: Conquest of Araucanian Indian territory; subsequent settlers include many Germans

1865: Welsh colony founded in Chubut region

1880–1900: Gradual settlement of Patagonia

1899–1902: Region subject of border dispute between Argentina and Chile

FALKLAND ISLANDS 1832: to Britain

1000 km
1000 miles

THE ECONOMIC REVOLUTION

RAPID INDUSTRIALIZATION occurred throughout most of Europe by the end of the 19th century. A stable currency and an effective private banking system were seen as essential to the growth and success of every industrializing nation. The major industrial nations also began to invest heavily overseas. Their aims were the discovery and exploitation of cheaper raw materials, balanced by the development of overseas markets for their products.

What connections does this map reveal between industrialization and imperialism?

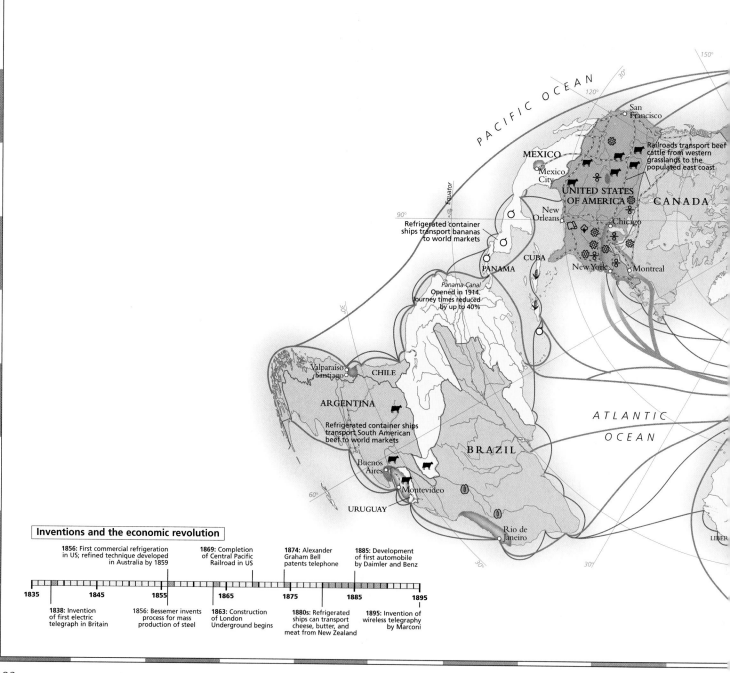

Railroads transport beef cattle from western grasslands to the populated east coast

Refrigerated container ships transport bananas to world markets

Panama Canal Opened in 1914. Journey times reduced by up to 40%

Refrigerated container ships transport South American beef to world markets

Inventions and the economic revolution

1856: First commercial refrigeration in US; refined technique developed in Australia by 1859

1869: Completion of Central Pacific Railroad in US

1874: Alexander Graham Bell patents telephone

1885: Development of first automobile by Daimler and Benz

1835   1845   1855   1865   1875   1885   1895

1838: Invention of first electric telegraph in Britain

1856: Bessemer invents process for mass production of steel

1863: Construction of London Underground begins

1880s: Refrigerated ships can transport cheese, butter, and meat from New Zealand

1895: Invention of wireless telegraphy by Marconi

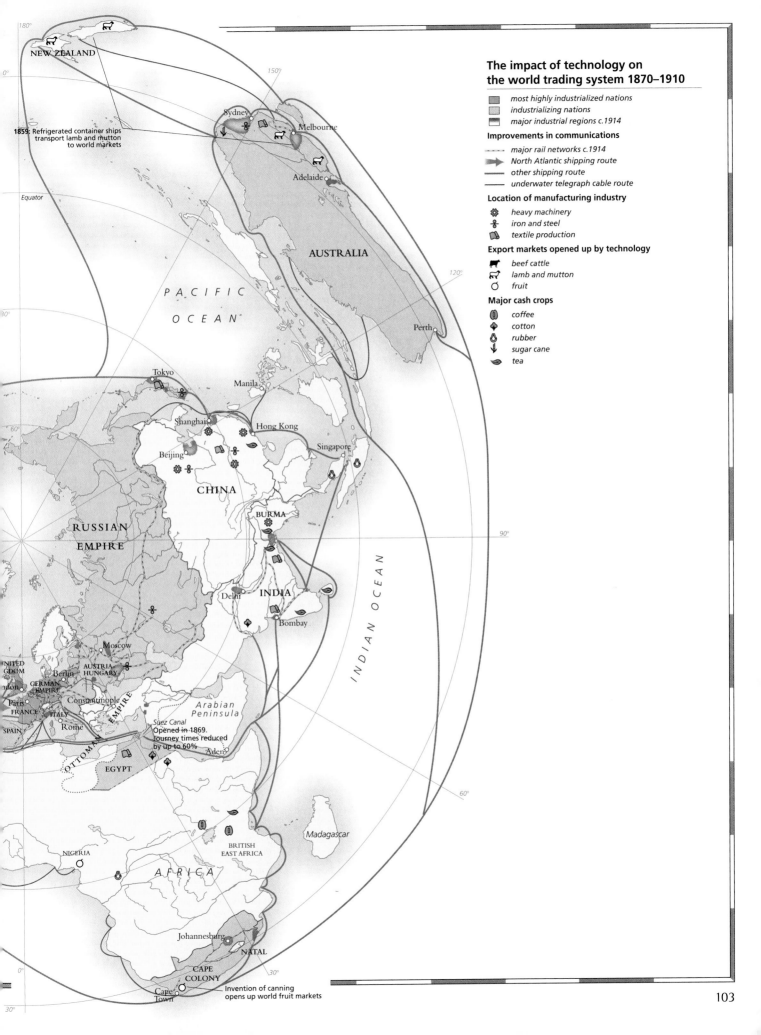

The impact of technology on the world trading system 1870–1910

- ▨ most highly industrialized nations
- ▨ industrializing nations
- ▭ major industrial regions c.1914

Improvements in communications
- ⋯⋯ major rail networks c.1914
- ➤ North Atlantic shipping route
- ── other shipping route
- ── underwater telegraph cable route

Location of manufacturing industry
- ⚙ heavy machinery
- ⚒ iron and steel
- ▨ textile production

Export markets opened up by technology
- 🐄 beef cattle
- 🐑 lamb and mutton
- ○ fruit

Major cash crops
- ◉ coffee
- ◈ cotton
- ◊ rubber
- ⬇ sugar cane
- 🍃 tea

NEW ZEALAND

1859: Refrigerated container ships transport lamb and mutton to world markets

Sydney

Melbourne

Adelaide

AUSTRALIA

Perth

PACIFIC OCEAN

Equator

Tokyo

Manila

Shanghai

Hong Kong

Beijing

Singapore

CHINA

BURMA

RUSSIAN EMPIRE

Delhi

INDIA

Bombay

INDIAN OCEAN

Moscow

AUSTRIA-HUNGARY

UNITED KINGDOM

Berlin

GERMAN EMPIRE

London

Paris

FRANCE

Constantinople

SPAIN

ITALY

Rome

OTTOMAN EMPIRE

Arabian Peninsula

Suez Canal
Opened in 1869.
Journey times reduced by up to 60%

Aden

EGYPT

Madagascar

NIGERIA

BRITISH EAST AFRICA

AFRICA

Johannesburg

NATAL

CAPE COLONY

Cape Town

Invention of canning opens up world fruit markets

THE WORLD IN 1900

BY 1900, the major European powers had extended their economic and political influence to the very ends of the globe, colonizing virtually all of Africa, most of South and Southeast Asia, and exploiting the fatal weaknesses of China's crumbling Qing dynasty.

Compare this map with the map on pages 96–97. What has changed?

Compare this map with the map on pages 96–97.

Europe

1854–56: Franco-British-Turkish alliance victorious against Russians in Crimea

1861: Abolition of serfdom in Russia

1862: Otto von Bismarck prime minister of Prussia

1867: Dual monarchy of Austria-Hungary established

1870: Franco-Prussian war; Prussian victory leads to collapse of Second Empire

1871: Rome becomes capital of united Italy; King Wilhelm I of Prussia declared German emperor

1887: Bulgaria, independent of Ottoman empire, becomes leading Balkan state

1896: Revival of Olympic Games at Athens, Greece

1850   1860   1870   1880   1890   1900

Map labels

Greenland

ICELA

Alaska

CANADA

NEWFOUNDLAND

BRIT

Great Lakes

St. Pierre and Miquelon

SP

Rocky Mountains

Chicago

St. Lawrence

PORTUGAL   Mac

UNITED STATES OF AMERICA

New York
Washington DC

Lisbon

Azores

GIBRALTAR   Ceut

Los Angeles

Appalachian Mountains

Mississippi

Bermuda

Madeira

MOROCCO

Rio Grande

ATLANTIC OCEAN

IFNI

MEXICO

Bahamas

Canary Islands

RIO DE ORO

S

Hawaiian Islands

Mexico

Havana

CUBA
US occupation

DOMINICAN REPUBLIC

Puerto Rico

Virgin Islands

St. Martin

LEEWARD ISLANDS

Jamaica   HAITI

Guadeloupe

CAPE VERDE ISLANDS

Senegal

BRITISH HONDURAS
HONDURAS

West Indies

Martinique

GAMBIA

S

PACIFIC OCEAN

GUATEMALA
SALVADOR

NICARAGUA

Curaçao

BARBADOS

WINDWARD ISLANDS

PORTUGUESE GUINEA

a

COSTA RICA

TRINIDAD AND TOBAGO

SIERRA LEONE

GO
COAS

Christmas Island

VENEZUELA

BRITISH GUIANA
DUTCH GUIANA
FRENCH GUIANA

LIBERIA

COLOMBIA

Orinoco

Guiana Highlands

Phoenix Islands

Galapagos Islands to Ecuador

ECUADOR

Amazon

Amazon Basin

Ascension

Marquesas Islands

BRAZIL

ACRE

São Francisco

Samoa

Tuamotu Islands

Lima

PERU

ST. HELENA

Society Islands   Tahiti

TONGA ISLANDS

BOLIVIA

Andes

Atacama Desert

Rio de Janeiro
São Paulo

Pitcairn Island

PARAGUAY

Paraná

Kermadec Islands

CHILE

ARGENTINA

URUGUAY

Santiago

Buenos Aires

Patagonia

FALKLAND ISLANDS

The Americas

1858: Mexican Civil War between conservatives and liberals

1861–65: US Civil War

1864–70: Paraguayan War: Brazil, Argentina, and Uruguay defeat Paraguay

1867: Canada becomes a British dominion

1876: Battle of Little Bighorn; Sioux warriors kill 250 US soldiers

1879–83: War of Pacific; Chile, Peru, and Bolivia fight for control of Atacama Desert

1898: Spanish-American War. US occupies Cuba, and gains control of Philippines

1850   1860   1870   1880   1890   1900

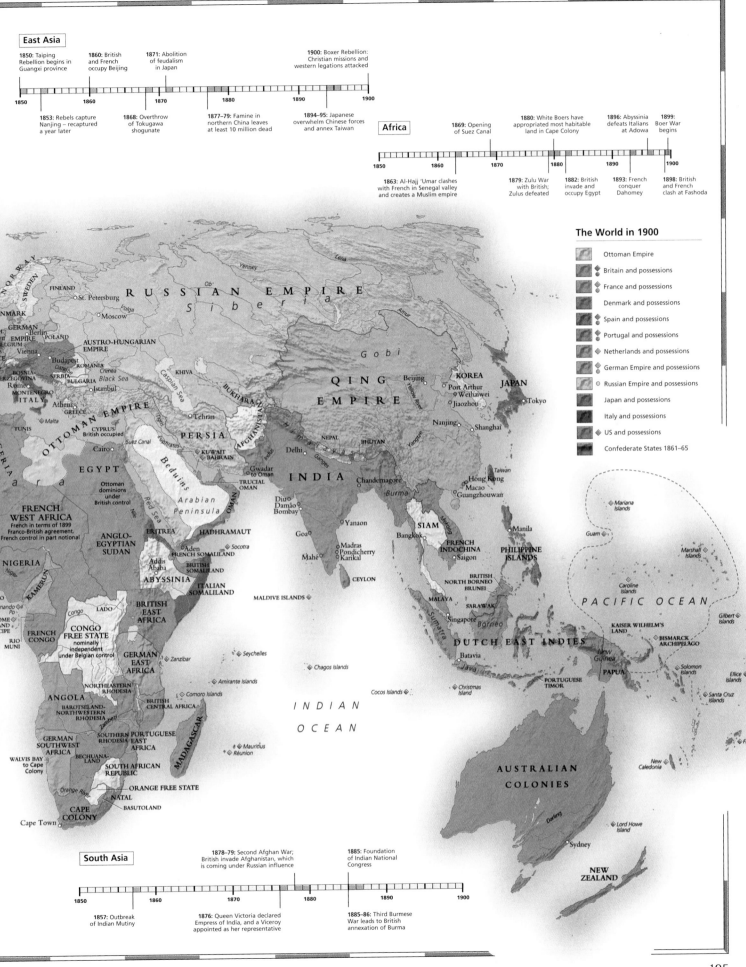

East Asia

1850: Taiping Rebellion begins in Guangxi province

1860: British and French occupy Beijing

1871: Abolition of feudalism in Japan

1900: Boxer Rebellion: Christian missions and western legations attacked

1850 — 1860 — 1870 — 1880 — 1890 — 1900

1853: Rebels capture Nanjing – recaptured a year later

1868: Overthrow of Tokugawa shogunate

1877–79: Famine in northern China leaves at least 10 million dead

1894–95: Japanese overwhelm Chinese forces and annex Taiwan

Africa

1869: Opening of Suez Canal

1880: White Boers have appropriated most habitable land in Cape Colony

1896: Abyssinia defeats Italians at Adowa

1899: Boer War begins

1850 — 1860 — 1870 — 1880 — 1890 — 1900

1863: Al-Hajj 'Umar clashes with French in Senegal valley and creates a Muslim empire

1879: Zulu War with British; Zulus defeated

1882: British invade and occupy Egypt

1893: French conquer Dahomey

1898: British and French clash at Fashoda

The World in 1900

- Ottoman Empire
- Britain and possessions
- France and possessions
- Denmark and possessions
- Spain and possessions
- Portugal and possessions
- Netherlands and possessions
- German Empire and possessions
- Russian Empire and possessions
- Japan and possessions
- Italy and possessions
- US and possessions
- Confederate States 1861–65

Map labels

NORWAY, SWEDEN, FINLAND, DENMARK, GERMAN EMPIRE, BELGIUM, POLAND, AUSTRO-HUNGARIAN EMPIRE, BOSNIA-HERZEGOVINA, SERBIA, BULGARIA, MONTENEGRO, ITALY, ROMANIA, GREECE, Berlin, Vienna, Budapest, Rome, Athens, Malta, TUNIS, St. Petersburg, Moscow, Volga

RUSSIAN EMPIRE, Siberia, Yenisey, Ob, Lena, Amur

Black Sea, Crimea, Istanbul, Caspian Sea, KHIVA, BUKHARA, Gobi

QING EMPIRE, Beijing, Port Arthur, Weihaiwei, Jiaozhou, Yellow River, KOREA, JAPAN, Tokyo, Nanjing, Shanghai, Yangtze, Taiwan, Hong Kong, Macao, Guangzhouwan

OTTOMAN EMPIRE, CYPRUS British occupied, Suez Canal, Cairo, EGYPT, Tehran, PERSIA, AFGHANISTAN, Tigris, Euphrates, KUWAIT, BAHRAIN, Gwadar to Oman, TRUCIAL OMAN, OMAN, Beduins, Arabian Peninsula, Red Sea, Nile, Ottoman dominions under British control

NEPAL, BHUTAN, Himalayas, Indus, Delhi, Ganges, INDIA, Chandernagore, Burma, Diu, Damão, Bombay, Goa, Yanaon, Madras, Pondicherry, Karikal, Mahé, CEYLON, SIAM, Bangkok, Mekong

FRENCH WEST AFRICA (French in terms of 1899 Franco-British agreement. French control in part notional), NIGERIA, Niger, ANGLO-EGYPTIAN SUDAN, ERITREA, HADHRAMAUT, Aden, FRENCH SOMALILAND, Addis Ababa, BRITISH SOMALILAND, ABYSSINIA, ITALIAN SOMALILAND, KAMERUN, FERNANDO PO, SÃO TOMÉ AND PRÍNCIPE, RIO MUNI, FRENCH CONGO, Congo, CONGO FREE STATE nominally independent under Belgian control, BRITISH EAST AFRICA, GERMAN EAST AFRICA, Zanzibar, Seychelles, MALDIVE ISLANDS, Chagos Islands, Amirante Islands, Comoro Islands

NORTHEASTERN RHODESIA, ANGOLA, BAROTSELAND-NORTHWESTERN RHODESIA, Zambezi, BRITISH CENTRAL AFRICA, GERMAN SOUTHWEST AFRICA, SOUTHERN RHODESIA, PORTUGUESE EAST AFRICA, MADAGASCAR, Mauritius, Réunion, WALVIS BAY to Cape Colony, BECHUANALAND, SOUTH AFRICAN REPUBLIC, ORANGE FREE STATE, Orange River, NATAL, BASUTOLAND, CAPE COLONY, Cape Town

FRENCH INDOCHINA, Saigon, PHILIPPINE ISLANDS, Manila, MALAYA, Singapore, BRITISH NORTH BORNEO, BRUNEI, SARAWAK, Borneo, Sumatra, DUTCH EAST INDIES, Batavia, Java, Christmas Island, Cocos Islands, PORTUGUESE TIMOR

PACIFIC OCEAN, Mariana Islands, Guam, Marshall Islands, Caroline Islands, Gilbert Islands, KAISER WILHELM'S LAND, New Guinea, PAPUA, BISMARCK ARCHIPELAGO, Solomon Islands, Ellice Islands, Santa Cruz Islands, Fiji, New Caledonia

INDIAN OCEAN, AUSTRALIAN COLONIES, Darling, Sydney, Lord Howe Island, NEW ZEALAND

South Asia

1878–79: Second Afghan War; British invade Afghanistan, which is coming under Russian influence

1885: Foundation of Indian National Congress

1850 — 1860 — 1870 — 1880 — 1890 — 1900

1857: Outbreak of Indian Mutiny

1876: Queen Victoria declared Empress of India, and a Viceroy appointed as her representative

1885–86: Third Burmese War leads to British annexation of Burma

GLOBAL MIGRATION

THE TECHNICAL INNOVATIONS of the Industrial Revolution made the 19th-century world a much smaller place. More than 80 million people emigrated from their country of origin during the 19th and early 20th centuries. Over half of them moved across the Atlantic to North and South America. In the Russian Empire, movement was eastward from European Russia into Siberia and the Caspian region. Europeans moved south and east to take up employment in the colonies, while indentured laborers from China and India traveled to the Americas, Africa, and Southeast Asia.

What were the factors that led so many people to migrate during the 19th and early 20th centuries?

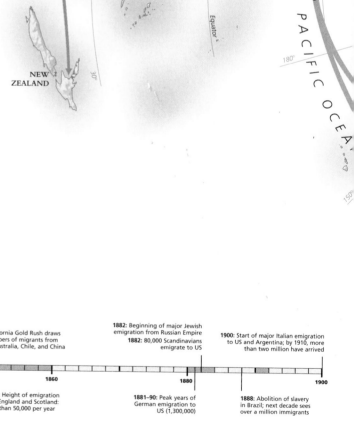

World migration c.1860–1920

Transatlantic migration

- to North America
- to South America and the Caribbean
- to Europe from the Americas

Other European migration

- to Australia and New Zealand
- to North Africa

Asian migration

- to the Americas and Australia
- Russian migration into Siberia
- Indian inter-colonial migration

- transcontinental railroad
- major exporters of people
- major importers of people

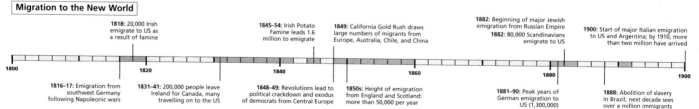

Migration to the New World

1816–17: Emigration from southwest Germany following Napoleonic wars

1818: 20,000 Irish emigrate to US as a result of famine

1831–41: 200,000 people leave Ireland for Canada, many travelling on to the US

1845–54: Irish Potato Famine leads 1.6 million to emigrate

1848–49: Revolutions lead to political crackdown and exodus of democrats from Central Europe

1849: California Gold Rush draws large numbers of migrants from Europe, Australia, Chile, and China

1850s: Height of emigration from England and Scotland: more than 50,000 per year

1881–90: Peak years of German emigration to US (1,300,000)

1882: Beginning of major Jewish emigration from Russian Empire

1882: 80,000 Scandinavians emigrate to US

1888: Abolition of slavery in Brazil; next decade sees over a million immigrants

1900: Start of major Italian emigration to US and Argentina; by 1910, more than two million have arrived

1800   1820   1840   1860   1880   1900

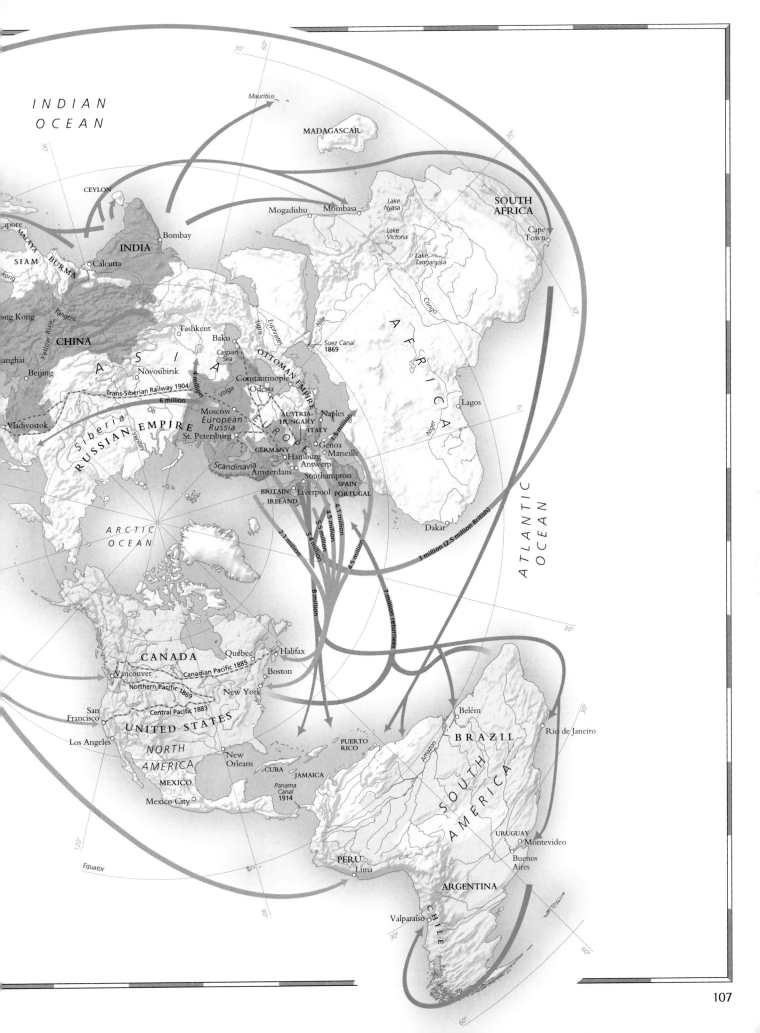

INDIAN
OCEAN

Mauritius

MADAGASCAR

SOUTH
AFRICA

CEYLON

Mogadishu Mombasa

*Lake
Nyasa*

Cape
Town

Bombay

INDIA

*Lake
Victoria*

SIAM

BURMA

Calcutta

*Lake
Tanganyika*

A F R I C A

Congo

ong Kong

Yangtze

Tashkent

Baku

*Suez Canal
1869*

CHINA

Yellow River

A S I A

Novosibirsk

*Caspian
Sea*

OTTOMAN EMPIRE

Beijing

Nile

anghai

Constantinople

4 million

Volga

Odessa

Trans-Siberian Railway 1904

Lagos

6 million

Moscow

AUSTRIA-
HUNGARY

Naples

Vladivostok

Siberia

RUSSIAN EMPIRE

*European
Russia*

ITALY

1.5 million

Ob

St. Petersburg

GERMANY

Genoa

Niger

Yenisey

Marseille

Hamburg

ATLANTIC
OCEAN

Scandinavia

Antwerp

Amsterdam

Southampton

ARCTIC
OCEAN

BRITAIN Liverpool

SPAIN

IRELAND

PORTUGAL

Dakar

2.1 million

3.4 million

5.5 million

4.5 million

4.1 million

4.5 million

3 million (2.5 million British)

8 million

1 million returnees

CANADA

Québec Halifax

Vancouver

Canadian Pacific 1885

Boston

Northern Pacific 1869

New York

Belém

Central Pacific 1883

San
Francisco

BRAZIL

Rio de Janeiro

UNITED STATES

NORTH

Los Angeles

New
Orleans

Amazon

PUERTO
RICO

AMERICA

MEXICO

CUBA

JAMAICA

S O U T H

MEXICO CITY

*Panama
Canal
1914*

A M E R I C A

URUGUAY

Montevideo

PERU

Buenos
Aires

Lima

ARGENTINA

Valparaíso

CHILE

Equator

MOVEMENTS AGAINST COLONIAL RULE 1880–1920

THE AGGRESSIVE SCRAMBLE FOR EMPIRE provoked determined armed resistance across Africa and Asia. Local peoples rose up to repel the European intruders, but in most cases they had to submit when faced by superior firepower.

How is foreign rule the catalyst for nationalistic struggles?

1916: Easter Rising
BRITAIN
NETHERLANDS
GERMANY
FRANCE
PORTUGAL
ITALY
SPAIN
RUSSIAN EMPIRE
1919–26: Rif war between Spain and Rif and Jibala tribes
1911: Jeliaz incident
OTTOMAN EMPIRE
1916: Large-scale revolt in Central Asia
QING EMPIRE
MOROCCO
1915–16: Rebellion against French
TUNISIA
1881–82: Arabi Pasha leads nationalist uprising
1905–09: Persian revolution
1899–1900: Boxer rebellion
SPANISH SAHARA
ALGERIA
1912–13: Sanusi war
1906: Dinshaway incident
PERSIA
KUWAIT
1891: Anti-western riots in Wuchang
Tropic of Cancer
LIBYA
EGYPT
NEJD
1911–12: Chinese revolution
PACIFIC OCEAN
Tropic of Cancer
FRENCH WEST AFRICA
1897–1900: Rabih leads resistance against French
1881–98: Mahdiyya jihad against British and Egyptian rule
INDIA
BURMA
1883–88, 1883–1913: Guerrilla warfare against French
1905–09: Terrorist campaigns in Maharashtra and Bengal
FRENCH INDO-CHINA
1884–98: Manda resistance
NIGERIA
1904: Anyang rebellion
FRENCH EQUATORIAL AFRICA
ANGLO-EGYPTIAN SUDAN
1896: Italian defeat at Adowa
BRITISH SOMALILAND
1886–91: War against British rule
SIAM
1898–1902: Aguinaldo leads nationalist revolt
1900: Ashanti rebellion
ABYSSINIA
1891–1920: Sayyid Muhammad resists British and Italian rule
1885–87, 1916: Rebellions against French rule
ANNAM
1885–86: Revolts against French rule
PHILIPPINE ISLANDS
GOLD COAST
CAMEROON
Equator
1890–98: Bunyoro resistance
UGANDA
1895–1905: Nandi resistance
INDIAN OCEAN
1898–1913: Moro resistance
Equator
ATLANTIC OCEAN
FRENCH CONGO
BELGIAN CONGO
1911–17: Tutsi and Hutu resistance
GERMAN EAST AFRICA
BRITISH EAST AFRICA
1888–89: Abushiri resistance
1891–98: Hehe resistance
1881–1908: Jihad against Dutch
DUTCH EAST INDIES
1905–07: Maji-Maji resistance
BRITISH CENTRAL AFRICA (NYASALAND)
Sumatra
ANGOLA
NORTHERN RHODESIA
Java
1890, 1914–17: Uprising by Saminist peasant movements
1881–94: Rebellions against Dutch
1913: Risings against Portuguese rule
1896: Revolts by Matabele and Mashona
PORTUGUESE EAST AFRICA
MADAGASCAR
1898–1904: Anti-French risings
GERMAN SOUTHWEST AFRICA
BECHUANALAND
SOUTHERN RHODESIA
Tropic of Capricorn
Tropic of Capricorn
1904–06: Risings by Herero and Hottentots
1906: Zulu revolt
UNION OF SOUTH AFRICA
1899–1902: Boer war between Britain and two Boer republics

1000 km

1000 miles

Movements against colonial rule, 1880–1920

Anti-colonial uprisings and incidents

- anti-British
- anti-Dutch
- anti-French
- anti-German
- anti-Italian
- anti-Portugal
- anti-Russian
- anti-Spanish
- anti-US

Other partly anti-western rebellions

- Persia
- area of Chinese revolution 1911–12
- — boundary at 1914

JAPANESE MODERNIZATION

BY 1900, Japan was a prosperous, sophisticated society – socially developed, universally literate, ready for modernization – and keen to dominate East Asian affairs.

What is the relationship between modernization and militarization?

Asahikawa
Otaru
Hokkaido

Goryokaku
27 Jun 1869
Hakodate

Oct 1868–May 1869: besieged by imperial forces

Aomori
AOMORI

AKITA
Akita
Morioka
IWATE

Sakata
YAMAGATA
Yamagata
MIYAGI
Sendai

Niigata
NIIGATA
Fukushima

ISHIKAWA
Fukui
Takaoka
Kanazawa
TOYAMA
NAGANO
Nagano
GUNMA
Maebashi
TOCHIGI

Sea of Japan

Sado

1864, 1865: Bakufu forces repulsed

Okayama
Kyoto
Nagoya
SHIMANE
TOTTORI
HIROSHIMA
Hiroshima
OKAYAMA
HYOGO
Kobe
KYOTO
FUKUI
SHIGA
Gifu
GIFU
AICHI SHIZUOKA
YAMANASHI
IBARAKI
Edo

1853: US Commodore Perry forces trade agreements
Jan 1868: renamed Tokyo

Tsushima Strait
Hamada
Shimonoseki
Kure
Matsuyama
KAGAWA
OSAKA
Osaka
NARA
Ise
MIE
Toyohashi
Shizuoka
SHIZUOKA
Chiba
CHIBA

Yamata
Fukuoka
Moji
Saseho
SAGA
NAGASAKI
OITA
EHIME
TOKUSHIMA
Shikoku
Kochi
KOCHI
Wakayama
WAKAYAMA
Fushimi
27 Jan 1868

Yokohama

Nagasaki
Kumamoto
Kyushu
KUMAMOTO
MIYAZAKI

Osaka

Kagoshima
KAGOSHIMA

Inland Sea

PACIFIC OCEAN

200 km
200 miles

◀ Japanese modernization 1868–1918

Boshin War 1868–69

- imperial (anti-Bakufu) alliance
- → route of imperial army
- ✕ battle, with date

Modernization under the Meiji

- KOCHI prefectures established 1871
- main industrial areas by 1918
- railways built 1868–1918

Traditional industries

- ⚱ ceramics
- textiles
- silk

Industries developed after 1868

- manufacturing
- ❈ machine-building
- ⚓ shipbuilding
- chemicals
- ● city of over 500,000 in 1918
- ◦ city of over 100,000 in 1918
- ○ other major city

1854: First foreign trade treaties

1877: Satsuma rebellion, led by reformer Saigo Takamori, in defence of traditional values

1904–05: Russo–Japanese War consolidates influence in Korea and Manchuria

1919: League of Nations accords German Pacific territories under mandate to Japan

1840   1860   1880   1900   1920

1868–69: Boshin War; Tokugawa Bakufu defeated by modernizing imperialists

1889: New constitution balances imperial authority with parliamentary government

1894–95: Sino–Japanese War; increases sphere of influence on mainland

1918: Japan occupies areas of Russia during civil war

Beijing
MANCHURIA
Mukden
Yingkou
Xiuyan
Andong
Yalu River
17 Aug 1894
Liaodong Peninsula
Port Arthur
Dairen
Anju
Pyongyang
16 Sep 1894
Shandong Peninsula
Weihaiwei
12 Feb 1895
Wonsan
Inchon
Seoul
Tangjin
29 Jul 1894

QING CHINA
Feb 1895– May 1898: Japanese occupation

Yellow Sea
KOREA
Pusan
Sea of Japan

Quelpart Island (Cheju-do)

Tsushima Strait
Hiroshima
Shimonoseki
Saseho
Honshu
JAPAN
Kyushu

17 Apr 1895: Peace Treaty signed

200 km
200 miles

▲ The Sino-Japanese War 1894–95

- area of Tonghak rebellion
- → Japanese advance
- ✕ Japanese victory
- area leased to Japan 1895

The Russo-Japanese War 1904–05 ▶

- Qing China
- to Russia 1897, to Japan 1905
- area leased to Japan 1895
- → Japanese advances 1904–05
- → route of Russian Baltic fleet
- ✕ Japanese victory, with date

Harbin
Chinese Eastern Railway
Mukden
1–10 Mar 1905
Liaoyang
Aug–Sep 1904
Changchun
Jilin
Dashiqiao
Manchurian Railway
Beijing
Funing
Yingkou
Fushun
MANCHURIA
RUSSIA
Vladivostok

1898: Russia occupies Japanese leased territory
Liaodong Peninsula
Daguzhan
Dairen
Piziwo
Weihaiwei to Britain
Qingdao to Germany
Port Arthur
Aug 1904–Jan 1905
8 Feb 1904: Japanese bombard Russian fleet
Hoeryong

1897: occupied by Russia
1905: occupied by Japan

Wonsan
Seoul
KOREA
1905: Japanese protectorate
1910: Crown Colony

Sea of Japan

QING CHINA
Yellow Sea
Mokpo
Pusan
Tsushima
17 May 1905
Honshu
Hiroshima
Shimonoseki
JAPAN

200 km
200 miles

WORLD WAR I

WORLD WAR I is one of history's watersheds. The conflict mobilized 65 million troops, of whom nine million died and over one-third were wounded. The war was won by the Allied Powers, but at great cost. The German, Austro-Hungarian, Ottoman, and Russian empires were destroyed; European political and financial supremacy ended; and by 1918 the US had emerged as the greatest power in the world. The disillusionment that followed paved the way for the extremist forces of the left and right that emerged in the 1920s and 1930s.

How did the effects of World War I destabilize Europe?

The Western Front 1914–1918

→	German invasion of France and Belgium, 1914
▲▲	furthest extent of German advance, 1914
→	German retreat
▬▬	line from end of 1914–Jul 1916
- - -	Hindenburg line
▒	gains by Allied powers 1916–17
→	Kaiserschlacht (the Kaiser's battles') 1918
▲▲	German offensive Mar–Jul 1918
→	Allied counter-attacks, 1918
▬▬	line at the Armistice 11 Nov 1918

Major battles

✾	1914
✾	1915
✾	1916
✾	1917
✾	1918

The Western Front 1914–16

The Western Front 1916–18

The Western Front

Aug 1914: Battle of the Frontiers

Oct 1914: The 'race to the sea'

May 1916: Battle of Jutland in North Sea

Feb–Mar 1917: Germans withdraw to Hindenburg Line

Apr–May 1917: Allied offensives

Mar–Jul 1918: German offensives on Somme, Aisne, Noyon-Mondidier and Champagne-Marne lines

Sep 1914: Battle of the Marne; first battle of the Aisne

Feb–Dec 1916: Battle of Verdun

Jul–Nov 1916: Battle of the Somme

Apr 1917: US declares war on Central powers

Aug–Nov 1917: Third battle of Ypres

Jul–Oct 1918: Counter-offensives by Allies

Nov 1918: Armistice ends war on Western Front

The Eastern Front

FINLAND
6 Dec 1917: declared independence from Russian Empire

The Eastern Front

- ➤ Russian advances, 1914
- ▲▲ front line in 1914–15 (limit of Russian advance)
- ▲ limit of Austro–German advances, 1915–16
- ➤ Brusilov offensives, 1916
- ▒ Armistice line Dec 1917
- ➤ German landings, 1917–18
- ➤ German offensives into Russia 1918
- ▲ German penetration into Russia by Jun 1918
- ⬚ Area occupied by Central Powers under Treaty of Brest–Litovsk

Major battles:
- 🔥 1914   🔥 1916
- 🔥 1915   🔥 1917

250 km
250 miles

NORWAY

SWEDEN

Vyborg
Lovisa
Helsingfors
Hango
Gulf of Finland
St. Petersburg
Lake Ladoga

Dagö
Gulf of Riga
Pskov

RUSSIAN EMPIRE

Vindava
Libava
Riga
Mitava
Ösel
Shavli
Memel
Jakobstadt
Dvina
Dvinsk
Smolensk
Lake Naroch
Vilna
Königsberg
Danzig
Gumbinnen
Masurian Lakes
Grodno
Minsk
Mogilev
Berezina

GERMANY
Tannenberg
Thorn
Vistula
POLAND
Narev
Pinsk
Baranovichi
Pripet
Pripet Marshes
Desna

Kalish
Lodz
Warsaw
Pilitsa
Brest-Litovsk
Lublin
Oder
Breslau
Krasnik
San
Komarow
Lutsk
Kiev
Vorskla
Don

Cracow
Tarnow
Brody
Lemberg
Jul 1917: failed Russian offensive
Yekaterinoslav
Gorlice
Przemysl
GALICIA
Stanislau
Dnieper
Don
Rostov
Danube
Czernowitz
Dniester
Bug
Donetz

Budapest
MOLDAVIA
Pruth
BESSARABIA
Kishinev
Nikolayev
Sea of Azov

AUSTRIA–HUNGARY
Odessa
Crimea
Sevastopol

SERBIA
1915: Conquered by Germany
Belgrade
ROMANIA
1916: Conquered by Germany
Black Sea

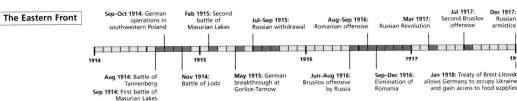

The Eastern Front

Sep–Oct 1914: German operations in southwestern Poland
Feb 1915: Second battle of Masurian Lakes
Jul–Sep 1915: Russian withdrawal
Aug–Sep 1916: Romanian offensive
Mar 1917: Russian Revolution
Jul 1917: Second Brusilov offensive
Dec 1917: Russian armistice

1914 — 1915 — 1916 — 1917 — 1918

Aug 1914: Battle of Tannenberg
Sep 1914: First battle of Masurian Lakes
Nov 1914: Battle of Lodz
May 1915: German breakthrough at Gorlice-Tarnow
Jun–Aug 1916: Brusilov offensive by Russia
Sep–Dec 1916: Elimination of Romania
Jan 1918: Treaty of Brest-Litovsk allows Germany to occupy Ukraine and gain access to food supplies

Europe after the First World War

European empires in 1914
- ━ German Empire
- ━ Austro-Hungarian Empire
- ━ Russian Empire
- ━ frontiers 1923
- ▨ new states

500 km
500 miles

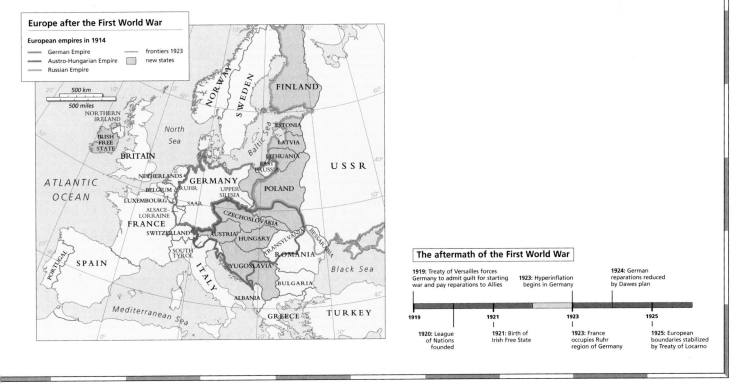

NORWAY
SWEDEN
FINLAND
North Sea
Baltic Sea
ESTONIA
LATVIA
LITHUANIA
EAST PRUSSIA
USSR
NORTHERN IRELAND
IRISH FREE STATE
BRITAIN
NETHERLANDS
BELGIUM
LUXEMBOURG
GERMANY
RUHR
SAAR
UPPER SILESIA
POLAND
ATLANTIC OCEAN
ALSACE-LORRAINE
FRANCE
SWITZERLAND
AUSTRIA
CZECHOSLOVAKIA
HUNGARY
TRANSYLVANIA
BESSARABIA
SOUTH TYROL
ITALY
ROMANIA
Black Sea
YUGOSLAVIA
BULGARIA
PORTUGAL
SPAIN
ALBANIA
Mediterranean Sea
GREECE
TURKEY

The aftermath of the First World War

1919: Treaty of Versailles forces Germany to admit guilt for starting war and pay reparations to Allies
1923: Hyperinflation begins in Germany
1924: German reparations reduced by Dawes plan

1919 — 1921 — 1923 — 1925

1920: League of Nations founded
1921: Birth of Irish Free State
1923: France occupies Ruhr region of Germany
1925: European boundaries stabilized by Treaty of Locarno

WORLD WAR II

World War II was a protracted struggle by a host of Allied nations to contain and eventually destroy the Axis, a small group of extreme nationalist (fascist) states led by Germany and Japan. Its human costs were enormous, and its conclusion – the detonation of two atomic bombs over Japan – heralded the Nuclear Age.

Why is World War II known as a "Total War"?

The Second World War, Sep 1939–Dec 1941

— political boundaries in 1939
▨ Axis and its allies in Mar 1940
▨ Allies in May 1940
▨ Allies by Dec 1941
▤ Axis territorial expansion by Jun 1940
▤ Axis territorial expansion by Dec 1941
◆ Axis satellites following the German invasion of France, May 1940
☐ neutral state

The Second World War, Dec 1941–Jul 1943

▤ extent of Axis powers Dec 1942
▨ Allies Jul 1943
▨ Axis powers Jul 1943
☐ neutral state
● Allied base
● Axis base
⚔ major battle

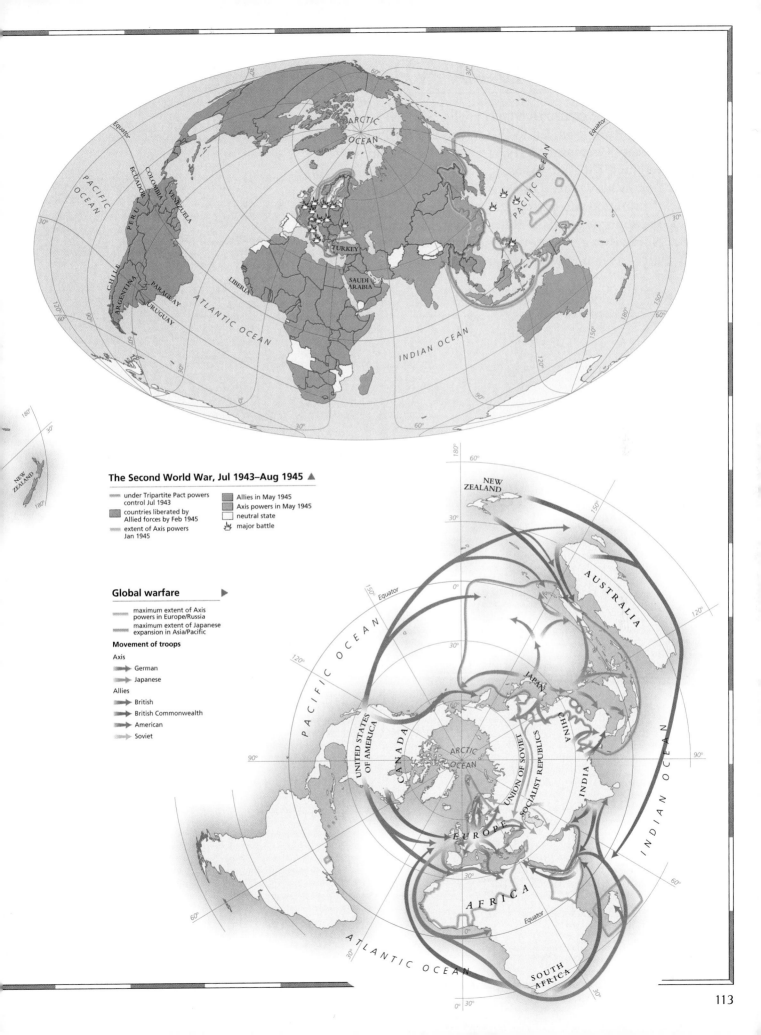

The Second World War, Jul 1943–Aug 1945 ▲

- under Tripartite Pact powers control Jul 1943
- countries liberated by Allied forces by Feb 1945
- extent of Axis powers Jan 1945
- Allies in May 1945
- Axis powers in May 1945
- neutral state
- major battle

Global warfare ▶

- maximum extent of Axis powers in Europe/Russia
- maximum extent of Japanese expansion in Asia/Pacific

Movement of troops

Axis
- German
- Japanese

Allies
- British
- British Commonwealth
- American
- Soviet

THE COLD WAR

DEEPENING US-SOVIET HOSTILITY, plus Western Europe's inability to defend itself, led to the creation of the North Atlantic Treaty Organization (NATO) in 1949; this in turn prompted the USSR and its satellite countries in Eastern Europe to form the Warsaw Pact. Thus the Cold War took shape, with the US committed to a policy of containment and the USSR intent on supporting anti-Western movements throughout the world. North Korea's invasion of the south in 1950 was immediately seen as a test of US credibility.

Why was the divide between Eastern and Western Europe known as an "Iron Curtain"?

▲ The Korean War 1950–53

	area controlled by North Korean forces 15 Sep 1950
▲▲▲	front line 15 Sep 1950
➡	US forces 16 Sep–24 Oct 1950
➡	Chinese forces Oct 1950
▲▲▲	front line 24 Nov 1950
▲▲▲	front line 25 Jan 1951
++++	cease-fire line 27 Jul 1953

The Cold War in Europe

1953: Widespread uprisings;
1961: Berlin Wall built

1944–47: Civil war;
1953: Strikes and riots

1968: Widespread demonstrations; reformist government crushed

1956: Widespread uprising; government withdraws from Warsaw Pact, Russian invasion

1964: Nominal independence declared

1955: Allied occupied partition ends

1948: Tito splits from Soviet alliance;
1955: Détente

1968: Government leaves Warsaw Pact

The Cold War in Europe

■	original NATO members in 1949
■	later NATO members (with dates)
■	Warsaw Pact members in 1955
□	neutral states

500 km
500 miles

The Cold War in Europe 1947–68

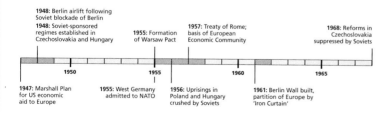

1948: Berlin airlift following Soviet blockade of Berlin

1948: Soviet-sponsored regimes established in Czechoslovakia and Hungary

1955: Formation of Warsaw Pact

1957: Treaty of Rome; basis of European Economic Community

1968: Reforms in Czechoslovakia suppressed by Soviets

1947: Marshall Plan for US economic aid to Europe

1955: West Germany admitted to NATO

1956: Uprisings in Poland and Hungary crushed by Soviets

1961: Berlin Wall built, partition of Europe by 'Iron Curtain'

DECOLONIZATION OF AFRICA / THE PALESTINIAN PROBLEM

MOST INDEPENDENT AFRICAN STATES were territorially identical to the colonies they replaced. The new leaders often became dictators; many governments were corrupt and a number of countries were devastated by war.

How has the legacy of colonialism affected African politics?

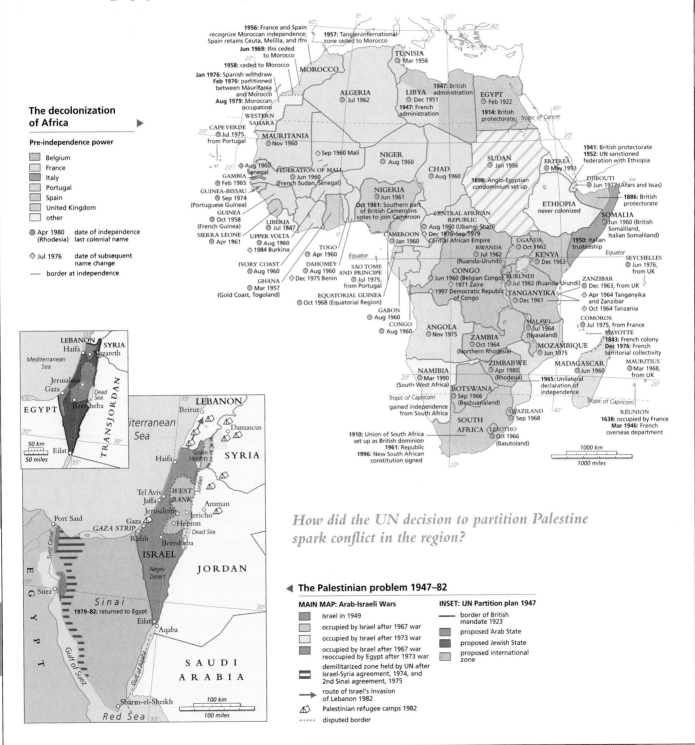

The decolonization of Africa ▶

Pre-independence power

- Belgium
- France
- Italy
- Portugal
- Spain
- United Kingdom
- other

● Apr 1980   date of independence
(Rhodesia)   last colonial name

◇ Jul 1976   date of subsequent name change

— border at independence

1956: France and Spain recognize Moroccan independence; Spain retains Ceuta, Melilla, and Ifni
Jun 1969: Ifni ceded to Morocco
1958: ceded to Morocco
Jan 1976: Spanish withdraw
Feb 1976: partitioned between Mauritania and Morocco
Aug 1979: Moroccan occupation
WESTERN SAHARA
CAPE VERDE ● Jul 1975, from Portugal

1957: Tangier international zone ceded to Morocco

TUNISIA ● Mar 1956
MOROCCO
ALGERIA ● Jul 1962
LIBYA ● Dec 1951
1947: French administration
1947: British administration
EGYPT ● Feb 1922
1914: British protectorate
MAURITANIA ● Nov 1960
NIGER ● Aug 1960
SUDAN ● Jan 1956
1898: Anglo-Egyptian condominium set up
ERITREA ● May 1993
1941: British protectorate
1952: UN sanctioned federation with Ethiopia
DJIBOUTI ● Jun 1977 (Afars and Issas)
1886: British protectorate
◇ Sep 1960 Mali
◇ Aug 1960 Senegal
FEDERATION OF MALI ● Jun 1960 (French Sudan, Senegal)
GAMBIA ● Feb 1965
GUINEA-BISSAU ● Sep 1974 (Portuguese Guinea)
GUINEA ● Oct 1958 (French Guinea)
SIERRA LEONE ● Apr 1961
LIBERIA ● Jul 1847
UPPER VOLTA ● Aug 1960 ◇ 1984 Burkina
IVORY COAST ● Aug 1960
GHANA ● Mar 1957 (Gold Coast, Togoland)
TOGO ● Apr 1960
DAHOMEY ● Aug 1960 ◇ Dec 1975 Benin
CHAD ● Aug 1960
NIGERIA ● Jun 1961
Oct 1961: Southern part of British Cameroons votes to join Cameroon
CENTRAL AFRICAN REPUBLIC ● Aug 1960 (Ubangi-Shari) ◇ Dec 1976–Sep 1979 Central African Empire
CAMEROON ● Jan 1960
ETHIOPIA never colonized
SOMALIA ● Jun 1960 (British Somaliland, Italian Somaliland)
1950: Italian trusteeship
UGANDA ● Oct 1962
RWANDA ● Jul 1962 (Ruanda-Urundi)
KENYA ● Dec 1963
SAO TOME AND PRINCIPE ● Jul 1975, from Portugal
EQUATORIAL GUINEA ● Oct 1968 (Equatorial Region)
CONGO ● Jun 1960 (Belgian Congo) ◇ 1971 Zaire ◇ 1997 Democratic Republic of Congo
BURUNDI ● Jul 1962 (Ruanda-Urundi)
TANGANYIKA ● Dec 1961
ZANZIBAR ● Dec 1963, from UK ◇ Apr 1964 Tanganyika and Zanzibar ◇ Oct 1964 Tanzania
SEYCHELLES ● Jun 1976, from UK
GABON ● Aug 1960
CONGO ● Aug 1960
ANGOLA ● Nov 1975
ZAMBIA ● Oct 1964 (Northern Rhodesia)
MALAWI ● Jul 1964 (Nyasaland)
MOZAMBIQUE ● Jun 1975
COMOROS ● Jul 1975, from France
MAYOTTE **1843:** French colony **Dec 1976:** French territorial collectivity
NAMIBIA ● Mar 1990 (South-West Africa)
ZIMBABWE ● Apr 1980 (Rhodesia)
1965: Unilateral declaration of independence
MADAGASCAR ● Jun 1960
MAURITIUS ● Mar 1968, from UK
BOTSWANA ● Sep 1966 (Bechuanaland) gained independence from South Africa
SWAZILAND ● Sep 1968
RÉUNION **1638:** occupied by France **Mar 1946:** French overseas department
1910: Union of South Africa set up as British dominion
1961: Republic
1996: New South African constitution signed
SOUTH AFRICA
LESOTHO ● Oct 1966 (Basutoland)

1000 km
1000 miles

How did the UN decision to partition Palestine spark conflict in the region?

◀ **The Palestinian problem 1947–82**

MAIN MAP: Arab-Israeli Wars
- Israel in 1949
- occupied by Israel after 1967 war
- occupied by Israel after 1973 war
- occupied by Israel after 1967 war reoccupied by Egypt after 1973 war
- ▭ demilitarized zone held by UN after Israel-Syria agreement, 1974, and 2nd Sinai agreement, 1975
- → route of Israel's invasion of Lebanon 1982
- ⛺ Palestinian refugee camps 1982
- +++++ disputed border

INSET: UN Partition plan 1947
- — border of British mandate 1923
- proposed Arab State
- proposed Jewish State
- proposed international zone

Inset maps (Palestine)

LEBANON — Haifa — SYRIA — Nazareth
Mediterranean Sea
Jerusalem — Gaza
Dead Sea
EGYPT — Beersheba
TRANSJORDAN
50 km / 50 miles
Eilat

LEBANON — Beirut
Mediterranean Sea — Damascus
Haifa — Golan Heights
SYRIA
Tel Aviv — Jaffa — WEST BANK — Amman
Jerusalem — Jericho
GAZA STRIP — Gaza — Hebron
Rafah — Dead Sea
Beersheba
Port Said
ISRAEL
Negev Desert
JORDAN
EGYPT
Suez Canal
Suez
1979–82: returned to Egypt
Sinai
Eilat — Aqaba
Gulf of Suez — Gulf of Aqaba
SAUDI ARABIA
Sharm-el-Sheikh
Red Sea
100 km / 100 miles

DECOLONIZATION OF SOUTH AND SOUTHEAST ASIA

THE GLOBAL WAVE of decolonization swept over the region with remarkable speed. Independence, however, did not always mean freedom from foreign presence, as Britain, France, and the US all sought to retain control, both commercially and through the maintenance of military bases.

How did the end of colonial rule effect South and Southeast Asia?

Nov 1946: French naval bombardment drives Viet Minh from city, precipitating first attack on French

Aug 1964: North Vietnamese attacks reported on US destroyers. Gulf of Tongking Resolution, commits US forces to war

1965–69: Communist-controlled areas bombed by US

1954: North-South Demarcation Line agreed at Geneva Conference

Mar 1965: First US ground forces arrive in Vietnam, ostensibly to protect air base

Mar 1968: Notorious massacre of 300-400 South Vietnamese civilians by US soldiers in My Lai

Apr 1975: North Vietnamese Army encircles city. US civilians are evacuated by helicopter from embassy rooftop. Final surrender

The decolonization of South and Southeast Asia

Former colonial powers

United Kingdom	US	1948 end of colonial/dependent status
France	Portugal	member of British Commonwealth 1971
Netherlands	Australia	

KASHMIR
1949: Status disputed by India and Pakistan leading to military conflict
1949: Ceasefire agreed

PAKISTAN (WEST PAKISTAN) 1947
1972: left British Commonwealth
1989: readmitted

1971: independence from Pakistan and renamed Bangladesh

1949–71: Indian administration

PAKISTAN (EAST PAKISTAN) 1947

INDIA 1947

Diu 1961
Daman 1961
Goa 1961
Mahé 1954
Pondicherry 1954
Karikal 1954
Yanam 1954
Chandernagore 1951

CEYLON 1948

MALDIVES 1965

BURMA 1948

LAOS 1954

VIETNAM 1954

CAMBODIA 1954

THAILAND

Macao 1999
Hong Kong 1997

PHILIPPINES 1948
Philippines:
1935: Commonwealth of Philippines established as transitional step to independence
1941–45: occupied by Japanese

Andaman Islands to India
Nicobar Islands to India

Malaya:
1942–45: Japanese occupation
1948: State of emergency protracted period of anti-British insurgency.
1963: Federation of Malaysia (incorporating Singapore, Sarawak, Sabah).
1965: Singapore leaves

1941–45: occupied by Japanese
1945–63: reverts to status of British protectorate

BRUNEI 1984
BRITISH NORTH BORNEO (SABAH) 1963

MALAYSIA
MALAYA 1957
SARAWAK 1963
SINGAPORE 1963

INDONESIA 1949
Indonesia:
1942–45: occupied by Japanese
1945–49: Nationalist guerrilla war with Dutch

Netherlands cede colony to Indonesia

IRIAN JAYA 1963

1973: Granted self-government as transitional step to independence

PAPUA NEW GUINEA 1975

EAST TIMOR
1976: occupied by Indonesia

The Vietnam War ▲

The First Vietnam War, 1946–54
× major battle
French border posts, captured by Viet Minh 1951

The Second Vietnam War, 1964–75
Major battles with US involvement:
× 1965–66
× 1967–69
western limit of Pathet Lao areas, 1967
Tet offensive 1968
Viet Cong Eastertide offensive, 1972
Final offensive, 1974–75

Communist supply lines
→ Ho Chi Minh trail
→ Sihanouk trail

Political changes in Southeast Asia

1945: Sukarno and Ho Chi Minh declare independence for Indonesia and Vietnam respectively

1954: Geneva accords allow separate governments in North and South Vietnam

1957: Malaya granted independence, despite ongoing Communist insurrection

1963: Federation of Malaysia incorporates Singapore, Sarawak, and Sabah, along with Malaya

1975: Communist regimes come to power in South Vietnam, Laos, and Cambodia

1946: Philippines obtain their independence

1954: Sukarno abrogates union with Dutch and declares unitary state of Indonesia

1964: Gulf of Tonkin resolution authorizes US air strikes against North Vietnam and Viet Cong; war soon spreads to Laos and Cambodia

1945   1955   1965   1975

OIL PRODUCTION AND CONFLICT IN THE GULF

THE HISTORY OF WEST ASIA since World War II has been dominated by three factors: oil, the creation of the state of Israel, and Islamic fundamentalism.

Why is the Gulf region so volatile?

Conflict in the Gulf ▼

Iran-Iraq War (1980–88)

▨	territory captured by Iraq Sep–Dec 1980
▨	territory captured by Iran Oct 1984
→	Iraqi invasion force Sep–Nov 1980
→	Iranian invasion force Oct 1984
✈	air strike 1980–88

The Gulf War (1990–91)

→	Iraqi invasion of Kuwait 1–2 Aug 1990
⊕	Iraqi air base
⊕	Allied air base
⬊	SCUD installation
☢	Iraqi nuclear/chemical/biological weapons plant
⚓	US battleship
⚓	US aircraft carrier
◀	Allied amphibious attack
→	Allied ground invasion force
→	Allied airborne attack
→	SCUD missile attack
▨	Kurdish region

Oil production ▶

■	oil field
■	gas field
🏭	oil refinery/terminal
—	pipeline
Asab	oil field name
1958	date oil first discovered
★	Arab League member

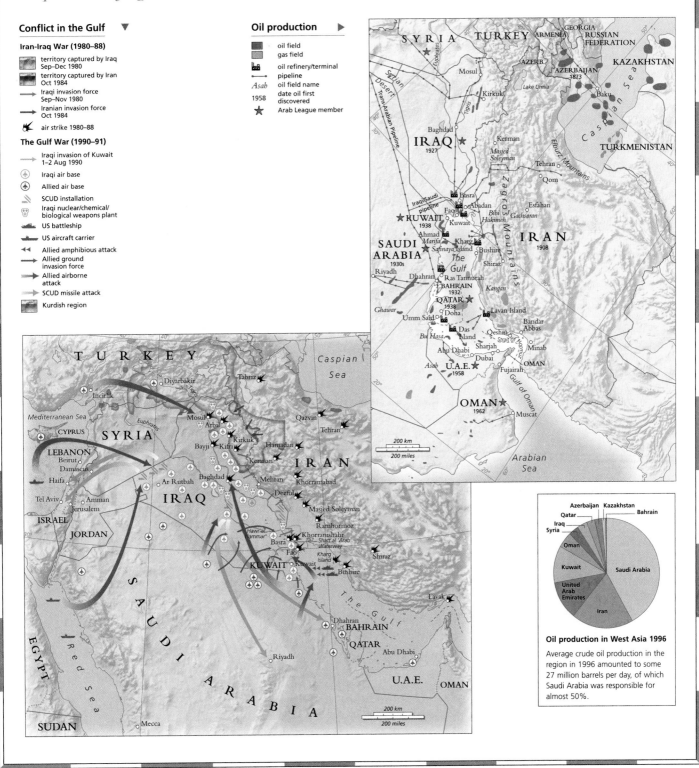

Oil production in West Asia 1996

Average crude oil production in the region in 1996 amounted to some 27 million barrels per day, of which Saudi Arabia was responsible for almost 50%.

POSTWAR NORTH AMERICA

IN THE 1950s, the US was labeled "the affluent society." This phrase reflected the experience of unprecedented economic prosperity and social progress in the years since World War II. The people of Mexico, Central America, and the Caribbean continued to have a much lower standard of living than the US and Canada. And within the US itself, not all regions and social groups experienced equal advances in affluence and status.

Scale varies with perspective

9230 km (5730 miles)

9390 km (5830 miles)

1971–81: Migration from Japan and China to Canada c.890,000

1971–91: South Asian migration to Canada c.620,000

1980 onwards: Migration from Korea and Southeast Asia to US

1980–90: Mexican and Central American migration to US and Canada c.3,000,000

1980–90: Caribbean migration to US c.660,000

1962: US economic and political blockade began

1981–91: Caribbean migration to Canada c.120,000

Postwar North America

- ❖ economy largely dependent on local raw materials
- 💻 high-tech industry
- 🏭 *maquilladora*
- ⚓ tourism crucial to economy

GNP per capita mid-1990s

- over $25,000
- $19,000–25,000
- $10,000–19,000
- $2,000–10,000
- Less than $2,000
- — US interstate highways
- — major roads and highways

What has been the effect of US prosperity on the other countries of North America?

POLITICAL CHANGE IN SOUTH AMERICA FROM 1930

POLITICAL AND ECONOMIC INSTABILITY have plagued South America since the 1930s. Various factors, including a sharp rise in population and rapid urbanization and industrialization, exerted great pressures on the weak democratic institutions of most nations.

Why has South America been more unstable than North America?

Scale varies with perspective

4450 km (2770 miles)

1987: Fighting almost erupts over maritime border dispute in the Gulf of Venezuela

1966: Independence from UK

TRINIDAD AND TOBAGO Iron, oil, and gold rich area claimed by Venezuela

1975: Independence from Netherlands

French overseas department

VENEZUELA
- 1908–35 Gómez
- 1945, 1948
- 1952–58 Pérez Jiménez
- 1958
- 1959

Maracaibo
Caracas
San Cristóbal
PANAMA

GUYANA
1966

SURINAM
- 1980
- 1980–87
- 1990
- 1991

Georgetown
Paramaribo
Cayenne
FRENCH GUIANA

Hostilities mainly over illegal gold prospecting

claimed by Surinam

claimed by Surinam

COLOMBIA
- 1930
- 1953
- 1953–57 Rojas Pinilla
- 1957
- from 1964

Bogotá
Cali
Macapá
Belém
São Luís
Natal

ECUADOR
- 1930
- 1944, 1947, 1963
- 1963–66, 1972–79
- 1979

Quito
Guayaquil
Leticia

Previously claimed by Ecuador

1998: Delineation of 77 km stretch of border between Peru and Ecuador; intended to give Ecuador navigation and trade rights in the Amazon region

BRAZIL
- 1930
- 1937–45 Vargas' Estado Novo
- 1945, 1964
- 1960s, early 1970s
- 1964–85
- 1985

Porto Velho
Manaus
Amazon Basin
Brasília
Recife
Aracaju
Salvador

PERU
- 1930
- 1936–39 Benavides
- 1948–56 Odría
- 1962 Ayacucho
- 1968
- 1968–75 General Velasco
- 1968–80
- 1980
- from 1980 Shining Path

Trujillo
Callao
Lima
Rio Branco

BOLIVIA
- 1930 1952
- 1936 1964
- 1940 1964–82
- 1943 1967 Che Guevara
- 1946 1969, 1971, 1978, 1979, 1981
- 1951 1982

La Paz
Lake Titicaca
Sucre
Cuiabá
Belo Horizonte

Bolivia had negotiated with Chile and Peru for corridor to Pacific Ocean since Atacama area was lost to Chile in 1884

Chaco War 1932–35 (see Map 2)

Campo Grande
Rio de Janeiro
São Paulo
Tropic of Capricorn

Short section of boundary has not been precisely delimited

PARAGUAY
- 1930
- 1936, 1937, 1940
- 1940–48 Morínigo
- 1948, 1954
- 1954–89 Stroessner
- 1989
- 1989

Asunción

Short section of boundary disputed

Short section of boundary disputed

CHILE
- 1936
- 1973
- 1974–90 under General Pinochet
- 1990

Valparaíso
Santiago
Córdoba
Montevideo

1982: allow UK to use ports during Falklands War

URUGUAY
- 1930
- 1933–38 President Terra (soft dictatorship)
- 1963–72 Tupamaros
- 1976
- 1976–84
- 1985

ARGENTINA
- 1930, 1943
- 1943–45
- 1946–55 Perón
- 1955
- 1955–58
- 1962, 1966
- 1966–73
- 1969–79 Montoneros and 1970–77 People's Revolutionary Army
- 1976
- 1976–83
- 1983

Buenos Aires

1982: Chile gives clandestine communications information and support to British forces during Falklands War

1978: Territorial dispute with Chile over islands in Beagle Channel almost leads to war; settled 1984 with Vatican mediation

FALKLAND ISLANDS to UK claimed by Argentina

Falklands War
1982: Argentina attempt to take Falklands from UK by military action

Political change in South America from 1930

- 🌿 civilian-led revolution
- 🌿 social revolution
- ⟳ democratic government
- border/ territorial dispute
- full-scale war
- ⭥ successful military coup
- personal dictatorship
- military regime
- guerrilla activity
- — frontiers 1999
- ☐ capital city

Urban population as a percentage of total population, 1995
- 0–49%
- 50–69%
- 70–80%
- over 80%

Political development from 1930

1937: 'New State' in Brazil launched by Vargas

1968: Tupamaros urban guerilla group founded in Uruguay
1968: Military junta take over Peru

1974: Brutal dictatorship of Pinochet in Chile

1980s: Many countries return to democracy

1930 1940 1950 1960 1970 1980

1932: Chaco War begins between Bolivia and Paraguay

1946: Peron comes to power in Argentina

1976: 15,000 political subversives killed during 'Dirty War', by military and right-wing death squads in Argentina

1982: Argentina occupies South Georgia and Falkland Islands; surrenders to UK forces

TIGER ECONOMIES AND CHINESE DEVELOPMENT

WHILE CHINA TOOK THE PATH of centralization and collectivization, between 1960 and 1998 Japan rebuilt and enjoyed an unprecedented economic boom. Spurred by the Japanese example, this success spread around the Pacific Rim, including China.

What factors account for East Asia's economic growth since World War II?

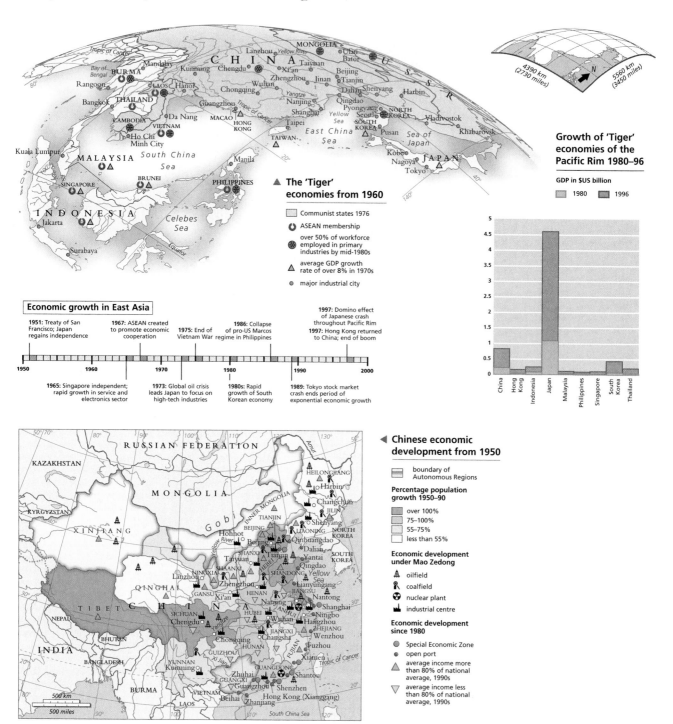

The 'Tiger' economies from 1960

Communist states 1976

⟳ ASEAN membership

⚙ over 50% of workforce employed in primary industries by mid-1980s

△ average GDP growth rate of over 8% in 1970s

● major industrial city

Growth of 'Tiger' economies of the Pacific Rim 1980–96

GDP in $US billion

☐ 1980   ☐ 1996

Economic growth in East Asia

1951: Treaty of San Francisco; Japan regains independence

1967: ASEAN created to promote economic cooperation

1975: End of Vietnam War

1986: Collapse of pro-US Marcos regime in Philippines

1997: Domino effect of Japanese crash throughout Pacific Rim

1997: Hong Kong returned to China; end of boom

1965: Singapore independent; rapid growth in service and electronics sector

1973: Global oil crisis leads Japan to focus on high-tech industries

1980s: Rapid growth of South Korean economy

1989: Tokyo stock market crash ends period of exponential economic growth

Chinese economic development from 1950

☐ boundary of Autonomous Regions

Percentage population growth 1950–90

☐ over 100%
☐ 75–100%
☐ 55–75%
☐ less than 55%

Economic development under Mao Zedong

⚒ oilfield
⚒ coalfield
☢ nuclear plant
⚒ industrial centre

Economic development since 1980

● Special Economic Zone
● open port
△ average income more than 80% of national average, 1990s
▽ average income less than 80% of national average, 1990s

CHINESE EXPANSION AND ASIAN NATIONALISM

Expansionism has characterized Chinese foreign policy since 1949, evidenced most notably by the invasion of Tibet in 1950. In Central Asia, Islam has survived suppression and political change to reemerge as a vital force, accompanied by a resurgence of traditional ethnic rivalries.

How does the revitalization of Islam affect Asian politics?

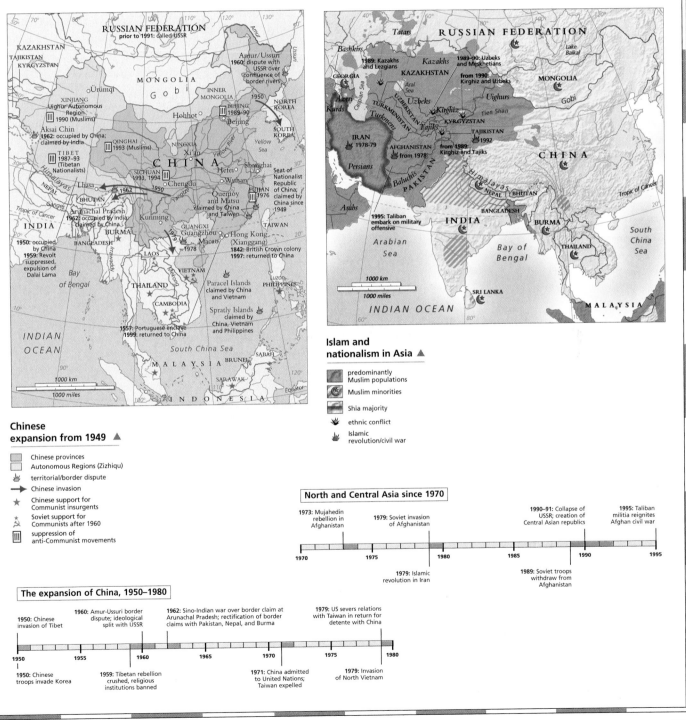

Chinese expansion from 1949 ▲

- Chinese provinces
- Autonomous Regions (Zizhiqu)
- 🕱 territorial/border dispute
- → Chinese invasion
- ★ Chinese support for Communist insurgents
- 🕱 Soviet support for Communists after 1960
- 🏛 suppression of anti-Communist movements

Islam and nationalism in Asia ▲

- predominantly Muslim populations
- Muslim minorities
- Shia majority
- 🔥 ethnic conflict
- 🔥 Islamic revolution/civil war

North and Central Asia since 1970

- **1973:** Mujahedin rebellion in Afghanistan
- **1979:** Soviet invasion of Afghanistan
- **1990–91:** Collapse of USSR; creation of Central Asian republics
- **1995:** Taliban militia reignites Afghan civil war
- **1979:** Islamic revolution in Iran
- **1989:** Soviet troops withdraw from Afghanistan

1970 | 1975 | 1980 | 1985 | 1990 | 1995

The expansion of China, 1950–1980

- **1950:** Chinese invasion of Tibet
- **1960:** Amur-Ussuri border dispute; ideological split with USSR
- **1962:** Sino-Indian war over border claim at Arunachal Pradesh; rectification of border claims with Pakistan, Nepal, and Burma
- **1979:** US severs relations with Taiwan in return for detente with China
- **1950:** Chinese troops invade Korea
- **1959:** Tibetan rebellion crushed, religious institutions banned
- **1971:** China admitted to United Nations; Taiwan expelled
- **1979:** Invasion of North Vietnam

1950 | 1955 | 1960 | 1965 | 1970 | 1975 | 1980

COMMUNISM AND THE EU

THE EUROPEAN ECONOMIC COMMUNITY was established in 1957 to guarantee the economic success of its members, and to develop a political union of states in an attempt to alleviate the risk of war. In December 1991 the European Union (EU) was created, which committed the members to a single currency. From an initial six members in 1957, by 2004 the EU had 25 member states. In 1989, the fall of the Berlin Wall signaled the end of the Cold War and the collapse of communism in Eastern Europe and Russia.

What impact does the growth of the European Union have on Russia?

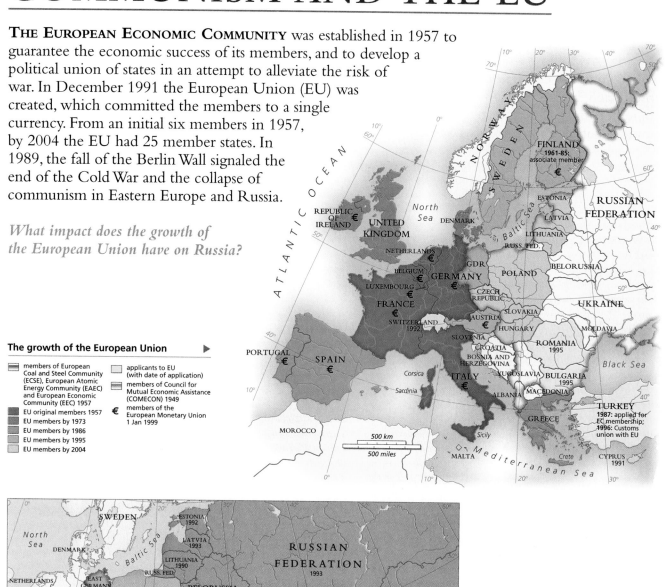

The growth of the European Union ▶

- members of European Coal and Steel Community (ECSE), European Atomic Energy Community (EAEC) and European Economic Community (EEC) 1957
- EU original members 1957
- EU members by 1973
- EU members by 1986
- EU members by 1995
- EU members by 2004
- applicants to EU (with date of application)
- members of Council for Mutual Economic Assistance (COMECON) 1949
- € members of the European Monetary Union 1 Jan 1999

▲ **The collapse of Communism in Eastern Europe**

- Soviet Union to 1991
- Soviet-dominated Eastern Europe to 1989
- German Democratic Republic (GDR), united with Federal Republic of Germany 1990
- Czechoslovakia to Dec 1992
- Yugoslavia to 1991
- other Communist state before 1991
- 1990 date of first free election

THE PANISLAMIC WORLD

THE WORLD AT THE END of the 20th century was increasingly globalized, reinforced by digital technology and the spread of telecommunications. At the same time, links of ethnic origin, cultural affinity, or religious identity defined many communities, such as Islam, that transcended national boundaries.

The pan–Islamic World

Percentage of Muslims in population

- 91–100%
- 51–90%
- 21–50%
- 6–20%
- 1–5%
- less than 1%

Official status of Islam

- ☾ formally designated Islamic republic
- ⬤ secular state where population is more then 50% Muslim
- 🕌 established religion is Islam
- ✳ membership of Organization of the Islamic Conference (OIC)
- 🔥 active conflict involving militant Islam

Is globalization incompatible with cultural and religious identity?

THE MODERN WORLD

RAPID POPULATION GROWTH, environmental degradation, ethnic conflicts, global terrorism, and nuclear proliferation mark the beginning of the 21st century.

How is humanity responding to the challenges that confront the world today?

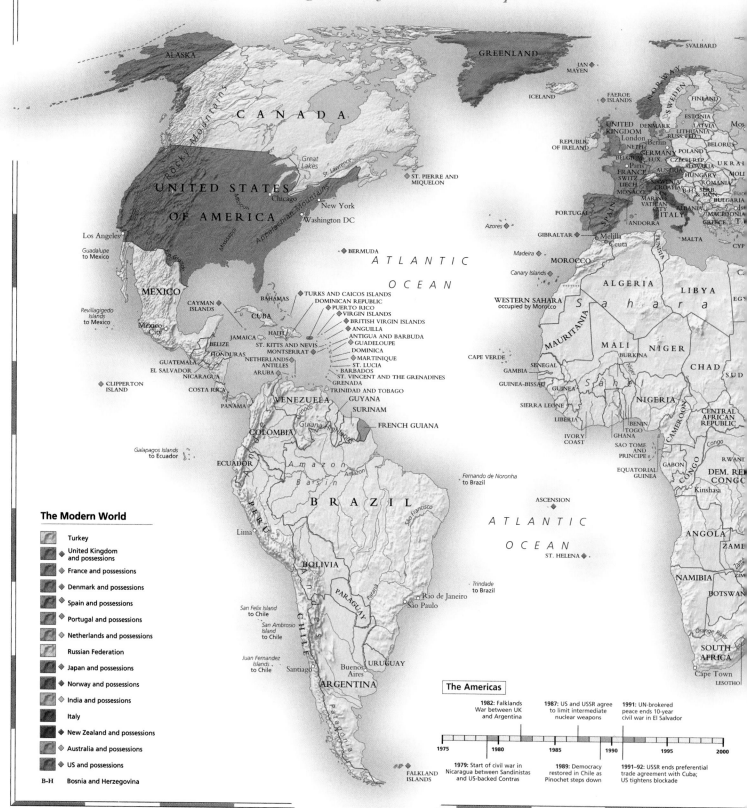

The Modern World

- Turkey
- ◆ United Kingdom and possessions
- ◆ France and possessions
- ◆ Denmark and possessions
- ◆ Spain and possessions
- ◆ Portugal and possessions
- ◆ Netherlands and possessions
- Russian Federation
- ◆ Japan and possessions
- ◆ Norway and possessions
- ◆ India and possessions
- Italy
- ◆ New Zealand and possessions
- ◆ Australia and possessions
- ◆ US and possessions
- **B-H** Bosnia and Herzegovina

The Americas

1982: Falklands War between UK and Argentina	**1987:** US and USSR agree to limit intermediate nuclear weapons	**1991:** UN-brokered peace ends 10-year civil war in El Salvador

1975 — 1980 — 1985 — 1990 — 1995 — 2000

1979: Start of civil war in Nicaragua between Sandinistas and US-backed Contras	**1989:** Democracy restored in Chile as Pinochet steps down	**1991–92:** USSR ends preferential trade agreement with Cuba; US tightens blockade

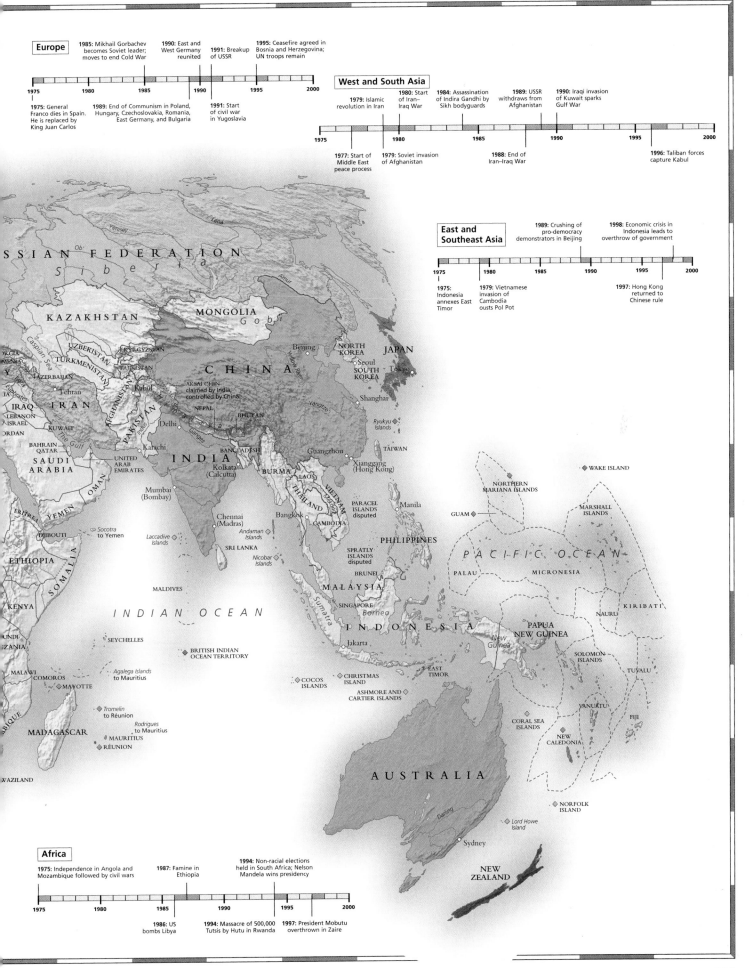

Europe

1985: Mikhail Gorbachev becomes Soviet leader; moves to end Cold War

1990: East and West Germany reunited

1991: Breakup of USSR

1995: Ceasefire agreed in Bosnia and Herzegovina; UN troops remain

1975   1980   1985   1990   1995   2000

1975: General Franco dies in Spain. He is replaced by King Juan Carlos

1989: End of Communism in Poland, Hungary, Czechoslovakia, Romania, East Germany, and Bulgaria

1991: Start of civil war in Yugoslavia

West and South Asia

1979: Islamic revolution in Iran

1980: Start of Iran–Iraq War

1984: Assassination of Indira Gandhi by Sikh bodyguards

1989: USSR withdraws from Afghanistan

1990: Iraqi invasion of Kuwait sparks Gulf War

1975   1980   1985   1990   1995   2000

1977: Start of Middle East peace process

1979: Soviet invasion of Afghanistan

1988: End of Iran–Iraq War

1996: Taliban forces capture Kabul

East and Southeast Asia

1989: Crushing of pro-democracy demonstrators in Beijing

1998: Economic crisis in Indonesia leads to overthrow of government

1975   1980   1985   1990   1995   2000

1975: Indonesia annexes East Timor

1979: Vietnamese invasion of Cambodia ousts Pol Pot

1997: Hong Kong returned to Chinese rule

Africa

1975: Independence in Angola and Mozambique followed by civil wars

1987: Famine in Ethiopia

1994: Non-racial elections held in South Africa; Nelson Mandela wins presidency

1975   1980   1985   1990   1995   2000

1986: US bombs Libya

1994: Massacre of 500,000 Tutsis by Hutu in Rwanda

1997: President Mobutu overthrown in Zaire

INDEX

REGION

TOPIC

Agriculture: 12-13, 14-15, 16-17, 18-19, 20-21, 22-23, 25, 95

Biological Exchange: 62-64, 69

Empire/Colonization: 28-29, 32-33, 36-37, 38-39, 42-43, 48-49, 50, 53, 54, 58-59, 64-65, 66, 67, 68-69, 70-71, 72-73, 75, 76, 78-79, 81, 84, 85, 88-89, 90, 91, 92, 93, 94, 95, 96-97, 100, 104-105, 108-109, 115, 116

Environment: 6-7, 8-9. 10-11, 12013, 14-15, 16-17, 22-23, 25, 52, 53, 62-63, 67, 69, 87, 95, 98-99, 102-103

Human Evolution: 6-8

Migration: 8-9, 10-11, 12-13, 14-15, 24, 33, 48, 98-99, 106-107

Religion: 38, 46, 48, 51, 52, 56-57, 74, 115, 123

Slavery: 82-83

Trade/Industry: 26, 34-35, 40-41, 52, 60-61, 72, 73, 82-83, 84, 85, 87, 100, 101, 102-103, 109, 117, 118, 120, 122

Urbanization: 20-21, 22, 25, 26-27, 30-31, 77, 87, 119, 120

NOTES